CRAZY

C R A Z Y

A Father's Search Through
America's Mental Health Madness

PETE EARLEY

G. P. Putnam's Sons
New York

G. P. PUTNAM'S SONS
Publishers Since 1838
Published by the Penguin Group
Penguin Group (USA) Inc., 375 Hudson Street, New York, New York 10014, USA • Penguin
Group (Canada), 90 Eglinton Avenue East, Suite 700, Toronto, Ontario M4P 2Y3, Canada (a division of Pearson
Penguin Canada Inc.) • Penguin Books Ltd, 80 Strand, London WC2R 0RL, England • Penguin Ireland,
25 St Stephen's Green, Dublin 2, Ireland (a division of Penguin Books Ltd) • Penguin Group (Australia),
250 Camberwell Road, Camberwell, Victoria 3124, Australia (a division of Pearson Australia Group Pty Ltd) •
Penguin Books India Pvt Ltd, 11 Community Centre, Panchsheel Park, New Delhi–110 017, India • Penguin Group
(NZ), Cnr Airborne and Rosedale Roads, Albany, Auckland 1310, New Zealand (a division of Pearson New Zealand
Ltd) • Penguin Books (South Africa) (Pty) Ltd, 24 Sturdee Avenue, Rosebank, Johannesburg 2196, South Africa

Penguin Books Ltd, Registered Offices:
80 Strand, London WC2R 0RL, England

Library of Congress Cataloging-in-Publication Data

Earley, Pete.
Crazy : a father's search through America's mental health madness / Pete Earley.
p.   cm.
ISBN 0-399-15313-6
1. Mentally ill—Biography.   2. Mental illness—Case studies.   3. Mentally ill—
Family relationships.   4. Mental illness.   5. Parent and child.   I. Title.
RC 463.E27   2006   2005050986
362.1'092—dc22
[B]

Printed in the United States of America
1 3 5 7 9 10 8 6 4 2

Book design by Stephanie Huntwork

While the author has made every effort to provide accurate telephone numbers and Internet addresses at the time of
publication, neither the publisher nor the author assumes any responsibility for errors, or for changes that occur after
publication. Further, the publisher does not have any control over and does not assume any responsibility for author or
third-party websites or their content.

This book is dedicated to persons with mental illness and those who love them. I would like to thank specifically these individuals who helped my son:

Hossein Bakhtar
Nawathip Boulom
Il Nam Cho
Dr. James F. Dee
Donald Graham
Penny Hinkle
Barbara Hunter
Dr. Don Infeld
Susan Infeld
Andrew Kersey
Patti Luzi
William Luzi
Jay Myerson
Robert Straub
Mike Wallace

I will never forget your kindness.

CONTENTS

MAJOR PLAYERS

Mike Earley   *Author's son*

Alice Ann Collyer   *Diagnosis: schizophrenia*

April Hernandez   *Diagnosis: schizoaffective*

Ted Jackson   *Diagnosis: bipolar disorder*

Judge Steven Leifman   *Judicial reformer*

Tom Mullen   *Director, treatment program*

Dr. Joseph Poitier   *Miami jail psychiatrist*

Judy Robinson   *Advocate*

Deidra Sanbourne   *Diagnosis: schizoaffective*

PREFACE

had no idea.

I've been a journalist for more than thirty years, a reporter for *The Washington Post*, the author of several nonfiction books about crime and punishment and society, some of them award-winning, even best-selling. I've interviewed murderers and spies, judges and prosecutors, always seeking the truth and attempting to convey it so that readers can see the people and the events for themselves—can understand not only what happened, also why.

But I was always on the outside looking in. I had no idea what it was like to be on the inside looking out. Until my son Mike was declared mentally ill.

If my son had broken his leg, most doctors would have agreed on the diagnosis and treatment. "Sir, your son's leg is broken into two pieces. The bone needs to be reattached, the wound closed, and the body allowed to heal." But that wasn't what happened with Mike. One psychiatrist said he had bipolar disorder, another said he showed early stages of schizophrenia, a third said he had schizoaffective disorder. They prescribed a dizzying range of different drugs and different therapies, and even worse, because he was an adult, I couldn't simply swoop in and make medical decisions for him. An array of incompatible laws about patient rights stood in my way, like a line of trees.

But even that was nothing compared with what happened when Mike, suffering delusions, committed a crime and was arrested. Suddenly, the line of trees became a forest. The contradictions, the disparities, the Catch-22s multiplied, until I began to despair.

"I just feel so damn helpless," I told my wife, Patti, one night. "I want to do something, but I don't know how to help him."

"Then do what you do best," she said. "You're a journalist. You make your living investigating stories. So investigate this. Pete Earley, the journalist, can dig out information that Pete Earley, the father, would never be able to get. If you want to help Mike, and others like him, then write about what he is going through, and find out why the mental health system in this country seems to be in such a mess."

I hesitated. I didn't know how Mike would feel about it, and I didn't want to risk writing something that might anger the people who'd be dealing with his case. I was also scared about what I might find. In the past, it wouldn't have bothered me if I'd discovered alarming conditions in the mental health system. Now this disease wore a recognizable face.

I decided to do some preliminary digging, and the more I dug, the clearer it became: What was happening to Mike was not an oddity. It was a tiny piece in a bigger story. A major shift had occurred in our country. The mentally ill, who used to be treated in state mental hospitals, were now being arrested. Our nation's jails and prisons were our new asylums.

In 1955, some 560,000 Americans were being treated for mental problems in state hospitals. Between 1955 and 2000, our nation's population increased from 166 million to 276 million. If you took the patient-per-capita ratio that existed in 1955 and extrapolated it on the basis of the new population, you'd expect to find 930,000 patients in state mental hospitals.

But there are fewer than 55,000 in them today. Where are the others? Nearly 300,000 are in jails and prisons. Another half million are on court-ordered probation. The largest public mental health facility in America is not a hospital. It's the Los Angeles County jail. On any given day, it houses 3,000 mentally disturbed inmates.

These statistics gave me an idea, but before I pursued it, I wanted to talk with Mike.

"I'm thinking about writing a book about the criminalization of the mentally ill," I told him.

"Okay," he replied.

"Mike, I want to make certain you understand what I'm going to do. I want to write about you and how you got into trouble with the law."

"Do you think people will want to read that?" He sounded surprised.

"It would be more than just your story."

I outlined my plan. I would write about his mental breakdown and how it had led to his being arrested, but I'd fold his personal story into a much larger one—an examination of the mental health system in America today. In order to do this, I'd find a jail in a major city far away from where Mike had been arrested, and I'd spend time inside its cell blocks, observing mentally ill prisoners. I'd select individual inmates to shadow, monitor their criminal cases through the courts, and follow them into the community. I'd interview correctional officers, public defenders, prosecutors, judges, mental health care professionals, and the police. I'd talk to parents, siblings, and spouses. I'd consult historians about how the mentally ill have been treated over the decades and centuries, and I'd question the civil rights lawyers who fought to pass laws to protect them. I'd meet with legislators and state hospital administrators. But my main focus would always be on the jail and the prisoners there. I'd use it as a microcosm. It would serve as my hub, much like the center of an old western wagon wheel. The inmates whose lives I would chronicle would be the spokes jutting out from it.

Could I be objective? Probably not. I'm a father first, a journalist second. But I could be honest and thorough and relentless.

Mike was still taking strong doses of antipsychotic medication when I first mentioned my idea to him, and I could tell by his reaction that he was having trouble focusing on what I'd just said.

"You're more important than any book," I explained. "I don't want to write anything that might harm you or limit your future. I'll forget about doing this if you want me to."

He didn't seem to understand how a book might hurt him, so I explained that writing about his illness could stigmatize him. "I'm not interested in making you a poster child for mental illness."

He was quiet for several moments, and then said, "If a book will help other people understand what it's like to get sick and be arrested, then do it."

"Are you sure?"

"If it helps someone else, yes."

We talked about using his name. To my surprise, he wanted me to print it. "You've got to be honest," he said. But I was still hesitant. We compromised by agreeing to use his middle name. It would be a thin veil.

I was still nervous that Mike might not really understand the impact of what I was proposing. I couldn't predict what might happen in the future—five, ten years from now—after I outed him in this book.

"Dad," he said, "tell my story."

"I'll let you read it. You can go over the parts about you."

"No! I don't want to do that," he replied firmly. "I trust you to tell the truth."

T his book tells two stories. The first is Mike's. The second describes what I learned during a yearlong investigation inside the Miami-Dade County jail in Miami, Florida, a city that's home to a larger percentage of mentally ill residents than any other major metropolitan area in America. I was given the complete run of the jail, its inmates and employees, with no restrictions. Although the portrait that follows was taken from a single jail, it could just as easily have been a snapshot of any community in America.

For privacy reasons, I have used pseudonyms to identify most of the inmates. The exceptions are my son and prisoners whose cases have already been heavily publicized. All the characters in this book are real, and I have not changed any other facts about them. Their voices, and those of all the other people in this book—lawyers, law-enforcement officials, doctors, social workers, family—who are attempting to thread their way through the mental health maze in America, are reported accurately.

There have been many books by professionals and journalists writing from the outside looking in. There have been many books by patients and inmates writing from the inside looking out. This book attempts to do both.

If you belong to any of the groups mentioned above, I hope the book provides some extra light and clarity to the situations you face every day. If you do not, I hope it will inspire you to action, for the stories told here, in this day and age, are extraordinary, and worthy of your attention.

If it could happen to my family, it could happen to yours.

M i k e ' s   S t o r y :   1

How would you feel, Dad," Mike asked, "if someone you loved killed himself?"

It was not a threat, delivered in anger. Rather, my son's voice was tired. I was speeding south along Interstate 95, driving from New York City to Virginia. We were a couple of miles north of Baltimore. For the past few hours, I had been begging Mike to take Zyprexa, a medicine prescribed for mental disorders.

"Pills are poison," Mike snapped. "Doctors don't know what they're talking about. I just think differently."

I had first learned that he was slipping earlier that morning. "Something's wrong," his older brother had telephoned from Manhattan to tell me. Since that call, I'd discovered Mike's dementia actually had become obvious several weeks before, when he'd found a videocassette on the sidewalk while walking to a subway near Times Square. It was Oliver Stone's movie Heaven and Earth, a gut-wrenching account by a Vietnamese woman about the fighting there and its aftermath. Mike had watched it three times, and he had become convinced it contained a secret message aimed at him.

"As soon as you see it, everything will make sense," he told me. "You'll see."

I pressed harder on the gas pedal and again suggested he take a Zyprexa tablet.

"Okay," he finally declared. "I'll take your damn pill." *But he paused just before he slipped the tablet into his mouth.*

Please, God! I silently prayed. Swallow it!

As I watched, he took a gulp of water from a plastic bottle that I'd given him, but when he wiped his lips dry with his sleeve, I noticed his hand drop down next to the car seat, and he shook it.

Was that the pill?

"No one dies unless God wants him dead," *he announced.*

"Did Patti's first husband choose to die?" *I asked.*

Patti was my wife, his stepmother. Her first husband had died from cancer, making her a widow with four children. My question annoyed him. So he ignored me. For several moments, neither of us spoke, and then, suddenly, his thoughts came in rapid fire, bouncing from topic to topic without any apparent connection.

God. Capitalism. Satan. Comic books. Sex. Spontaneous laughter.

Mike saw an encrypted message in a bumper sticker on the blue sedan ahead of us: "Believe in Him!" It was a signal from God, he told me. They were everywhere. But only he could interpret them.

Just as quickly, Mike began to cry. Tears flowed from his eyes and he moaned as if he were an injured animal that had been struck by a car and knocked sprawling into a roadside ditch. The last time I'd seen him in such agony was when he was five years old and he got smacked in the head with a stick while playing with friends. A one-inch gash in his scalp had turned his silky blond hair crimson and sent him screaming to find me.

Now he was twenty-three.

"Why are you crying?"

"I can't tell you."

"Why can't you tell me?"

"Because you'll hate me forever."

Patti had already alerted the emergency room at Inova Fairfax Hospital, near where we lived. It was where we'd gone when he'd suffered his first psychotic episode. That was when I first heard the words bipolar *disorder. It was a mood disorder that caused its victims to switch in seconds from feeling euphoric to feeling suicidal. Hospital security guards had to wrestle him down the first time we took him there. But I shoved that memory aside and drove. My speedometer registered 95 mph. I wanted to stop and use a bathroom, but I was afraid.*

What if Mike took off? He had run from me before when he had been delusional.

I couldn't risk it. My needs would have to wait.

Mike began laughing.

"Dog God!" Ha ha ha. "God Dog! Get it?"

Hang on, son! I thought. The doctors will know what to do.

It was 8 P.M. by the time we reached the emergency entrance. An intake nurse rolled her eyes when Mike tried to convince her that he was perfectly sane. She snapped a white plastic ID around his wrist and led us down a hallway into a room, where another nurse soon appeared and questioned him again. She asked me about Mike's psychiatric history. While I gave her the abbreviated version, he sat unconcerned on an examination table, ignoring our conversation and glancing through an old copy of The New Yorker.

Mike's first psychotic breakdown occurred during his senior year at a university in Brooklyn. I have since learned this is not an uncommon time for mental illness to strike young men and women, because of stress. He had been about to graduate and was having a difficult time finding a job. I had never suspected that he might have a mental illness. There was no family history of it, at least that I'd been told of. The first hint that *something was wrong came one weekend during a phone call. We spoke every Sunday, and he mentioned that he'd taken five homeless men to McDonald's that morning for breakfast.*

"Why'd you do that?" I asked.

"They were hungry and I wanted to talk to them."

I didn't understand, but then fathers often don't understand why their sons and daughters do certain things in college.

Later that night, Mike called me again. He wanted to clarify his story. Now he wasn't certain if he had actually taken them to breakfast or if he had just dreamt that he had. He said he was having difficulty eating. Everything tasted bad. He'd been vomiting a lot. He started to cry, and I told him that I'd come up to New York in the morning.

"Everything will be okay," I assured him.

Before hanging up, he added that he'd gone to a party in the dormitory the night before, and it occurred to me that he might have been given or taken some hallucinatory drug. The next morning while I drove to Brooklyn, Patti telephoned several Manhattan psychiatrists and found one who was willing to see Mike immediately. I found my son waiting for me in his room. He didn't want to talk to a shrink, but after an hour I persuaded him.

"Let's hope it's drugs," the psychiatrist said after interviewing Mike.

"What!" I replied, clearly shocked.

"It's better than the alternative," he explained. "Your son might be mentally ill."

Mike and I spent that day talking in his dorm room. I told him that we'd find a way to make everything okay. We hugged. I drove home on autopilot. He went to see the psychiatrist two more times, but then he stopped. There was simply too much schoolwork. Besides, he said, he felt fine. "I'm not crazy!" he told me. "I just need to eat better."

And he had seemed okay when we talked on the following Sundays. Now, looking back, I should have known better. How could I have been so stupid? There'd been lots of clues. But I'd wanted to believe the psychiatrist had overreacted. I'd wanted to believe Mike was just nervous about graduating. Besides, I had my own daily problems to juggle. Life had gone on, and the few times that I'd reminded him of the McDonald's incident, he complained, "Stop asking me about that! It was no big deal! Everything is under control."

And then his mind broke.

Five months after Mike had taken the homeless men to breakfast, one of his college friends had driven him home to me.

"He's not right," his buddy said.

Mike hadn't slept for five nights. He'd spent most of his days wandering aimlessly through Manhattan. He'd walked twenty miles one day going nowhere. He'd also become fixated on a friend named Jen, only she didn't know it. He was convinced they'd soon be married. He told me his plans shortly after his friend dropped him off.

"I've got to save her," Mike said. "I've got to save Jen."

"From what?"

"Evil."

Because he hadn't eaten, we drove to an International House of Pancakes, his favorite place for morning food. Mike looked exhausted, but when he talked, he seemed rational about everything—except for Jen. Whenever I asked about her, he'd become giddy and tell me how much he was in love and how he and Jen would be married soon. When we got back home after eating, I persuaded him to go to bed and left him in his bedroom. I slipped into my study and called the psychiatrist in Manhattan for advice. Before the doctor came on the line, I heard the front door open and slam shut. I looked out the window. Mike was walking away. I hung up the receiver and ran after him.

"Where are you going?"

"To save Jen. She's in danger."

"This is nuts," I said. "Come home."

He started walking faster.

"You're acting weird. Do I have to call the cops?"

Mike shot me a glaring look and started running. I tried to keep up, but couldn't. I turned back toward the house, jumped into my car, and began searching for him. An hour later, he came home. He couldn't find Jen, he said.

"We need to go to the hospital," I told him. "You need to see a doctor."

"I'm not going to see a doctor."

"Jen wants you to go," I tried.

"She's there?" he asked, his face suddenly brightening.

"Yes," I replied.

"Hurry!" he demanded. "Take me."

Patti called the hospital while Mike and I were en route. Two security guards met us at the door. A doctor gave him an injection of Haldol, a powerful antipsychotic. Incredibly, within an hour, he was calm.

"I'm sorry," he said. At that point, Mike agreed to enter Dominion Hospital, a private mental institution. He recognized something was wrong. Four days later, his psychiatrist told us that our insurance company was pressuring him to discharge Mike. Although confused, Mike seemed to be thinking rationally. We brought him home. Two days after that, he got up early before everyone, slipped outside, and decided to go for a drive. About a mile from the house, he let go of the steering wheel and shut his eyes. He told me later that he'd not been sure if he was awake or dreaming. He figured the quickest way to find out was to turn loose the wheel.

The car crashed into a parked sedan. Hearing the noise, its owners called the police. A sympathetic officer telephoned us.

"Your son is crazy," he simply said.

I'll never forget those words.

Crazy.

But Mike wasn't arrested.

Instead, I was allowed to take him back to Dominion. This time around, our insurance company let him stay an entire week. When he was discharged, I asked him what he'd remembered about the past several days.

"There were two of me: one sane, one insane," he explained, "but the sane one couldn't do anything but watch the insane one."

We decided Mike needed to stay home for a while and not return to New York until he was better. He hadn't wanted to see a psychiatrist or a therapist, but we forced him to go. His doctor had prescribed Zyprexa and Depakote. Mike didn't like the pills. I couldn't blame him. He put on thirty pounds. The medication turned his mouth dry, made him sluggish, and killed his sex drive. One afternoon while he was out, I sneaked into his bedroom and counted the tablets. There were too many in the bottle. He hadn't been taking them. I confronted him as soon as he returned.

"There's nothing wrong with me," he insisted. "I don't need pills. I stayed up for five days in New York. That's what caused this. I just freaked out. Stop making such a big deal out of it. I'm not sick!"

I reacted exactly the way his therapist had told me to: with tough love. I drew a line. "Take your medicine or you can't live here."

Mike stormed out and moved in with his mother, my ex-wife. For the next four months, Mike, indeed, seemed fine. When he announced that he was going back to New York, even I thought maybe we'd overreacted. Maybe his breakdown was a onetime event. Maybe it had been brought on by exhaustion. Maybe the doctors were wrong and Mike wasn't really mentally ill.

As we'd always done, Mike and I spoke every Sunday on the telephone after he returned to Brooklyn. But Mike always kept our talks brief. He realized I was upset because he still wasn't taking his antipsychotic pills. Even so, he had done well. He'd finished school and found a job.

And then his brother called me. Mike had started acting odd again.

*T*he nurse who listened to me describe Mike's psychiatric history said a doctor would be in shortly to examine him.

At least this time I've gotten him to a hospital before he was too far gone!

I thought. At least this time, he won't be driving down a road and closing his eyes to see if he is awake or asleep. He'll get help.

I looked at Mike, who was still thumbing through the well-used New Yorker, *and I wondered if he knew what was happening*

For the next two hours, we waited. No one came to help us. No one poked a head in to ask if we were okay. Mike was still reading the same magazine. He was starting to discern secret messages in the text. I was beginning to seethe.

"This is incredible," he said. He giggled.

Another hour passed and then, unbelievably, another. I'd always prided myself on being polite, patient. But four hours! It was midnight now. I couldn't believe we were still waiting. What was the holdup?

"I'm leaving," Mike announced.

"Just a minute," I said. I rushed into the hall and waved down a nurse. A few minutes later, a doctor entered the room. He was in his thirties, clean-cut, and all business. As he came in, he raised both hands as if he were surrendering to enemy troops.

"Sorry you've had to wait, but we're busy, and there's not going to be much I can do for you," he said.

I thought: You haven't even examined my son! But the doctor explained that the intake nurse had already warned him that my son believed all medicines were poison.

The doctor asked Mike, "Do you know who I am?"

"You're the witch doctor. Ow-ee-ow-ah-ah."

The doctor grinned. This isn't funny, I thought. I blurted out, "He's been diagnosed as having bipolar disorder." I began to explain how Mike had been hospitalized at Dominion Hospital twice and how he had not been taking his antipsychotic medicine for at least five months.

But the doctor cut me short. "What's happened before this moment doesn't really matter," he declared.

I was stunned. "It doesn't matter?" Would he say this to a patient complaining of any other illness?

"On the drive here from New York, Mike asked me how I'd feel if someone I loved killed himself," I said. I wanted this doctor to understand how serious this was.

He turned to face Mike and asked, "Are you going to hurt yourself or anyone else?"

"No!"

The doctor glanced back at me and shrugged.

I couldn't believe this was happening.

"He's delusional!" I exclaimed. "For godsakes, he's been reading the same magazine page for four hours."

With an irritated look, the doctor asked Mike, "Who's the president of the United States?"

"That idiot George Bush."

"What day is it today?"

Other questions followed: "Can you count backwards by sevens from a hundred? What does the phrase 'Don't cry over spilled milk' mean? How about the words 'a heavy heart'?"

Mike answered each question easily. Then he explained that he was God's personal messenger and that he was indestructible.

The doctor said, "Virginia law is very specific. Unless a patient is in imminent danger to himself or others, I cannot treat him unless he voluntarily agrees to be treated." Before I could reply, he asked Mike, "Will you take medicines if I offer them to you?"

"No, I don't believe in your poisons," Mike said. "Can I leave now?"

"Yes," the doctor answered without consulting me. Mike jumped off the patient's table and hurried out the door. I started after him, but stopped and decided to try one last time to reason with the doctor.

"My son's bipolar, he's off his meds, he has a history of psychotic behavior. You've got to do something! He's sick! Help him, please!"

He said, "Your son is an adult, and while he is clearly acting odd, he has a right under the law to refuse treatment."

"Then you take him home with you tonight!" I exclaimed.

Before the doctor could respond, we both heard a commotion in the hallway. Mike was screaming at his mother because she had told him that he needed to take his medicine. "You drink beer, why not take your medicine?" she'd asked. "Alcohol is a drug."

My son was so out of control that a nurse called hospital security. I was glad. Maybe now they will medicate him, I thought. But before the security guard arrived, Mike dashed outside, cursing loudly. I went after him. Meanwhile, the doctor told my ex-wife that it was not illegal for someone to be mentally ill in Virginia. But it was illegal for him to treat them unless they consented. There was nothing he could do.

"Even if he's psychotic?" she asked.

"Yes."

Mike couldn't forcibly be treated, the doctor elaborated, until he hurt himself or someone else.

Afraid to take him home where Patti and my other children were waiting, I drove to my office, which was in a ranch-style house where I'd lived briefly after my divorce. I bolt-locked the doors and hid the keys. While Mike was taking a shower, I found his old medication, crushed a Zyprexa tablet, and spiked the milk shake that I made him. He drank it and went to bed. But I was too worried to sleep. I didn't want him slipping out, so I placed a chair in his doorway and spent the night sitting in it.

The next morning, he insisted I watch Heaven and Earth. *"You'll understand then," he said. Patti arrived and tried to reason with him, but he wouldn't listen to logic. Without warning, he'd burst into tears. "There's so much pain. I just want the pain to go away."*

Patti had already called the therapist and the psychiatrist who had treated him after his first breakdown, but neither had seen him in months. Unless Mike wanted to talk to them voluntarily, they both said, there was nothing they could do to help. "Try taking him to a different emergency room," the psychiatrist suggested.

I couldn't believe this was happening. My son was crazy and getting worse with each passing moment! Yet I couldn't get anyone to help him.

I asked Mike, "Will you go see your former psychiatrist?"

"No. You took me to the hospital and the doctor there let me go, didn't he? That means I'm fine."

Unsure what to do next, I slipped into my office and called the Fairfax County police.

"Until he breaks the law, we can't get involved," a dispatcher told me.

Patti telephoned a friend whose daughter has bipolar disorder. The friend told her, "I had the same problem when we took our daughter to the hospital. I yelled at her doctor, 'Do I have to wait for my daughter to hang herself before you'll treat her?' And he said, 'Yes. If she attempts suicide, then we can do something. Sorry, but it's the law.'"

It was 2 P.M. now, and during the past twenty-four hours I'd watched Mike slip deeper and deeper into his own delusional world. Because it was his mind that was sick, I was being told that I had to back off and leave him to face his madness alone. I had to watch as he gradually continued to lose all touch with reality.

This can't get any worse, I thought.

But I soon discovered it could.

Mike's Story: 2

What's this?" Mike asked as he flipped the spoon in his dish, causing several pink flecks floating on the milk to swirl between Frosted Flakes.

We were having cereal for lunch. I knew what the pink flecks were. I'd mixed a crushed tablet of Depakote into his bowl, but the pill's hard outer shell had refused to dissolve.

Mike recognized it. "You're trying to poison me with medicine!" he shouted. He started for the front door.

"Wait!" I yelled. "Please! Don't run away!"

"Then take me to my mom's!"

I was exhausted. Frustrated. Angry. And completely confused about what to do to help him. Mike was upset too—at me. He was mad because I had taken him from New York directly to Inova Fairfax Hospital. He was irked because I'd watched Oliver Stone's Heaven and Earth and I still didn't understand the secret message that seemed so apparent to him.

I followed him out to my car.

"Mike, you're mentally ill," I said, starting the engine. "Please, please, just take your medicine. It will help you think more clearly. Then we can go see a doctor."

"We saw a doctor yesterday," he replied, as I backed the car out of the driveway.

"But that doctor was a jerk. He should have admitted you to the hospital. He should've treated you."

Mike exploded. "STOP TRYING TO FUCKING CONTROL MY LIFE!"

"I'm your father!" I replied. "What do you expect me to do? Sit by and let you wander the streets like a crazy person?"

"Get the fuck out of my life!"

I lost my temper. I wasn't used to being spoken to like this. We began to argue. About halfway to his mother's house, Mike grabbed the car's door handle even though we were going thirty miles an hour. I hit the brakes and reached for his shoulder to keep him from leaping out. But he pulled away and jumped before the car had reached a full stop. I heard the screech of brakes behind me and expected to be rear-ended, but the vehicle swerved around us and the driver flipped me an obscene gesture as he shot by. Meanwhile, Mike had started marching down the sidewalk. I grabbed my cell phone and called my ex-wife.

"He's on his way to your house on foot," I explained, quickly recounting what had happened.

"He jumped from your car?" she asked. "Doesn't that prove he's dangerous? Maybe that's enough to force him into the hospital."

"I'll call the police and ask."

"I want to talk to him first."

I pulled into a strip mall, parked, waited.

Fifteen minutes later, my ex-wife called. "He's really angry at you and we've just had a big argument. He's really out of control. I'm scared. I think you should call the police."

I did, and by the time I reached her house, two Fairfax County police officers were parked outside. I hurried over to the squad car, figuring Mike would be handcuffed in the back seat. But he was nowhere to be seen.

The officer said my ex-wife had changed her mind. She'd refused to let them enter her house to question Mike. As the police car pulled away, I stormed up the sidewalk and pounded on her front door.

She stepped out so Mike couldn't hear us argue and explained that I'd already alienated him. What happened if he blamed her for calling the police, and the hospital turned him away again? she asked, adding, "Then he won't trust either of us. He'll run away."

"What he thinks doesn't matter," I replied. "He's out of his head."

I drove home fuming. Unsure what to do next, Patti and I called a nurse who was a close family friend. She told us about a treatment program at the Northwest Center for Community Mental Health run by Penny Hinkle. Although it was Labor Day weekend, I called Hinkle at her home, and she agreed to talk with Mike as quickly as we could arrange it.

"I'm pretty good at convincing people to join our program," she said.

I returned to my ex-wife's house, where Mike was watching television, only now he'd wrapped aluminum foil around his head so no one could read his thoughts. He wouldn't speak to me. If he weren't my son, I might have laughed at the absurdity of the moment. But he was. This was Mike.

My ex-wife promised to call Penny Hinkle, and for the first time since Mike had been turned away from the emergency room, I felt hopeful.

"It's going to be okay," my wife Patti assured me. "We'll get him into Penny's program and he'll get help."

The next morning, I was awakened by a call from the Fairfax police.

Mike was being driven to the Woodburn Center for Community Mental Health. It was less than one mile from the Inova Fairfax Hospital emergency room where I'd taken him Friday night, begging for help. The dispatcher wouldn't tell me why he had been arrested.

A tall, thin uniformed officer was waiting outside when I pulled up to the center. Police Officer Vern Albert said Mike had gotten up early at his mother's house and had walked to a nearby Starbucks coffee shop. He'd removed a glass water bottle from a shelf there, hoisted it up into the air, and *announced to the store's customers that it wouldn't break if he dropped it because he had supernatural powers. He had let the bottle fall, and it had shattered at his feet. Mike had bolted from the store. But a clerk had recognized him from their high school days together and telephoned the police. While Officer Albert and his partner were interviewing her, they received a call from their dispatcher. A burglar alarm had gone off a few blocks away.*

It was Mike. From Starbucks, he'd run into a residential area, entered the backyard of a house, climbed onto its wooden deck, and hurled a patio chair through the plate-glass door, setting off the alarm.

"Luckily, the homeowners were away for the long holiday weekend," Officer Albert said.

Ignoring the piercing sound, Mike had ducked inside the house, switched on a stereo CD player to drown out the racket, and begun rummaging through the kitchen cabinets. He'd then made his way upstairs, where he'd gone from bathroom to bathroom, turning on the taps. After checking the bedrooms and discovering no one was around, Mike had stripped and taken a bubble bath.

By this time, Albert and several other police officers had arrived outside. But they were reluctant to enter the house. Completely by chance, two sheriff's deputies in an adjoining county had been shot to death the day before while they were arresting a mentally ill man. His parents had tried repeatedly to get their son psychiatric help, but doctors had refused to treat him— just as I had been unable to get help for Mike. I later learned the gunman's father and mother had heard the exact same thing I'd been told: It wasn't against the law to be crazy, and until their son harmed either himself or others, there was nothing that could be done. The result: two dead deputies and a mentally ill man's future ruined.

Not wanting a repeat of those fatalities, Albert and the other Fairfax officers waited until a canine officer arrived. The officers burst in after releasing the dog. Mike had finished his bath and had dressed. He was stepping into a bedroom when the animal sprang. As trained, the dog locked its teeth into Mike's upper arm. Even though the dog was biting him, Mike hadn't surrendered. He'd wrestled with the officers, and it had taken five of them to finally handcuff him.

When Officer Albert finished telling me his story, I apologized: "I'm sorry my son fought with you. He's never been in any trouble like this. Thank you for not shooting him."

"He's not thinking right," Officer Albert said. He then offered me advice. "Listen, even though your son has broken into a house, unless you tell the medical personnel inside that he's threatened to kill you, they aren't going to treat him. We'll end up taking him to jail, and you don't want that to happen. You don't want him in jail in his mental condition."

"But he hasn't threatened to kill me."

Albert shot me an exasperated look.

As I stepped into the Woodburn facility, I thought, None of this would've happened if that damn doctor had helped him. Mike could've been killed, and now I'm being told this still isn't enough to get him help.

"I want my son put into the hospital," I blurted out when a psychiatric social worker appeared. "He's threatening to kill me, and I'm afraid for my life."

It was a blatant lie, and I was afraid she could tell. But thankfully, she accepted my statement without asking any questions. She left to fill out a Temporary Detention Order that would get my son admitted into a hospital psychiatric ward. While she prepared the paperwork, Officer Albert escorted me into a tiny room where his partner was watching Mike. My son was handcuffed and nervously rocking back and forth on a chair. His arm had been bandaged by paramedics where the police dog had snared him.

"Do you know who this is?" Albert asked.

"My dad," Mike replied, but he didn't look at me.

I felt physically ill, but Mike was giddy. Ignoring me, he asked Albert's partner, "Do you know about karma? You come back an animal. I'll be a bird. Dove, probably. Man, Bob Marley is great. You ever listen to rap? I eat a lot of spaghetti. My dad fixes it. He's angry at me right now."

Albert's partner looked at me, shook his head, and smirked.

Within ten minutes, the paperwork had been signed. Albert and his partner drove Mike to the psychiatric unit at Mount Vernon Hospital rather than jail. I learned the hospital was part of the same Inova Hospital network as the emergency room where Mike and I had been refused help. At this point, I was so angry that I wanted to find the doctor who'd turned us away and let him have it. The officers had told me that I couldn't go with my son in the squad car, so I was still at Woodburn. I was about to leave, when the psychiatric nurse told me that under Virginia law, I had to appear before a special justice within forty-eight hours to explain why Mike needed to be hospitalized. If I wasn't able to convince the judge that Mike was dangerous, he would be turned loose.

"How long does it take antipsychotic medicines to work?" I asked.

The nurse seemed surprised. "I'm sorry," she said, "but just because your son is being admitted into the hospital doesn't mean he's going to be treated there."

"What?" I couldn't believe I'd heard her correctly. "They won't treat him?"

"They can't give him medicine unless he agrees to take it. That's the law."

"But he thinks medicines are poison."

I was confused. What was wrong with the law? This was insanity!

I called Penny Hinkle, and she said she'd never heard from my ex-wife. That's why she'd not spoken to Mike. A short time later, I got a telephone call from an attorney whom I'd never met. She'd been appointed by the state to represent Mike at his commitment hearing. At first, I was excited because I naïvely thought she was going to help us get Mike treatment. But she said her job was to represent Mike and get him released from the hospital if that's what he wanted.

"But he's not thinking clearly!" I exclaimed. "He just broke into a house. He doesn't know what's best for him. I'm his father, for godsakes!"

The attorney had never met Mike. She didn't know anything about his medical past, our relationship, or our family. But she was now stepping in to defend his civil rights and to protect his best interests.

"But you don't love him," I said. "I do."

"I understand, but the court wants someone impartial to make sure his civil rights are protected."

"I'm not impartial," I replied. "I want him treated. I want him sane. What happens after the hearing? What happens if you get him out of the hospital and he's not treated?" I didn't give her time to reply. "I'll tell you what happens: You'll go on with your life and forget about him. But not me. I'll still be here trying to get him help. Please help me get him treatment."

"I'm a lawyer, not a doctor," she replied. "If he doesn't want to stay in the hospital, then it's my job to get him out."

I continued my harangue, and she promised to talk to Mike. An hour later, she telephoned and said he had agreed to voluntarily commit himself. I called our family attorney, Jay Myerson, and he told me that Mike's decision was great news, because in spite of everything that Mike had done, it still would have been difficult for us to have forcibly committed him against his will.

"Even though he broke into a house to take a bubble bath?" I asked incredulously.

"Yes," Myerson replied. He then warned me that this was far from over. The hospital could hold Mike a maximum of only five days—if that long. After that Mike could check himself out anytime, Myerson explained, because he was a voluntary patient.

Myerson added that the commitment hearing would take less than five minutes. "It's routine paper signing."

Routine? Five minutes! Mike's life!

I drove to Mount Vernon Hospital that night to visit Mike in the psychiatric ward, and at one point, when he stepped away from the visiting room to use the bathroom, a friendly nurse hurried over. "Twenty years ago, you could get someone committed into a mental hospital just by accusing them of being crazy," she told me. "But now the law has swung so far the other way that you can't get them help even though you know they will thank you later."

In a burst of pent-up emotion, I confessed, "Mike never threatened to kill me!"

"So you lied. Big deal." She sighed. "I've told parents to wait outside the hospital's front entrance and as soon as their child is discharged, to accuse them of threatening their lives so they can be arrested and brought right back in here. You've got to do what you've got to do when you are a parent to save your child."

The next morning, there were three other sets of parents and an elderly mother waiting for commitment hearings. I'd been warned that the special judge wanted to finish quickly, because he was allowed to eat breakfast free in the hospital dining room—it was one of the perks of his job—but the cafeteria stopped serving breakfast in less than an hour.

The hearing was held in a classroom on the same floor as the locked mental ward. Children's drawings of stick figures decorated the walls. The special judge was a private attorney who did these hearings as a side job. He had a reputation for interpreting the law strictly, which meant that he released patients who were not visibly a danger to themselves or anyone else, even if they were clearly psychotic.

"Why are you voluntarily committing yourself?" the judge asked Mike when he was brought into the hearing.

"Because I'm having a relapse and my parents want me somewhere safe," he replied.

I was looking at Mike, but he avoided eye contact. I was surprised at how calm and lucid he was. Thankfully, he had voluntarily taken Zyprexa and Depakote tablets after he had been admitted into the unit, and he'd taken additional medication this morning.

"Does anyone object to this voluntary commitment?" the special justice asked. He was directing his question to Mike's court-appointed attorney. She shook her head.

"I do!" I said.

My outburst surprised everyone, including Mike.

"I understand there is nothing I can do legally to stop you from releasing my son in five days," I said, reading a prepared statement that I'd written the night before. "But my son told me last night that as soon as he is released, he will stop taking medicine and not cooperate in any treatment program." Suddenly, I couldn't continue. My voice cracked, tears welled. My display of emotion seemed to make everyone in the room uncomfortable. The special justice explained that his hands were tied by Virginia law. "If your son wants to leave and is not a danger to himself or others, then he will be allowed to go," he said.

I replied, "My lawyer has told me that. But please, I'm speaking to you not as a judge, but as one father to another father. Please don't release my son until he is mentally stable."

In a compassionate gesture, the justice asked Mike if he had heard what I'd said. Mike said he had. Then it was over. Mike was escorted back to the mental ward.

I returned eight hours later, when visiting hours began. It was my birthday. I was fifty-one years old, but Patti and our children had decided to postpone the celebration. We'd been too busy scrambling to arrange for Mike to go directly from the hospital into Penny Hinkle's treatment program. She'd told us that if Mike continued to take his medicine while he was in the hospital, there was a good chance that he'd agree to enter her program voluntarily so she could teach him how to manage his mental illness. But if he didn't take his medicine voluntarily and he was released from Mount Vernon before the drugs could help alleviate his symptoms, in her words, "He'll probably have another episode."

Mike seemed happy to see me when he was brought into the visiting room, in part because I was holding a box of Kentucky Fried Chicken. I knew he wouldn't like hospital food. When he sat down at a table across from me, he handed me a sheet of paper. It was a hand-drawn birthday card. He'd re-

membered. He also had written down several past events that we'd done together. That list was his present to me. "Good Times with Dad and Me" was scribbled across the page. He began reading the events out loud.

"Remember when I fell off the cliff?" he asked.

I did. We had been fishing in the Black Hills of South Dakota, where his grandparents lived. But five-year-olds have no patience, and Mike had wandered too close to a ravine. The dirt at the edge gave way and he tumbled one-third of the way down the embankment before he grabbed a bush and clung on, hollering for help, his chest scraped and bleeding. I'd made my way down to him, but he wouldn't let go of the bush until I'd promised that I'd protect him. Over the years, the story had grown. The gully had become a hundred-foot-high cliff. In sixth grade, he'd written an essay about how I'd saved his life by climbing down to rescue him. That was when he was little and I was still his hero.

After he finished his fried chicken, we talked about happier times. Neither of us mentioned the morning commitment hearing or how he had told me only a few days ago to stay the fuck out of his life.

When it was time for me to leave, we hugged. I'd been warned by a nurse on his ward that mentally ill patients who go off their medicines often become alcohol and drug abusers. Somehow both helped them cope. The nurses called it "self-medication." Other bipolar patients became so depressed that they killed themselves to escape the pain. As I drove home that night, I told myself: Not my son. Not Mike!

The next morning, the hospital psychiatrist, Dr. James Dee, called with disturbing news. A pill had been found on the floor in Mike's room. Apparently, Mike had spit it out and tried to hide it. Mike had told Dr. Dee that medicines were poison.

When I visited Mike that night, I pleaded with him to take his medicines. He ignored me and asked me instead why his arm was bandaged.

"Don't you remember?" I asked. "The police dog bit you."

"I thought it was just a bad dream. Sometimes I think all of this is a *dream—even you sitting here now. I keep waiting to wake up and find my-self back in New York. I can't tell anymore what is real or what I'm dream-ing. Am I dreaming now, or are you really here?"*

I reached over and touched his hand. "This is real. You're in the hospital. Take your medicines."

The next morning, Dr. Dee called again. Mike had agreed to take his pills after I'd gone last night. Mike had told him that he wanted to get better, but now we had a new problem. Dr. Dee said our insurance company had started pressuring the hospital to release Mike sometime today. According to the company's graphs and charts, three to four days should be enough for a patient to become stable enough for discharge. I was furious. I immediately called the insurance company, but the person who answered my call was both unrelenting and unsympathetic.

"If your son isn't going to hurt you or someone else, he doesn't need to be in a locked mental ward," the woman explained. "He can recover at home, and the law requires that he be held in the least restrictive environment possible."

"That's unacceptable!" I replied. And then I did something that I had never done before in my career. I told the woman that I was a former re-porter with the Washington Post, and if the insurance company pushed Mike out of the hospital before he was mentally stable, I'd write about it. It was a threat and I meant it to be. It was a violation of journalistic ethics. But I didn't care. I mentioned that I knew CBS investigative reporter Mike Wallace of 60 Minutes. I would call him, too. She got my point.

Dr. Dee telephoned me a few hours later and said the insurance com-pany had backed off. Mike could stay until he said it was okay for him to be discharged. That night, I learned how lucky I was. A young girl who'd stabbed herself in the neck with a pencil during a psychotic breakdown had been discharged that afternoon after two days in the hospital. After they drove her home, she told her parents that she wanted to go on a walk. Now she was missing. Her parents were frantic.

My attorney friend Jay Myerson called me the next day with a suggestion. "If someone broke into my house," he said, "I'd want someone to tell me they were sorry." He also thought there would be less of a chance that the homeowners would demand vengeance if I personally apologized. "In our litigious society, it would not only be the right thing to do, but a smart one."

I was truly sorry. And embarrassed. And nervous when I went to see the homeowners later that same day. They lived about a half mile from the Starbucks where Mike had dropped a bottle of water on the floor. I was afraid that they might not want to talk to me if I called them on the telephone, so I arrived unannounced. There was a sports car parked outside a two-car garage. The landscaping around the two-level colonial had been done meticulously. This could have been any upper-middle-class home in any comfortable suburb.

A teenager answered the bell, and I asked to speak to his father. The man who next appeared was tall, fit, and dressed in a polo shirt, khakis, and loafers. He was a decade younger than I.

"My son broke into your house," I stammered.

He hesitated, but then invited me inside. His wife joined us in their family room. She forced a smile. I noticed a sheet of plywood where the patio-door glass had been. It was where Mike had broken inside.

"I want to apologize," I said. I told them how Mike had been attending college in Brooklyn when his illness had first surfaced. My voice cracked. Tears welled in my eyes. I paused to bring myself under control.

"I can't imagine how I'd feel if it were my son," the man said sympathetically.

But his wife seemed suspicious. Where was Mike now? Why had he chosen their house? What had he said about the break-in?

She told me that Mike had flipped over the photographs of their children on the fireplace mantel, placing them facedown. Why? He'd opened a bottle of expensive liquor and drunk a glass. Why? He'd dropped an heirloom dish *that she said had been handed down through her family. Why? The carpet was wet upstairs, and when she'd bent down to examine it, she was certain that she'd smelled urine.*

"He peed on our carpet," she said tersely.

Continuing, she said the bedspread in the master bedroom had been damp from Mike sitting on it after his bubble bath. She'd tossed it in the trash. Mike had forgotten to turn off the spigots, and water had overflowed onto the hardwood floors. Their insurance agent had already inspected the damage and issued them a check to replace—not clean, but replace—all their upstairs carpet and to remove and replace the hardwood floors. It seemed extreme to me, but I kept silent.

I couldn't answer most of her "whys." My son had been psychotic. How do you explain the actions of a mentally ill person? But I apologized again, and then again. But she wasn't finished. What if Mike came back? She said she was frightened for her teenage daughter. Mike had taken his bubble bath in the bathroom that the girl used. Her daughter was scared, too. The woman said her family had loved this house. It had been their dream home. Now none of them felt safe in it. Whenever she heard a noise, she wondered: Is someone breaking in? Is it a crazed person?

I told her I had two daughters. I told her that I understood why she was afraid. But I also reminded her—as gently as I could—that Mike had not been himself, he'd been psychotic. He had never harmed anyone.

"He's a great kid. Really, he is."

Her husband appeared sympathetic. But not her. She asked me for a photograph of Mike so she'd be able to recognize him if he ever came near the house again. Her husband added that he'd already spoken to an attorney about suing Mike. He'd mentioned it to a lawyer while playing golf. But because Mike was legally on his own and didn't have any money, the attorney had warned him that there wasn't much point—unless they could find a reason to sue his mother and me.

When I got ready to leave, the husband said, "Your son is lucky we weren't home." He explained that he had a gun. "What would you have done if you woke up and found a crazy man inside your kitchen?" he asked. Without waiting for my reply, he said, "I would have shot your son."

I typed up notes about our conversation after I got home. Somehow writing it down helped. I also decided to write the couple a letter. I reminded them that Mike still didn't know their names, that he'd chosen their house at random, that he was getting help in the hospital and was now taking his medicine. I explained he had no history of violence and he would not be living anywhere near them after he was released. I asked them to forgive him and added that as soon as he was released from the hospital, he would begin attending a day treatment program so he could learn how to cope with his mental illness.

Mike stayed in the hospital for fourteen days. A nurse told me that she couldn't remember when a bipolar patient had been allowed to remain in the mental ward for that long. Of course, Mike was eager to get home. All of us wanted him home too, but Penny Hinkle urged us to reconsider our plans. She suggested that we refuse to pick Mike up at the hospital when he was discharged. She said we needed to declare him indigent. That would force the hospital to send him by taxi to a county-run homeless shelter. Fairfax County would then have to provide Mike with his expensive antipsychotic medicines and a place to live, and help him find a job after he completed Hinkle's treatment program. If either his mother or I took him into our homes, he'd be put at the end of the line when it came to getting county-provided services. And it was a very, very long line.

Dr. Dee gave us completely different advice. He was afraid Mike would stop taking his medication and run away to New York City if we refused to let him move back home. My ex-wife said she couldn't risk that. She was also afraid that Hinkle's plan would send Mike the wrong message: that we didn't care. Although I trusted Hinkle, I agreed with my ex-wife. We couldn't risk putting Mike into a homeless shelter.

On the morning when he was discharged, I met Mike at the hospital and we stopped at a restaurant for lunch. He was still confused about everything that had happened. He was still having trouble deciding what was real and what was imaginary. The drugs that he was taking were still making him feel sluggish. He told me that he was having trouble concentrating. After we finished eating, I drove him to his mother's house. He had decided that he wanted to live with her for a while. I went to my office, where piles of paperwork were stacked up. But now I was the one who was having trouble focusing. All I could think about was Mike. I fought the urge to call and check on him. I was afraid that he was going to wander off.

A few days later the phone rang and I checked the caller ID. It was the Fairfax County police. As I reached for it, I noticed my hand was trembling.

"Mr. Earley," a woman said, "I'm Detective V. O. Armel of the Reston substation. I'm calling to tell you two felony warrants have been issued for your son's arrest."

I didn't understand. "Is he okay?" I asked. "What's he done?"

"These charges are from the home break-in," Detective Armel explained. Mike was being charged with violating Virginia Sec. 18.2-137 (intentionally destroying, defacing, and damaging property in excess of $100) and Sec. 18.2-91 (breaking and entering in the daytime with the intent to commit larceny). Both carried up to $10,000 in fines, as well as five-year prison sentences.

Prison. Five years.

I was stunned. Officer Albert had told me that the county probably wouldn't file any criminal charges against Mike, because he was obviously out of his mind at the time. "But Mike's mentally ill," I stammered. "He's in a day treatment program right now. He didn't know what he was doing when he broke into that house! What's the point of prosecuting him?"

"I understand that he's in a treatment program," Detective Armel replied, "and that's good, but I just got off the phone with the Fairfax County commonwealth attorney's office, and the prosecutor handling this case said that just because your son is mentally ill doesn't mean he can't be charged with breaking the law."

"But why?" I repeated. "Why are you doing this now?"

*"The woman who owns the house has signed a complaint against him,"
she said. "You need to bring him into the station so we can book him, otherwise we'll have to send officers to get him."*

I was still in shock.

*"You'll need to hire an attorney," she continued. Then she added, "The
fact your son was arrested inside the house is going to make it difficult for
him to claim he's innocent."*

*Because Mike was attending a day treatment program, Detective Armel
was willing to recommend that he be released into our custody. This way, he
could continue in the program rather than be stuck in jail until his case was
heard. Detective Armel was telling me this on a Friday afternoon. She suggested that I bring Mike into the jail on Monday morning.*

*I had no idea how Mike would react to being accused of two felonies—or
if he would even understand how they threatened his future. He still acted
much like a zombie. Dr. Dee had warned us that it might take weeks for Mike
to adjust to the powerful antipsychotic medication that he was being given.
The young man whom I saw daily didn't seem like my son. The face was the
same, but his expression was blank, his brown eyes hollow, his voice robotic.
He'd regressed to a vocabulary that consisted of three words: yes, no, okay.*

"Are you hungry?"

"No."

"It's time for bed."

"Okay."

*Having been betrayed by his own mind, Mike had lost his confidence in
making decisions. He second-guessed himself. "What do you think I should
do?" he asked constantly.*

*I telephoned Jay Myerson and asked if he would represent Mike. But
Myerson begged off. If Mike was convicted, it could damage our friendship,
he said. Just the same, he offered advice. "Usually, the prosecutor's office
will agree to drop one felony charge if a defendant will plead guilty to the*

second charge to avoid a trial." As a former newspaper reporter, I knew that only a handful of criminal cases ever went to trial. Most were settled through plea negotiations worked out in advance. But I didn't want to assume anything, so I asked, "What happens if Mike pleads guilty to one felony count?"

After a long pause, Myerson explained that Mike would probably not be sentenced to prison, because this was his first arrest. Instead, he would be placed on a year of probation and ordered to continue getting psychiatric treatment. That was it. Only it really wasn't so simple. Continuing, Myerson said convicted felons lose many of their civil rights. They can't vote, can't run for a political office, can't own a firearm or serve in the military. Mike could be ordered to surrender his driver's license. But the most frightening punishment was none of that. It was the impact that a felony conviction would have on Mike's future employment. Few companies were willing to hire convicted felons, and Mike would be automatically barred from entering a number of professions, including the career that he had just spent four years in college getting ready to enter. If Mike pleaded guilty to both or even one felony, he'd never be able to work in his chosen field. Ever.

"Can you expunge a felony?" I asked.

It was unlikely, Myerson replied.

I couldn't sleep Friday night. I lost my appetite. When I was around Mike on Saturday, I pretended to be confident, optimistic. But all I could think about was Monday and Mike's being locked in jail, Mike's being forced to plead guilty to a felony, Mike's being barred from a career that he hoped to enter. It all felt so damn unfair.

Patti tried to reassure me. Mike would be booked and released Monday morning, just as Detective Armel had promised, she said. He would not be thrown in jail. Somehow, we would find a way to get the two felony charges filed against him reduced. The doctors would be able to help Mike get his bipolar disorder symptoms under control. He'd live a normal life.

"You've got to remember this is horrible for us," she said, "but it's routine

for the police and for the doctors. They've seen all this before. Mike is not the first to go through this."

As promised, Detective Armel was waiting when Mike and I reported to the jail. She handcuffed him and they disappeared behind a thick steel door. A half hour later, she brought him back into the lobby.

As we walked to the county jail's parking lot, I thought: Patti was right. It is all routine to them. It is business as usual. And somehow that made it even more troubling.

I t was then that I first got the idea for this book. I began contacting jails in Los Angeles, New York City, Baltimore, Washington, D.C., Chicago, and Miami, thinking that I'd choose the facility that would be the most representative and also give me the most unrestricted access. Taking care of Mike was paramount, but the wheels of justice move slowly, and I knew there would be times during the coming weeks and months when I could be away. One person in the mental health grapevine particularly urged me to contact Judge Steven Leifman in Miami. I'd heard of Leifman. Since taking the bench, he had earned a national reputation as a reformer.

It was Leifman who convinced me to go to Miami. The chief psychiatrist at the Miami-Dade County jail, Dr. Joseph Poitier, would be expecting my call.

PART ONE

THE NINTH FLOOR

If you ask most people today where the mentally ill are in our society, they will tell you they're in state mental hospitals. They're wrong. . . . They are in our jails and prisons.

—*Judge Steven Leifman*
Eleventh Judicial Circuit
Miami, Florida

C h a p t e r   1

The Miami-Dade County Pretrial Detention Center, which is the official name of the city's main jail, sits behind the Richard E. Gerstein Justice Building, a twelve-story, rectangular courthouse in a poor Miami neighborhood known as Overtown. A better description would have been "*overlooked* town." It is miles away from the city's famous beaches, cruise ships, nightlife, and multimillion-dollar Spanish-style mansions.

The courthouse is the hub of Florida's Eleventh Judicial Circuit. The state has twenty circuits, and this is its largest. The judges here—there are 112 of them—dispense justice for a population of 2 million within a 2,000-square-mile area. In an average year, some 800,000 criminal cases are heard in the Gerstein courthouse, including disputed traffic tickets. That makes the Eleventh Circuit the fourth-largest trial court in the nation.

The jail is directly across a narrow street from the courthouse and is two stories shorter. In Miami, avenues run north and south, and streets go east and west. The city uses numbers to identify addresses in both directions. Because of this, the jail sits at the corner of Thirteenth Avenue and Thirteenth Street. Twice unlucky.

From the sky, the jail resembles a giant Y. Three wings extend from its center core. In typical bureaucratic fashion, the wings are identified only by letters. "A wing" points southeast, "B wing" extends southwest, and "C wing" looks north. A faded pink concrete wall topped by razor wire encircles all the wings except at the jail's front.

Dr. Joseph Poitier, the center's chief psychiatrist, was waiting for me outside the entrance. He was wearing dark slacks, a white long-sleeved shirt, a loose tie, and a maroon sweater-vest. A pleasant-looking man at a husky six feet, two inches tall, he had just turned fifty. I would quickly come to appreciate his kind, unassuming manner and insightful comments.

Leading me inside, he suggested we begin by taking a quick tour. A television was hanging from the lobby ceiling, supposedly to display rules for visitors. But someone had switched the channel to Telemundo. There was no carpet on the white tile floor to muffle the sound, and since the TV's volume had been ratcheted up, visitors had to shout to be heard.

According to a brass plaque bolted onto the red brick walls, the facility had been completed and dedicated in 1960. Though clean, it showed its age, both in design and wear. A poster on the opposite wall announced that inmates would be charged a $2-per-day "subsistence" fee to help defray the cost of their imprisonment. There were also extra charges if they needed to see a doctor ($5) or a nurse ($3). No one would be released until the fees were paid, the sign warned. But Dr. Poitier told me those charges didn't apply to psychotic prisoners.

Two correctional officers were sitting in the lobby's control booth behind bullet-resistant glass. I'd spent enough time in prisons to know that you didn't refer to them as "guards." That was an insult. They were correctional officers. A nearby poster spelled out the department's Code of Professional Conduct.

Our mission is to provide caring and compassionate services to those entrusted to our care and to protect the public we serve.

There was only one doorway from the lobby into the jail's interior. It was protected by a gate made of reinforced steel bars wrapped with a wire mesh so thick that it was nearly impossible to peer through. The gate had been painted gunmetal gray so many times that it was now coated with a thick shell. It opened only when an officer in the control booth pushed a button, causing a warning buzzer to sound. Then there was a loud *snap*— as the electronic deadbolt drew back—followed by a *pop*, which meant the door was ready to be tugged open. Dr. Poitier pulled the gate toward us, and we slipped into a narrow alcove. The gate slammed shut.

A second gate stood about twenty feet in front of us. These two barriers had been designed so they could never be opened at the same time—a precaution that guaranteed there would always be at least one gate between the "free world" and inmates. In an average year, 130,000 people were booked into the jail. But they didn't come inside through the lobby as we had. They were brought in handcuffs through a heavily guarded door at the back of the facility. Most prisoners didn't stay long. They were freed after bail was posted. Those who couldn't bond out were locked up until their cases were heard. Depending on the charges, that could take months. If an inmate was found guilty, he could serve his sentence in the jail, but only if it was for a year or less. Anything longer was supposed to earn the prisoner a trip to a state prison. But there were delaying tactics defense attorneys could use to keep a client in Miami so he could remain close to his home and avoid a distant prison. Some had stayed as long as five years here.

Officially, the facility had enough beds for 1,712 prisoners. But overcrowding was a common problem. Whenever that happened, inmates were issued mattresses and slept on the floor. Miami had four other jails, including a 375-bed women's detention center. On an average day, 7,000 prisoners were incarcerated in Miami-Dade County, making its jails the fourth-largest system in the nation.

The main jail that I had just entered was considered the most dangerous and the toughest. Fistfights between inmates were common, and so
were reports of beatings at the hands of the correctional staff. In 1996,
Miami Herald reporter Sydney P. Freedberg investigated brutality complaints and concluded that

> Brute force is a way of life in the Miami jail. Physical violence
> is used to keep order and . . . to punish inmates. . . . Violence be-
> hind jail walls is overlooked, downplayed, misreported and under-
> investigated. And the magnitude of the problem is immeasurable.

Even so, no correctional officer had ever been prosecuted. The un-
written "code of silence"—which forbids an officer to squeal on his
peers—makes it nearly impossible for prosecutors to punish the accused. That hadn't stopped prisoners from filing civil lawsuits. The largest payment was $500,000, awarded to an inmate who had been knocked
out by officers. When he woke up, he was on a hospital respirator with
a broken nose, a fractured eye, cracked ribs, dislocated shoulders, and
lungs filled with fluid.

The first floor held a booking area, a property room, an employee
cafeteria, an inmate dental office, and a medical screening room. A
chapel was located on the second floor near a courtroom where prisoners were arraigned each morning via a closed-circuit television system.
This allowed the judge to sit in his chamber across the street in the
courthouse and talk to prisoners over a microphone. Each new prisoner
was evaluated according to a point system that was based on his criminal record, his history of violence, and the seriousness of the charge filed
against him. The worst are issued bright-red jumpsuits and locked in
single-man cells.

The jail's "general population" inmates live on the third, fourth, fifth,
and sixth floors, and when we reached those levels, Dr. Poitier's pace

quickened. One of the reasons the jail has such a violent history is its antiquated design. Newer jails are built so officers can look into cells from a central location and see everything that is happening. But in Miami, inmates are locked in huge group cells, some holding as many as fifty men. These units sit back-to-back in the center of the A, B, and C wings. All the cells look out at the wing's exterior walls. This design permits sunlight to shine directly into them and air to circulate through the open windows. But it also makes it impossible for the officers on duty to see into the cells unless they patrol up and down the narrow corridor between the cell fronts and exterior walls. Most correctional officers don't. Instead, they sit in a control booth in the center of the Y where the three wings come together. From this vantage site, all they can actually see is the empty walkway that passes in front of the cells.

As Dr. Poitier and I hurried down a cell block, prisoners rushed toward the bars from the darkness, like fish rising suddenly from the murky waters of a lake.

"Hey, doc," one called.

"Hey, hey, hey. Come here! Come here!"

"Got a minute?"

We didn't stop. Otherwise, Dr. Poitier would have been stuck for hours talking to inmates who had nothing else to do to pass their time. Some prisoners had hung towels across the bars, making it impossible to look inside. Others had draped sheets in front of their bunks. The curtains hide whatever is happening. A Miami inmate was once gang-raped for three days in a cell before officers were tipped off by another prisoner and rescued him.

To avoid going into the cells, officers rely on a houseman. They are prisoners—usually the toughest in a cell—who've been chosen to keep order. The houseman decides who sleeps in what bunks and what cleaning chores each inmate performs. It's an old custom that is prone to abuse. Housemen frequently demand payment—in the form of commissary supplies or sexual favors—from weaker prisoners for such basic privileges as making a telephone call.

The seventh floor houses the administration offices. The eighth and tenth are where geriatric inmates and mentally ill prisoners who are "compliant" live. That means they are voluntarily taking their antipsychotic medication and are not considered suicidal.

On an average day, seven hundred inmates in the Miami jail system are taking antipsychotic drugs. Three hundred of them are housed in the main jail, and the most dangerous and unpredictable of those are locked on the ninth floor. Officially, it is known as the jail's "primary psychiatric unit." But it has a bleaker nickname. It's called "the forgotten floor," a cell block that is home to the lowest of the low.

It was our next stop.

Chapter 2

J ust like every other floor in the jail, the ninth has three wings. But C cell block is where the "suicide cells" are located, and it has its own unique configuration. Ten years earlier, its huge group cells were ripped out and new ones were built along its exterior walls. The traditional steel bars were replaced with shatter-resistant glass fronts.

I stood at C wing's entrance and looked inside.

There are ten cells on the right side of C wing. Nine on its left. They face each other. The center is open and is where the ninth-floor staff works. Because the cells now line the outer walls and have clear fronts, correctional officers can pace up and down the center and see into them. With little else to do, the inmates also spend hours standing at the front of their cells, peering out. The keepers and the kept, each watching the other.

I took a deep breath.

The air in C wing stinks. It is a putrefied scent, a blending of urine, expectorant, perspiration, excrement, blood, flatulence, and dried and discarded jailhouse food. When the jail's antiquated air conditioning breaks down during the summer, which it often does, some officers claim C wing's pink walls actually sweat. It's decades of filth and grime bubbling up, rising through coats of paint.

I listened.

C wing is noisy. Toilets flushed. Prisoners hacked, coughed, groaned, spat, sang. Correctional officers chattered, laughed, yelled. A jail trusty kicked a silver mop bucket, sending it sliding across the concrete, emitting a grating sound. Leg chains click-clacked against the hard surface as new prisoners were brought inside for processing. These are traditional sounds. Intermingled with them were strange asylum noises. A prisoner sobbed, another babbled at an unseen tormentor.

"Arrrghhhhh," an inmate yelled.

Thud, thud, thud. Then faster. Thudthudthud. Then louder. THUD. THUD. THUD. He was banging his forehead against a glass cell front.

"I ain't crazy!" he shouted.

"Then stop acting like you is," an officer called back.

I tried to take mental photographs so I could remember what I was seeing and thinking. A newly arrived prisoner was ordered to strip where he was standing in the center corridor. Inmates in the cells gawked at him. Once naked, he shielded himself with his hands while his clothing was stuffed into a brown paper bag. He was issued a white jumpsuit made of paper and led to a cell. Other prisoners in C wing were dressed in Ferguson gowns. They were navy blue, quilted safety smocks sewn of nylon backpack material that was difficult to shred and too bulky to tie into knots or to be used as a rope. The inmates wearing them looked as if they were about to umpire baseball games.

Five correctional officers were on duty. Three women, two men. They would later tell me that the jail hadn't offered them any special training about how to handle the mentally ill. Nor were they paid extra for working in C wing. Several of them were convinced they had been assigned to the ninth floor as punishment. "This is a dead end for them [the inmates] and for us," an officer later complained.

The five officers on duty were responsible for making certain none of the prisoners harmed or killed himself. Four of the officers were assigned to watch specific cells. Every fifteen minutes, they would sign a log, indicating that they had personally observed the inmates under their care and that none of them was in any danger.

There was a workstation in the middle of C wing that was U-shaped and rose chest-high. It was where the officers kept their supplies: extra handcuffs, bureaucratic forms, and boxes of disposable plastic gloves they were required to wear whenever they came into contact with an inmate. Directly behind the workstation was a narrow room that contained several desks. It had glass walls. The psychiatric social workers and nurses worked inside this cubicle and could be seen easily by the inmates whose exterior-wall cells encircled them. A recent salary study had revealed that nurses on the ninth floor earned an average of $2,000 per year less than their counterparts in Miami hospitals. That was because many of the workers on C wing were recent immigrants who had been trained in foreign schools. Most of the nurses and the correctional officers assigned to the ninth floor were women, and that caused specific problems. Inmates frequently masturbated in front of them. Jail officials had asked the state's attorney's office to prosecute prisoners for doing this. But state prosecutors didn't think the crime was worth pursuing. It was an occupational hazard.

The inmates in C wing were assigned cells based on how suicidal they were. The first six cells on the right wall were reserved for those who were the most intent on killing themselves. But a prisoner was not automatically put into a cell by himself just because he said he was suicidal. C wing was far too crowded for that. Two and sometimes three suicidal inmates were bunched together in a cell. Only inmates who had actually attempted to take their own life or had attacked other prisoners or correctional officers were rewarded with one-man cells.

Every inmate in C wing was supposed to wear either his own street clothes, a paper jumpsuit, or a Ferguson gown. But the suicidal prisoners in the first six cells were usually kept naked. This was just one of several regulations that were bent or ignored on the ninth floor. Its officers, I would learn, believed they knew more about how to handle psychotic prisoners than the jail's administrators. Most supervisors had never worked on the ninth floor, and none visited C wing during my stay there.

The first six "suicide" cells each contained a combination sink and stainless-steel commode. They also held a bright-blue hard-plastic bed that was built so prisoners could be strapped spread-eagled onto it. There were no sheets in these cells, no blankets, no pillows, no other creature comforts. There were no televisions, radios, magazines, books, or writing materials. A prisoner had nothing to do except sleep or watch the world outside the cell.

The remaining thirteen cells in C wing each contained two steel bunks that were bolted onto the walls. Some had thin mattresses, sheets, and wool blankets. These cells had been built to hold two inmates, but on most days they held at least three and sometimes four prisoners crowded inside them. In those instances, two inmates claimed the bunks. The others sat and slept on the floor.

The temperature inside C wing was kept chilly because of a design flaw. C wing's air vents were located at the rear of each cell along the exterior walls. Cool air was supposed to be blown across the cells into the center of the wing. Tiny holes had been punched into the front of each cell front near the ceiling so the air could slip through. But after several inmates threw urine and feces through these airholes at employees, the openings were sealed. This trapped the frigid air inside, causing temperatures to dip into the low fifties in the cells. But even before these holes were closed, the cells had been kept colder than anywhere else in the building. Administrators claimed the freezing temperature reduced the spread of germs. But there was another reason. It was done to keep inmates huddled under their blankets. "That way they're too damn cold to cause any trouble," an officer chuckled.

Dr. Poitier began most mornings by conducting rounds. Naomi Auerbach, a psychiatric social worker, and Evelyn Johnson, the head nurse on the ninth floor, usually joined him. A corrections officer was supposed to be part of the group, but none of them ever walked alongside Dr. Poitier. If he needed their help, he would call out to one of them.

Dr. Poitier always began at cell number one and moved counterclockwise through C wing. Because the cell fronts were thick glass and the doors were made of solid steel, Dr. Poitier had to unbolt the food slot—a rectangular opening used to pass meals through to inmates—in order to speak to the men. He would lean down in front of the cutout in order to hear what the inmates were saying. There was no privacy.

Dr. Poitier always addressed prisoners as "Mr." because he wanted to show them respect. He read their surnames either from a computer printout that he received each morning and carried with him, or from an 8-by-10-inch sheet of white paper that the officers had taped to the front of the cell. These ID papers displayed a photograph of each inmate in a cell and listed his name, date of birth, and jail case number. Jail officials had been warned that the ID sheets violated federal privacy regulations as spelled out under the Health Insurance Portability and Accountability Act of 1996, better known as HIPAA. But no one inside the jail had come up with a better way to keep track of inmates, and until they did, the sheets would continue to be stuck on the cell fronts for anyone to read.

"How you feeling today, Mr. Boreman?" Dr. Poitier asked the prisoner in cell one.

The thirty-two-year-old nude man locked inside ignored him. He'd been diagnosed with schizophrenia.

"You still having suicidal thoughts?"

Again there was no response.

"Will you take medicine today if I prescribe it for you, Mr. Boreman?"

The prisoner glared at Dr. Poitier and snapped, "I've already answered that damn question seventeen times: No, no, no, no, no, no, no—"

Dr. Poitier shut the food slot and moved on, leaving Mr. Boreman to continue chanting. When he reached the eighteenth "No," he stopped.

Mr. Boreman was a "regular." Since Dr. Poitier had become the jail's chief psychiatrist in 1993, he'd seen Mr. Boreman more than a dozen times. He'd been booked into jail this time by a Miami policeman who'd made what is known as a "mercy arrest." The cop had wanted to get Mr. Boreman off the street for his own safety, because he was about to be beaten by the owner of a sidewalk café in Miami's Little Havana neighborhood. Mr. Boreman had started dropping by the café at dinnertime. Because he was homeless, he never had money to buy anything. But he would sit in the sidewalk café and scream profanities at diners. The owner had complained numerous times, and the police had always ordered Mr. Boreman to move along. But after several nights of losing customers, the restaurateur had purchased a baseball bat and had threatened to use it on his unwanted guest. The police had arrested Mr. Boreman for trespassing, and he was supposed to be released from jail within twenty-four hours, but this morning, when a female officer had come to turn him loose, Mr. Boreman had sucker-punched her. Now he'd been charged with felony assault and had become so despondent that he had tried to kill himself.

"Most mentally ill inmates do stupid things, not bad things," Dr. Poitier explained as we walked to the next cell. "The police officer who arrested him thought he was doing him a favor, but now he's facing a very serious felony charge. He's a perfect example of why the mentally ill should not be put in jail. He needs help for his mental illness, and he won't get it in here."

Cell two contained another naked prisoner. He was rocking on his haunches in a corner near the commode. As soon as Dr. Poitier opened the food slot, a repugnant odor caused him and the rest of us to reel back. It smelled like human excrement and rotting garbage, but the cell was empty of both. It was the inmate who stank. He was mentally ill and an alcoholic, Dr. Poitier said. The prisoner was going through detoxification.

"How old are you?" Dr. Poitier asked in Spanish.

"*Veinte,*" the shaking inmate replied. Nurse Johnson and social worker Auerbach exchanged shocked glances. He looked much older than twenty. They checked the ID paper taped to the cell front. It listed the man's age as thirty-six.

"Do you know what day it is?"

"*Sábado,*" he answered. But it was not Saturday. It was Tuesday.

Dr. Poitier shut the food slot.

"We get a lot of inmates in here who are both mentally ill and ad-dicted to either drugs or alcohol," he explained.

"Bipolars love cocaine," Auerbach volunteered. "Schizophrenics tend to use more hallucinatory drugs. And nearly all of them smoke. The nicotine in cigarettes seems to calm their brains."

Dr. Poitier continued on. Each cell held its own story. The prisoner in cell six, who had been banging his head against the glass so hard that he now had a huge lump on it, complained that he'd been in jail for ninety days without shoes and his feet hurt. A prisoner in that same cell whispered through the slot that he hadn't been able to urinate since he'd been arrested some forty-eight hours earlier. "I can't pee with all of these people watching."

In cell seven, Dr. Poitier found an inmate who had been on C wing the week before but had seemed stable enough to be transferred to a group cell on the jail's fourth floor.

"Why are you back here?" Dr. Poitier asked.

The officers on that floor had forgotten to give him his antipsychotic medicine, so he had relapsed and had tried to hurt himself.

There were four prisoners locked in cell number eight, and when we reached it, Dr. Poitier became concerned because one of them was lying on the floor next to the toilet without moving. Another prisoner was peeing, and it was splashing onto the prone man. Dr. Poitier asked one of the other inmates inside the cell to jostle the prisoner. He was shoved several times until he finally opened his eyes, wiped his face, and stumbled toward the door.

"Are you okay?" Dr. Poitier asked.

The man answered, but his words were incoherent. He turned and lay back down on the grimy floor with his face next to the commode.

The next cell contained another "regular." Freddie Gilbert was a big man in his thirties with an uncombed afro. Some of the officers had nicknamed him "Hagrid" because he resembled Rubeus Hagrid, the giant friend of Harry Potter's in the movies made from that popular series.

"Why have you taken your clothes off?" Dr. Poitier asked.

Gilbert didn't reply.

"If you want him to talk, doc, you've got to offer him food," Clarence Clem, who had worked as a correctional officer on the ninth floor for eighteen years—longer than anyone else—called out from his seat on a nearby bench.

Dr. Poitier eyeballed Gilbert. "This is a really sad case," he told me. Gilbert had been arrested nearly twenty times in the past six years, usually for minor crimes associated with mental illness. This time, he'd been jailed for trespassing, panhandling, and being a "sanitary nuisance," which meant that he had been caught repeatedly urinating and defecating in public. Gilbert was homeless and chronically mentally ill, which meant he was so deeply disturbed that it was going to require long-term care to bring his illness under control.

Turning toward Officer Clem, Dr. Poitier said, "Let's try to get him to keep his clothes on."

Clem stepped forward and smacked the glass front with his open palm.

"Put your clothes on or you won't get any sandwiches," he warned. He lifted his hand to his mouth as if he were eating.

Gilbert stared for a moment and then reached for the Ferguson gown at his feet and slipped it on.

Before moving on, Dr. Poitier reviewed his notes. When he'd arrived at work, he'd been told that he needed to find space on C wing for four additional prisoners. Because the cell block was already overflowing, he would have to move four inmates to a different wing to accommodate the newcomers. So far, he had not seen anyone he thought was mentally stable enough to be transferred. He had nine more cells to check.

A white inmate in his early forties was waiting by the food slot in cell eleven.

"I don't belong here," he declared as soon as Dr. Poitier arrived.

"Are you having suicidal thoughts?"

"No," he replied, sounding insulted. "I'm telling you, there's been a mistake."

"Are you currently taking medications for mental illness?"

"Yes." The inmate spewed off the names of six antipsychotic drugs.

"Why were you arrested?"

"I got into a fistfight in this store. They said I was trying to steal clothes, but my friend was supposed to pay for them. He just was late getting there."

"Your friend?"

"President Bush. He was supposed to pay for my clothes but he got hung up somewhere. You know he's busy."

"Will you take medication if I give it to you?"

"Absolutely, if it will get me off this floor. There's nothing mentally wrong with me."

Dr. Poitier asked who the inmate's psychiatrist was on the street. He didn't know. He got his pills at a clinic.

Dr. Poitier told me that this was a common problem. "These guys aren't booked into jail carrying their medical records, and most of them don't see psychiatrists on any regular basis." Because of this, Dr. Poitier had to decide what sort of medication they needed to be prescribed based largely on what the inmates themselves told him. He didn't have the time or the legal authority to perform an in-depth mental examination. "What I do here is triage, similar to what a doctor does in an emergency room." In nearly every case, Dr. Poitier worked entirely from his hunches. The drugs this prisoner had cited were consistent with ones used to treat schizoaffective disorder, a combination of bipolar disorder and schizophrenia. With that tidbit and the inmate's confused demeanor, Dr. Poitier felt confident that he'd made the correct diagnosis.

"Have you ever tried to kill yourself?" Dr. Poitier asked.

"No."

Dr. Poitier decided it was safe to move this prisoner from C wing into A wing, which was less restrictive. It served as a transition point between the ninth and eighth floors. He had now found one of the openings that he needed. He had three to go.

An inmate in cell twelve asked Dr. Poitier for Zyprexa. "I'm bipolar," he volunteered.

"Have you ever taken Risperdal?" Dr. Poitier asked.

The Miami-Dade County Public Health Trust/Correctional Health Care Services, which was the governmental body that employed Dr. Poitier and oversaw the jail's medical operations, required Dr. Poitier to prescribe Risperdal first whenever possible—rather than Zyprexa, which is much more expensive. Switching medications can cause patients to relapse, but that's a chance Dr. Poitier's superiors were willing to take.

"Let's see how you do on Risperdal," Dr. Poitier said. He then asked the inmate if he felt suicidal.

"No," he answered. "I'd never do that."

"Would you like to move to a different cell block where you could watch TV?"

"Sure."

Dr. Poitier had found his second opening.

Officer Michael Urbistondo stepped forward when the doctor reached cell fourteen. "This kid is faking it," he said, pointing to the ID paper affixed to the cell front and a photograph of a twenty-one-year-old white inmate. "He's been doing push-ups and sit-ups in his cell. He's been bugging us to use the telephone so he can call his girlfriend. You tell me, doc, how many inmates up here do push-ups and have girlfriends? This guy is definitely hiding out."

I asked Urbistondo what he meant and he said that often prisoners are afraid they will be raped or beaten if they are put into the large, general-population cells on the floors below, so they threaten suicide in order to be locked in C wing, where they will be watched and protected. This is especially true when it comes to young white inmates, Urbistondo added, because the jail's population is overwhelmingly Hispanic and African-American. Both prey on whites. What inmates often didn't realize was that prisoners who are housed on the psychiatric floors spend six times longer in jail than any other inmates, even when they are charged with identical crimes. It is part of the stigma that comes with mental illness. Judges and prosecutors are hesitant to release them. So while a prisoner might think that he has found a clever way to stay safe in jail, he also has guaranteed himself a longer stint if he hides in C wing.

Dr. Poitier called the inmate to the front of the cell.

"Voices are telling me to hurt myself," the youth said. It was a cliché response, but that didn't mean it wasn't real.

"Have you ever tried to kill yourself?"

"No. I've only thought about it since I've been in jail."

Dr. Poitier asked him several more questions and quickly determined that he was *not* mentally ill. Just the same, Dr. Poitier decided not to transfer him out of C wing. Statistically, young white males are the most likely to kill themselves in jail, and they usually did it within twenty-four hours after they were arrested.

Instead, Dr. Poitier found another inmate in the same cell who could be moved. His name was "Mr. Adams," and he too was a C wing regular. As soon as Dr. Poitier brought up a transfer, he jumped at it. The reason was Sergeant Sebastian Garcia, the officer in charge of the eighth floor during the day shift.

"Sergeant Garcia treats me really nice," the inmate explained, grinning. "He's my friend."

"Okay, I'll move you," Dr. Poitier replied, "but you've got to stay on your medication."

"I promise," the prisoner chirped excitedly.

After Dr. Poitier shut the food slot in the cell door, he told me that Adams was mentally retarded and schizophrenic. "His mother lives in a tough area, and when we send him home, the drug dealers in his neighborhood take advantage of him. They steal his monthly subsistence checks and get him involved in doing things for them. Then he gets caught and put back here in jail. It's a cycle."

I watched as Mr. Adams got on his hands and knees and crawled under the bottom bunk in the cell. I dropped down to see what he was doing. He was chewing on a discarded orange peel from the previous night's meal. When he noticed me, he waved.

We continued on. In cell nineteen, Poitier found his fourth and last transfer. He was another familiar face. The inmate had first met Dr. Poitier more than two decades before, when he was doing his residency at a state forensic hospital. Since then, the prisoner had been arrested some fifty times. When asked, he jumped at the chance to leave C wing and move onto the eighth floor. But he said that he needed to be transferred within the next hour.

"What's your hurry?" Dr. Poitier asked.

"They serve lunch then," he replied. "If I go later, I'll miss it."

Dr. Poitier smiled. This inmate, he explained, was a chronic schizophrenic and often suffered delusions and hallucinations. Yet he was aware enough to know the jail's feeding schedule.

Having found four prisoners who could be moved, Dr. Poitier and the rest of us left C wing to continue morning rounds in A and B wings.

"A lot of people think someone who is mentally ill is going to get help if they are put in jail," he told me as we walked. "But the truth is that we don't help many people here with their psychosis. We can't." His first priority was making sure no one killed himself. His next task was trying to convince prisoners to take antipsychotic medication so they could become stable enough to be put on trial.

"Mentally ill people don't belong in jail," Dr. Poitier continued. "By its very design, a jail like ours is intended to dehumanize and humiliate a person. It's supposed to have a negative impact, to bring an inmate down, to make him not want to come back. This sort of atmosphere is counter to treatment or helping improve anyone's mental health—including the people who work here."

By the time he had finished his rounds, Dr. Poitier had either spoken with or visibly observed all of the ninety-two inmates on the ninth floor. I checked my watch. His rounds had taken nineteen and a half minutes to complete. That was an average of 12.7 seconds per inmate.

A fter visiting the ninth floor, I went to see Judge Steven Leifman across the street at the courthouse.

"Miami has a larger percentage of mentally ill residents than any other major metropolitan area," he said. The average for most cities is 3 percent, but Miami has three times that—a whopping 9 percent of its population is mentally ill. The city starts with the same 3 percent as everywhere else, but gains another 3 percent because of Florida's warm winter weather. The final jump can be traced to 1980, when Cuban dictator Fidel Castro emptied his mental hospitals into the waves of Cuban refugees fleeing to Florida from the port of Mariel.

When we met at the courthouse, I asked Judge Leifman if anyone in his family had a mental illness. A gregarious man in his forties, the judge had a national reputation for being an untiring advocate for the mentally ill, and I was curious why he was so concerned about them.

"No," he replied. The first time he'd met someone who was psychotic was when he was eighteen and working as an intern for a Florida state senator in 1977. A distraught constituent had complained that her son was being mistreated at a state mental hospital north of Miami, and Leifman had been sent to investigate. He still remembered the patient's name: Jonathan Petrosino. "I found him tied to a hospital bed. He'd been diagnosed as being schizophrenic." But it turned out that Petrosino actually had a developmental disorder, autism, and Leifman arranged for him to be moved from the hospital into a group home. "I remember thinking at the time that the Miami zoo treats its animals better than patients were being treated at that state hospital."

Leifman ended up earning his law degree in Washington, D.C., but returned to work in the Miami public defender's office. During his eight years there, he noticed that he was being assigned more and more clients who were clearly mentally ill. On his own, he sent a letter to the police, state prosecutors, area hospitals, and local mental health facilities to see if anyone would meet with him to discuss ways to help get the mentally ill out of jail and into treatment. It was an earnest effort, but not a single person or agency replied.

None.

Leifman ran for the Florida legislature in 1992 as a Democrat, but lost. His campaign caught the eye of local politicos, however, and when a county judge's job came open three years later, the Democratic governor appointed him to finish the unexpired term. Leifman didn't sit on the bench long, though. Miami Republicans ousted him a few months later. Still, he'd made an impression. *The Miami Herald*'s editorial page described his loss as an example of why electing judges was a lousy idea. As soon as another judicial opening appeared, the same Democratic governor appointed Leifman to fill it.

After he was sworn in, he sent out a second letter about the mentally ill, only this time he put his invitation on his judicial stationery. Everyone who got one showed up. He had discovered the clout that he could wield as a judge, and he was quick to use it. He told the group that mental illness affected all of them—the police, the courts, the hospitals, the business community, the jail, and social services. They were spending time and money dealing with the same deranged individuals, but no one was sharing information or coordinating their efforts. By the time that initial meeting ended, all the representatives had agreed to join Judge Leifman in creating a new oversight group. He called it the Eleventh Judicial Circuit Court Criminal Mental Health Project, and he immediately began applying for federal grant money under its name. He used the funds to fly in a team of outside advisers. They urged him to create a "misdemeanor diversion program." It took him two years of cajoling to set it up. Under the judge's program, a mentally ill inmate was supposed to be diverted from the jail into a local community treatment center within forty-eight hours after he was arrested. He would spend three to seven days there being "stabilized," and then would be brought back into court. In most cases, the minor charges filed against him would be dismissed as long as he promised to continue getting psychiatric help after he was freed. The judge's mantra became: "Jail should be the last resort, not the first."

After its first year of operation, Judge Leifman evaluated the diversion program and the results were staggering. Previously, 70 percent of mentally ill inmates who'd been jailed on minor charges had been arrested again. But after the diversion program was put into place, the recidivism rate plunged to *7 percent*.

Unfortunately, the program could be used only to divert inmates who had been accused of misdemeanor crimes, and that was a small number. Overall, 3,070 people with "severe and/or persistent mental illness" had been booked into the jail during the time period that Judge Leifman had studied. Most of them—2,828 people—had been accused of felonies. They hadn't qualified and had remained locked up.

"I wanted to reach more," he said. When he took another look at the statistics, he noticed an interesting fact. More than half of the 2,828 mentally ill inmates in jail had been charged with *third*-degree felonies. They were considered minor felonies. Half the inmates had been arrested for possession of illegal drugs. This mirrored national studies that showed that a high number of mentally ill persons in jails and prisons were substance abusers.

Armed with those additional figures, Judge Leifman tried to expand his diversion program to include third-degree, "nonviolent" felons. But he hadn't been able to persuade anyone else in the justice system that including felons in the diversion program was a good idea. At least not yet. "But we're going to get it approved at some point," he predicted.

That was only one of the reforms that Judge Leifman was advocating, and for nearly an hour he talked enthusiastically about them.

Finally, I interrupted. "Why are you doing this?" I asked. The question took him by surprise, so I elaborated. "I don't see what's in it for you. Those inmates I saw today on the ninth floor don't vote. One reason they're stuck there is that the public and politicians don't consider mental health a priority. So I don't see how being an advocate for them is going to help you get reelected."

Rather than giving me a direct answer, Judge Leifman told me about a criminal case that had been brought before him shortly after he had been appointed. A promising University of Miami student had been about to complete his medical residency in psychiatry when he himself had become stricken with schizophrenia and had been arrested because of his bizarre antics. "His parents came to see me and they begged me to help them get their son treatment—to force him into treatment," Judge Leifman recalled. When the defendant was brought into the courtroom, the judge interrogated him. "He told me his parents were impostors. He said they worked for the CIA." Even though Judge Leifman wanted to help, his hands were tied by civil rights statutes. He had to free the defendant. As soon as he was released, he disappeared. No one knew what ever happened to him, including his parents.

"I've never forgotten how desperate they were to get their son help," he said. "I kept thinking, What if he had been my brother or father or son? I decided there had to be a better way than what we were doing, and I wanted to do what I could by working in the system to bring about changes."

Later that night, I couldn't sleep, so I decided to walk to the jail, since I was staying in a hotel not far from it. I wasn't planning on going inside. I just wanted to stretch my legs. I stared up at the building's windows and found the ninth floor. They were lit, of course. They always were. I remembered the smells, the sights, the sounds from my morning tour. I thought about Freddie Gilbert, the Hagrid-looking inmate who'd put on his Ferguson gown only after he was promised a sandwich. I thought about Mr. Adams, who had curled up under the steel bunk to chew on a discarded orange peel.

As I turned the corner at Fourteenth Street on my way back to the motel, I noticed a lone figure sitting inside a glass-enclosed bus shelter. I had spotted him earlier when I'd first arrived at the jail. I'd been told that his name was Willie and that he was mentally ill. He could always be found sitting in the shelter, although he never caught a bus going anywhere.

I walked over to the enclosure.

"Willie?" I asked.

He was tearing a white napkin from a nearby McDonald's into tiny pieces and didn't look up or respond.

"They told me at the jail your name is Willie. I'm writing a book. I'd like to talk to you—maybe about why you are sitting here, what you are thinking."

He ignored me.

"You are Willie, right?"

"No," he quietly replied.

"Would you be willing to talk to me?"

"No."

I tried to persuade him, but after several minutes I gave up and left. Had I really believed it would be so easy?

A few minutes after 3 A.M., I woke up from a nightmare. In my dream, I'd been on the ninth floor, accompanying Dr. Poitier on his morning rounds through C wing. We'd stopped outside a cell swarming with psychotic inmates and I spotted one of them ducking under a bunk. Just as I had actually done during my real jail tour, I knelt down in my dream and peered through the smudged glass cell front at the prisoner curled up on the concrete. He was chewing on an orange peel, only the face that I saw in my dream looking back at me had not been Mr. Adams or Willie from the bus stop. It had been Mike.

expectancy had increased. And state hospitals had become a catchall for society's disposables—the elderly, the deaf, the blind, and the poor.

The psychiatrists who worked in them operated largely unchecked. Electroshock, insulin injections, Metrazol (induced seizures), hydrotherapy (wet sheets and continuous baths), and fever therapy (injecting patients with diseases to cause fevers) were common. In 1946, lobotomies were introduced. Performed by sticking an ice pick into the frontal lobes of the brain, the treatment was considered so promising that its inventor was awarded a Nobel Prize.

On May 6, 1946, *Life* magazine published a cover story titled "Bedlam: Most U.S. Mental Hospitals Are a Shame and a Disgrace," by Albert Q. Maisel. The investigative story began with a description of a mental patient being tortured to death by the hospital staff. Maisel then explained that murders in "dilapidated, overcrowded, undermanned state mental hospitals" were "hardly the most significant of the indignities heaped upon guiltless patient-prisoners held in over 180 state mental institutions.

We feed thousands a starvation diet, often dragged further below the low-budget standard by the withdrawal of the best food for the staff dining rooms. We jam-pack men, women and sometimes even children into hundred-year-old firetraps in wards so crowded that the floors cannot be seen between the rickety cots, while thousands more sleep on ticks, on blankets or on the bare floors. We give them little and shoddy clothing at best. Hundreds— of my own knowledge and sight—spend 24 hours a day in stark and filthy nakedness. Those who are well enough to work slave away in many institutions for 12 hours a day, often without a day's rest for years on end. . . . Thousands spend their days— often for weeks at a stretch—locked in devices euphemistically called "restraints," thick leather handcuffs, great canvas camisoles,

"muffs," "mitts," wristlets, locks and straps and restraining sheets.
Hundreds are confined in "lodges"—bare, bedless rooms reeking
with filth and feces—by day lit only through half-inch holes in steel-
plated windows, by night merely black tombs in which the cries
of the insane echo unheard from the peeling plaster of the walls.

Reader's Digest followed *Life*'s scandalous report with a condensation
of Mary Jane Ward's novel *The Snake Pit*, which described her hellish
experiences while she was confined in a state institution. Next came a
series of newspaper exposés by Mike Gorman, a reporter for *The Daily
Oklahoman*. Albert Deutsch, in *The Shame of the States*, compared the
conditions that he found in mental hospitals to those in Nazi concentra-
tion camps.

These revelations caused such a national uproar that Congress got
involved, and in late 1946, President Harry Truman signed a bill that
created the National Institute of Mental Health, or NIMH. Truman
urged it to find a "cure" for insanity.

At about this same time, psychiatry began to change. The teachings
of Sigmund Freud became popular. Rather than subjecting patients to
physical treatments, such as electroshock, doctors began leading group
therapy sessions where everyone—including other mental patients—was
encouraged to talk about his innermost feelings and emotions as part of
the "psychoanalytical therapeutic treatment process."

Just how many patients were actually helped over the years at state
mental hospitals—either by physical treatments or by talk therapy—is
impossible to determine. What is known, however, is that a discovery in
the 1950s completely revolutionized psychiatry and how the mentally
ill would forever be treated.

In 1952, a Paris surgeon named Henri Laborit began experimenting with a drug called chlorpromazine that had been developed by a
French manufacturer to treat allergies. Laborit was looking for a way to

sedate his patients before surgery, and he was surprised at how relaxed chlorpromazine made them feel. He decided to share his findings with French psychiatrists, who, he thought, might be able to use the drug to calm violent lunatics.

But none of the psychiatrists whom he contacted was interested. Like their American counterparts, they were convinced that Freudian psychoanalysis and behavior modification were the best hopes for treating insanity. While drugs might be useful as tranquilizers, they weren't thought to have any therapeutic value.

Laborit finally talked a psychiatrist named Pierre Deniker into giving chlorpromazine to several schizophrenic patients. The results shocked both men. Patients who had been so uncontrollable that they were kept bound in restraints suddenly became so placid that Deniker could speak to them and they could respond rationally.

Laborit and Deniker thought they had discovered a medical breakthrough, but neither of them was able to convince his medical peers. Meanwhile, the Rhone-Poulenc company, which had developed chlorpromazine, sold the rights to manufacture the drug to the Smith Kline pharmaceutical company. It flew Deniker to the United States to tell doctors about chlorpromazine. But American psychiatrists proved as closed-minded as their French colleagues. It was at this point that the drug company decided to try a different marketing approach. Rather than have Deniker meet with doctors, Smith Kline began sending him to talk with state legislators.

Why?

Money. Deniker claimed that chlorpromazine could save state legislators millions of tax dollars, because it would make mental patients well enough that they could be discharged. The states would no longer have to pay to house and treat them in asylums.

It was money, then, not necessarily compassion or concern for patients, that made it possible for the Smith Kline company to begin dispensing its new drug. It was marketed under the name Thorazine. Just as Deniker had promised, the results were staggering. Within a year, newsmagazines were calling Thorazine a "wonder drug" and reporters were claiming that a cure for most mental illnesses had been found. The first eight months that Thorazine was on the market, it was given to more than 2 million patients. In the next ten years, 50 million people worldwide would take it. Smith Kline's revenues would double three times in fifteen years, thanks entirely to Thorazine—a fact not lost on the pharmaceutical industry.

Thorazine's discovery forced psychiatrists to begin rethinking how they treated the insane. They slowly started abandoning Freud. While it would take years, psychiatrists would eventually decide that most mental disorders were caused by faulty chemistry in the brain, not bad parenting, bad morals, or horrible childhoods.

Thorazine's dramatic impact reached even into the White House. In 1961, when President John F. Kennedy was sworn in, he made mental illness a top priority, and Thorazine played a key role in his thinking. With Thorazine now available, did the nation really need costly state mental hospitals?

On October 31, 1963, Kennedy signed a national mental health law that authorized Congress to spend up to $3 *billion* in the coming decades to construct a national network of community mental health centers. These neighborhood clinics would replace the giant state hospitals and make it possible for even the most disturbed psychotics to live normal lives in their own hometowns—as long as they were given Thorazine.

At about this same time, the psychiatry profession came under attack. A Scottish doctor named Ronald David Laing published a book called *The Divided Self* that argued that patients in mental hospitals were not crazy—it was the psychiatrists treating them who were truly mad. Laing's book wasn't taken seriously at first, but in the mid-1960s it was embraced by America's mushrooming counterculture. Laing was joined by psychiatrist Thomas Szasz, who claimed in *The Myth of Mental Illness* that doctors who declared their patients mentally ill were no different from medieval witch hunters. "The practice of 'sane' men incarcerating their 'insane' fellow men in 'mental hospitals' can be compared to that of white men enslaving black men," he declared.

By themselves, Laing and Szasz might have appealed only to a fringe group, but a third book published in the 1960s tilted the balance. It convinced Middle America that psychiatry was, at best, a pseudoscience. It also undermined the public's already tainted image of state mental hospitals. The book was Ken Kesey's novel *One Flew Over the Cuckoo's Nest*, and it was soon made into one of the most influential films of the century. Starring Jack Nicholson as Randle Patrick McMurphy, the movie pitted a rebellious patient, who was pretending to be crazy, against the much-hated Nurse Ratched, chief nurse in a psychiatric hospital and the personification of a cold institutional superior. The film swept the Academy Awards in 1976, winning in *all* major categories—best picture, best director, best actor, best actress, and best screenplay.

It was the coming together of these events—the Bedlam exposés, the discovery of Thorazine, President Kennedy's call for building community mental health centers, and the emergence of the antipsychiatry movement—that started a massive antiasylum snowball rolling. As it raced downhill, it gained speed. Inspired by the 1960s civil rights movement, a new breed of attorneys began filing class-action lawsuits against states on behalf of patients who were being mistreated in asylums.

Even so, Dorothea Dix's network of state hospitals might have survived had it not been for the federal government. Congress began passing a series of laws that eventually made the mentally ill eligible for a variety of federal assistance programs, such as Medicaid, Medicare, Supplemental Security Income, Social Security Disability Insurance, food stamps, and federal housing subsidies. It was these programs that gave state legislators a way out. Faced with menacing class-action lawsuits and mounting public pressure to do something about the wretched conditions in mental hospitals, state legislators were happy to shift the burden of caring for the insane off the states' backs and onto Uncle Sam's assistance programs.

Once again, money was driving public policy.

Seemingly overnight, states began emptying their wards and boarding up mental hospitals. Between 1960 and 1980, the number of patients in state institutions plunged from more than 500,000 to under 100,000. This massive exit was called "deinstitutionalization."

So what happened to the mentally ill?

Tragically, deinstitutionalization turned out to be an unplanned social disaster. In most states, patients were discharged without any effort being made to link them to community services—if, in fact, there were any. President Kennedy's promise of $3 billion to create a safety net turned out to be a cruel lie. Congress turned its attention to other problems, primarily the Vietnam War and Watergate. In the coming years, mental health ended up going hungry when the federal pie was gobbled up. Congress never got around to financing community mental health centers.

Chronically mentally ill patients—psychotic and bewildered—began appearing on street corners. The few mental health centers that had been built were not equipped to help severely disturbed patients.

And what of Thorazine, that much ballyhooed wonder drug? It turned out to be less wonderful than had been predicted. It didn't always work, and it caused harmful side effects.

By the late 1980s, the mentally ill had started arriving in jails and prisons. By the 1990s, there were so many of them being locked up that a newly coined word began appearing in mental health publications. It was *transinstitutionalization*, bureaucratese for the "transfer" of the mentally ill from the old state hospitals into jails. It was why the Miami jail's ninth floor existed and why jails everywhere were now being overrun with psychotic prisoners. The emptying and closing of Dix's state hospitals had created a huge void in the system. Simply put, the mentally ill had nowhere else to go.

Dr. Poitier gestured toward the cells in C wing and then jabbed that same finger onto the cover of Professor Grob's book. "When you read about how the mentally ill were treated two hundred years ago and then you walk out there on C wing—" He didn't finish his sentence. He didn't have to. It was time for him to begin his morning rounds. His first stop would be at cell number one, where he'd find a deranged prisoner shivering naked in a freezing cell with nothing to occupy his time and little real hope of getting any treatment. Two hundred years had passed. What had changed?

Deinstitutionalization had led to hundreds of thousands of chronically mentally ill patients' being tossed into the streets. But there had to be more to solving this puzzle than the emptying of mental hospitals.

Renee Turolla had been one of the first in Miami to notice that its jail was being overrun with the mentally ill. In the early 1980s, she had spent two years investigating their criminalization. I decided to ask her why the ninth floor was still swarming with "lunatics."

enee Turolla blamed Fidel Castro.

R The Cuban dictator was the reason she got interested in Miami's mentally ill. For six months in 1980, Castro allowed 125,266 Cubans to flee their homeland in a flotilla. They came to Miami at the invitation of President Jimmy Carter, who said the United States would provide "an open heart and open arms to refugees seeking freedom from Communist domination." Castro took advantage of Carter's openness by flushing inmates from his prisons and patients from his mental asylums into the fleeing horde. The refugees became known as the Marielito Cubans, and although news stories would later routinely portray them as criminals, only 2 percent, roughly 2,505, had actually been released from Cuban prisons. How many came from mental hospitals was much harder to determine. Some experts claimed 3 percent. Others claimed 30 percent. What was undisputed was that most of them were young single men. Although the Marielitos were supposed to be resettled across America, more than 90,000 remained in Miami.

Within weeks after the boatlift ended, Cubans with obvious mental problems began appearing in Turolla's neighborhood. Although Miami Beach is currently a ritzy address, it hasn't always been. In the 1940s and 1950s, it was the United States' Riviera. But in the 1960s, tourism plunged, and by the time of the Cuban boatlift, many of the beach's hotels were nearly bankrupt. The Marielitos and other Third World refugees burrowed in. Crime jumped. Several of Turolla's friends were mugged. She got angry.

"I decided to do something," she said.

The daughter of a wealthy Canadian entrepreneur, she and her husband, Pino, had moved to Miami Beach in the 1950s to test a parachute that he'd designed with vents cut in its canopy. (The holes gave jumpers more control during descents.) They quickly became known as one of Miami's more exotic couples. In the 1960s, *The Miami Herald* published stories about scientific expeditions that Pino Turolla was leading into remote South American jungles in search of new medicines.

Renee Turolla joined the Citizens Crime Commission of Greater Miami, a volunteer public watchdog group, and began driving to the Gerstein courthouse every morning to monitor criminal cases. The petite brunette, who was then in her forties, had no legal background, but that didn't stop her from questioning prosecutors, defense attorneys, even judges, about their actions. She immediately noticed that the quality of justice meted out often depended on which judge heard a case. Her first impulse was to write a scathing report about the worst jurists. Instead, she issued an official Citizens Crime Commission report that highlighted the four best. "I hoped the lousy ones would learn by example." *The Miami Herald* published a story about her findings, and that publicity gave her new clout inside the courthouse.

Judge Howard Gross called her into his chambers one afternoon and thrust a letter at her.

"If you really want to make a contribution," he said, "then investigate this."

The letter was from a psychiatrist at the Florida State Hospital in Chattahoochee, where the criminally insane were imprisoned. It said a Miami defendant, who had been sent there, was now mentally competent and could be put on trial. But the physician warned the judge to hear the case quickly before the accused became mentally unstable again.

A defendant in a criminal case had to be competent enough to aid in his own defense and had to understand the charges filed against him, Judge Gross explained, otherwise he couldn't be put on trial.

"I send defendants to the hospital to be treated and they keep sending them back to me on medication," Judge Gross told Turolla. "As soon as they return to our jail, they stop taking their drugs, and by the time they get in front of the bench, they're climbing the walls. Then I have to send them back to the hospital again."

The letter from the Chattahoochee doctor was about a defendant who had spent *two years* shuttling between the jail and the hospital, and he still had not been put on trial because his mental condition kept deteriorating.

"Can you find out why these doctors keep sending these defendants back to my courtroom sick?" the judge asked Turolla. "They're supposed to come back treated."

Turolla agreed, and much to her surprise, the psychiatrists in Chattahoochee were delighted when she showed up there. No one from the Miami courthouse had ever come to hear their side of the story.

"Your judges think we are treating the defendants they send to us," a doctor explained. "But your judges don't understand the law."

His comment surprised her. "You're telling me that our *judges* don't understand the law?" she asked.

"That's right. The law doesn't require us to *treat* these people. Our job is to get them competent enough so they can be put on trial, and that's very different from actually treating someone's mental disorder."

The psychiatrist showed Turolla a mock courtroom inside the hospital. There were placards attached to each piece of furniture that identified where the judge, prosecutor, defense attorney, and jurors sat. The doctor told Turolla that patients were brought into the courtroom and the criminal charges filed against them were read out loud and explained. Then the patients were drilled by the hospital staff until they could answer ten questions. The doctor showed Turolla a sample:

> Question: What is a trial?
> Answer: A trial is where it is decided if you are not guilty, guilty, or
>   not guilty by reason of insanity of the charge.
> Q: Who represents you or defends you in court?
> A: My lawyer or public defender. My lawyer is chosen and hired by
>   me and the public defender is appointed by the state.
> Q: Who is against you?
> A: The state's attorney or prosecutor is against me.
> Q: What does he do?
> A: He tries to convict me, get me time, prove me guilty of the charge.

As soon as a defendant could answer the pro forma ten questions, he was hustled before a three-member competency review board. There were twelve criteria the patient had to meet in order for it to declare him competent. Again, the doctor gave Turolla a sample:

> Criterion Three: Does the defendant understand that (1) his
> attorney is trying to assist him, (2) the State's Attorney is trying
> to convict him, and (3) the judge and jury are impartial?

The doctor told Turolla, "We spend months getting these patients competent enough to pass our tests, and then your judges return them to us in horrible shape. What the hell is going on in the Miami jail? If you really want to help, find out what happens after we send these defendants home."

Turolla decided to do that. A hospital bus was driving several "competent patients" back to the Miami jail that same day, so she decided to follow it. She also picked a patient on the bus to shadow. She followed the bus in her car. The trip took *fourteen hours*, and Turolla noticed there was no air conditioning or medical staff on the bus. It was summer and blistering hot. By the time the bus arrived at the jail, several riders already had started acting strange.

Jail officials didn't know who Turolla was, so they stopped her from entering the jail compound. But she was determined to keep track of the defendant whom she was following. She telephoned Judge Gross, and he arranged for her to go inside. Turolla discovered that the doctors in Chattahoochee hadn't sent any antipsychotic medication with her patient. He was supposed to take his pills twice a day. The Chattahoochee doctors had assumed he'd get them in the jail. But it didn't have a full-time doctor, and three days passed before the defendant was examined and given medicine. Even then, he wasn't prescribed the same drug that he'd been taking. The jail used a cheaper substitute.

About a week after the defendant returned to Miami, he was taken before a judge, who ordered him to undergo a psychiatric exam. This was routine, Turolla learned. Judges never blindly accepted the findings of Chattahoochee doctors. Instead, they appointed three local psychiatrists to examine each defendant at a cost of $150 to each psychiatrist per exam. It took two months for these exams to be completed. During that time, the defendant was locked naked in an empty isolation cell. Not surprisingly, his mental condition slipped.

Another month went by before the defendant was taken into court again to hear the three psychiatrists' evaluations. Two of the doctors said he was competent, but the third said he wasn't. The judge scheduled a court date, but a few days later, the public defender asked for a continuance. He was busy with other cases. Another two months passed, and when the defendant was finally brought into the court for his trial, his behavior was so bizarre that the exasperated judge ordered that he be sent back to Chattahoochee.

Sadly, that wasn't the end of his story. Turolla discovered there was such a backlog of inmates waiting to be evaluated in Chattahoochee that the defendant sat in the Miami jail for another full year. By the time he was put on a bus for the trip to the hospital, he was close to catatonic.

Turolla had found an answer to Judge Gross's question. The justice system was completely overwhelmed with mentally ill inmates, and few of them were getting any actual treatment. Instead, they were being shuttled back and forth between the jail and the hospital, being made "competent."

Turolla decided to do more digging, and she learned from jail officials that the first wave of mentally ill defendants had started showing up in jail within days after Florida began "deinstitutionalization." But the facility hadn't been inundated until the Mariel boatlift in 1980. That year alone, the number of disturbed inmates in the Miami jail increased by 306 percent! Jail officials had been totally unprepared.

They still were three years later when Turolla arrived on the scene. There was no full-time jail psychiatrist. The only nurse who was on duty was responsible for monitoring 350 mentally disturbed prisoners. Antipsychotic medications were doled out by correctional officers who had no idea what sort of pills they were dispensing. But what troubled Turolla the most were the cells where many of the psychotic inmates were kept. Jail officials couldn't risk putting them in the facility's large group cell, because the other prisoners would prey on them. So the mentally ill were locked in isolation cells scattered throughout the building. These units were normally used to punish prisoners. There were no bunks, no mattresses, no blankets, no windows. Often the lights in them were turned off twenty-hour hours a day, leaving an inmate in total darkness—unless the solid door's food slot was left open.

"I looked into these dark cells and saw naked men crouching in empty rooms with no blankets," Turolla recalled. "They were cold and shivering and screaming. They'd loom forward from the darkness like wild animals. There was no feeling of sympathy, no effort to understand them, no special training for the guards. That jail was a hellhole."

How could the jail treat people like this? she wondered.

She began interviewing jail administrators, correctional officers, mental health professionals, and community activists. She pored over court records and spent months monitoring individual cases. No one was paying for her investigation, nor was anyone encouraging her to do it—except for her husband, Pino. At night, he listened to her descriptions of the horrific conditions. When she came home exhausted, frustrated, and sad, he urged her to keep probing.

Her research revealed that the jail had become a "revolving door." If a psychotic suspect was arrested for a minor crime, he was jailed for several days and then released—just as loony as he had been. If he was charged with a felony, he sat in jail until he could be sent to Chattahoochee, where he was "made competent" and then sent back without ever having received any actual help for his disorder. Even after an inmate was found not guilty by reason of insanity and sent to one of the state's few remaining mental hospitals, he still was not actually treated. Instead, he was shot full of drugs, stuck on a locked ward, and forgotten until he had served his time and was paroled.

Because he was still psychotic, he would soon be arrested and begin the revolving-door cycle again. "There was no treatment," Turolla said.

Turolla backed up her findings with case studies. One of them was a young inmate who had bipolar disorder. In 1982, he was arrested *51 times* for minor crimes associated with mental illness, such as loitering, panhandling, and trespassing. In 1983, he was arrested another *44 times*. One day, he was released from jail and arrested *twenty minutes later* less than one block away. At no time did anyone in the mental health system or justice system try to help him with his disorder. He simply kept being punished.

When Turolla asked jail officials why they weren't doing anything to treat mentally ill inmates, one of them snapped, "We're not here to treat 'em, our job is to keep 'em locked up."

Turolla decided the most effective way to show the public what was happening was to focus on a single inmate. She selected James Edward Tucker, because, as she would explain later in her report, "his odyssey through jails and courts, hospitals and community programs illustrates the well-beaten path taken by hundreds of mentally ill criminals in Dade County every year."

Tucker had been born in a poor black section of Miami called Liberty City. His father was a laborer. His mother, an alcoholic. Both were mentally ill, and so was Tucker. At age fourteen, he began hearing voices inside his head. He would later be diagnosed as having chronic schizophrenia.

Tucker was arrested for the first time in 1973, when he was fifteen. During the next eleven years, he would be arrested eighteen times on a variety of charges, including murder. During this period, he would spend two and a half years in jail awaiting trial and would be confined for three years in a state mental hospital. More than two dozen psychiatrists would examine him. Yet Tucker would never receive any treatment. *None.* When he was sent to Chattahoochee, the doctors there concentrated on making him competent. When he was sent to a state hospital, the psychiatrists kept him heavily sedated and then discharged him. Tucker was murdered in 1984 while standing outside his mother's house screaming obscenities at people walking by. He was hit with a shotgun blast in his chest. His killer was never found.

In her notes, Turolla wrote, "James Tucker was a young man who demonstrated from an early age that he had a personality disorder. . . . His bizarre behavior was noted by teachers, corrections officers, and, no doubt, his parents." And yet nothing had ever been done to actually help him deal with his mental illness. "The criminal justice system kept repackaging him with medication. Its priority was to make him look and sound competent so he could continue down the assembly line like so many widgets."

Turolla guessed that many Miami residents wouldn't care about the fate of a poor, black deranged man. But she thought Tucker's sorry fate might make them angry if she revealed how many tax dollars had been wasted in not helping him. She added up his court expenses and the price of keeping him in jail. Those two costs alone reached $135,662, or an average of $12,333 for each year Tucker was in trouble.

"What you have to remember," she wrote in her report, "is that James Tucker was simply one mentally ill criminal. Now consider how much the three thousand mentally ill inmates who revolve through the Miami-Dade County system each year are costing the public."

Turolla was nearly done with her probe when her husband Pino suffered a heart attack and died. She was devastated and considered abandoning her project. By this point, she had spent two years studying the mentally ill. *Why?* she asked herself. *Did anyone care?* She could have spent those two years with her husband.

But after his funeral, she pushed ahead. It was what Pino would have wanted her to do, and she felt obligated to the prisoners whom she'd seen languishing in jail.

In March 1985, Turolla released her study at a press conference. She titled her report *Mentally Ill Criminals in Dade County, Florida*, and although it was published under the Citizens Crime Commission's name, she had composed every word and had spent $5,000 from her own pocket getting the 400-page document printed. She dedicated it to Pino.

The Miami Herald called her investigation the most comprehensive study ever done about the plight of the mentally ill in jail. But Turolla wasn't finished. She organized a three-day workshop at Florida International University to discuss ways to solve the problems that she'd exposed.

She used the publicity that her report received to cajole jail officials, judges, hospital representatives, and other mental health experts into attending the seminar. "I didn't want my report stuck on a shelf somewhere and forgotten," she recalled.

"So what happened?" I asked.

Turolla closed her blue eyes and sighed. "My report was put on a shelf and forgotten—just as I'd feared. Nothing was done to help those poor men in the jail. Nothing was done to stop the justice system's revolving door."

Eight years after Turolla released her study, a mentally ill prisoner named Josue Mesidor was found dead in his jail cell. The police had arrested him because he'd been ranting on a street corner. He'd been in jail for fifteen days when his body was discovered in an isolation cell where he'd been left nude in frigid temperatures without a mattress or a blanket. An autopsy revealed that Mesidor had died of bacterial pneumonia, which he'd contracted in his filthy cell.

But the Miami-Dade County medical examiner's office also disclosed that several of his ribs had been cracked. At the time, high-pressure water hoses were used to wash cells, and a rumor spread through the jail that Mesidor had been shot with the hoses by correctional officers either for amusement, to make him obey their commands, or as punishment. Detectives were sent in to investigate, but no one was ever charged.

In an editorial titled "End Dade Jail's Hellhole," *The Miami Herald* noted that Mesidor would have "spent a day, maybe two, in jail" if he had been arrested for being drunk and yelling on a street corner. But because he was mentally ill, he'd been locked up for more than two weeks in "the jail's hellhole of a mental ward."

The newspaper mentioned Renee Turolla's 1985 cautionary report and how she had warned the public that mentally ill inmates were being held in barbaric conditions.

"Did I do all of that work for nothing?" the newspaper quoted her asking. "What's wrong with our community?"

A lawyer filed a class-action lawsuit against the jail because of Mesidor's death. To avoid a long trial, a Miami judge ordered county officials to negotiate a settlement. They agreed to hire three experts from outside Florida to tour the Miami jail and recommend improvements.

The three issued their grim findings a year later. Not surprisingly, they reached most of the same conclusions that Turolla had *nine years* earlier. The jail was a revolving door. "This ping-pong phenomenon between the jail and hospitals is well-known and it is hugely expensive for all concerned and harmful to persons with mental illness," the experts wrote.

Dr. Joseph A. Dvoskin, the head of the panel, made seventeen specific recommendations. He suggested that a separate room be built in the jail so inmates could speak privately with doctors or nurses. He called for special training for correctional officers assigned to oversee mentally ill inmates. He criticized the jail's policy of stripping inmates under "suicide watch" and removing mattresses and blankets from their isolation cells, especially when the temperature in their cells was kept near freezing. "I personally have never seen or heard of anyone making a serious suicide attempt or dying because of a foam mattress," he noted.

But what stunned the New York psychiatrist even more was the lack of trained medical staff. By 1993, the county had hired a full-time jail psychiatrist, but she was expected to monitor six hundred patients spread throughout the entire Miami jail system. "She is forced to choose between providing good care to a few or a small amount of care to as many as possible," Dvoskin warned.

Dvoskin said the jail needed to hire "six to eight" full-time psychiatrists. That would give each one an average of seventy patients per day to treat. While that was still too high a number, it would be better than the jail's current ratio of one doctor treating six hundred inmates.

Just as Turolla's report had been shelved, county officials chose to ignore all of the outside panel's recommendations except two. The ninth floor's C wing had been gutted and remodeled into its current configuration. And Dr. Joseph Poitier and a part-time doctor had been hired. This reduced the doctor-to-inmate ratio to one psychiatrist for every *two hundred* inmates—nearly three times higher than what Dvoskin had recommended.

I asked Turolla why so little had been done. After all, she had sounded an alarm in 1985, and Mesidor had died in 1993. What more did the public need to realize that mentally ill prisoners were living in wretched conditions inside the Miami jail?

"No one cares," she said bluntly. "These inmates don't have any political pull. Someone has to die before any changes are made. And even then, a Band-Aid is put on the problem."

Turolla had supplied another piece of the puzzle. In addition to deinstitutionalization, the Miami jail was overcrowded with psychotic inmates because few of them were actually being treated.

"Do you think the jail is still a big revolving door?" I asked. "Or have things improved? Are inmates now getting treatment?"

"You're spending time there," she said. "What have you seen?"

I compared my visit to the ninth floor with what the panel of experts had seen and criticized in 1994. They'd recommended that inmates not be held naked in cells. I'd seen them in C wing naked in cells. They'd recommended that inmates be issued blankets and mattresses. I'd seen them in C wing without blankets and mattresses. They'd recommended that inmates be allowed to speak to doctors in private. There was no privacy on the ninth floor. They'd recommended that the officers working there have special training. None of them had.

"Well," said Turolla, "are any of the recommendations that the experts made being done?"

I couldn't think of any.

"You want answers?" she said. "Then follow several people out of the jail and into the streets. Follow them as they make their way through the hospitals and clinics. See if they get treatment or if they bounce right back to jail without anyone ever really helping them. That's what I did for two years in the eighties. See for yourself if anything has changed now."

That's exactly what I plan to do, I said.

She smiled sadly and said, "Good luck."

Chapter 6

J ails run on routine. There's a time for inmate showers, for meals to be handed out, for medicines to be dispensed. Because of this, the days soon begin to blur together. There are no calendars, no clocks. Hours last sixty minutes but somehow seem longer. Most days are tedious. And then in the midst of the drudgery, a prisoner "goes off." A fistfight breaks out or someone tries to kill himself. For a few terrifying moments, the lull is forgotten, but then it returns.

Jails are transient facilities. Nearly all the prisoners in C wing would be moved somewhere else inside the building within a few days. An entirely new roster would take their places. This was especially true of inmates who voluntarily took antipsychotic medication. They would be brought in filthy and delusional. But most would soon start thinking much more clearly. The transformations were often dramatic. It wasn't unusual for a deranged inmate to be lapping water from a C-wing-cell toilet. A week later, he'd be watching MTV in an open recreational area on the eighth floor, interacting calmly with other prisoners.

There was an obvious exception. Freddie Gilbert, the inmate nicknamed Hagrid, showed no sign of improvement. He'd been brought to the ninth floor so mentally impaired that he couldn't speak. Instead, he grunted. While C wing was supposed to be reserved for prisoners who were suicidal, Gilbert had been put there for a different reason. He was so delusional that there was simply nowhere else in the jail he'd be safe. Other prisoners would have beaten or killed him. Because of his mammoth size, he was intimidating. But as far as anyone could tell, Gilbert didn't want to harm himself or anyone else, and that created a Catch-22 for Dr. Poitier. Because Gilbert wasn't in any obvious imminent danger or a threat, Dr. Poitier could not force him to take medication. The same civil rights laws that had kept the emergency room doctor at Inova Fairfax Hospital from treating my son Mike also prohibited Dr. Poitier from forcing medicine on Gilbert—even though drugs had proven to help him in the past. There was nothing Dr. Poitier could do legally but wait until Gilbert became so despondent from being locked in a cell all day that he hurled himself against its walls, attacked an officer, or miraculously agreed to begin taking his pills.

Each morning, the large black man would strip off his Ferguson gown, stand naked in the center of his cell, and stare out into the corridor. It was as if the cell's glass front wall that separated him from the rest of the cell block was a television screen and we were moving across it like actors in a confused drama. I began stopping by his cell each afternoon, intentionally inserting myself in his field of vision so that he had to make eye contact with me. I would smile and sometimes wave. But he never responded. His face remained blank.

One afternoon, Officer Clarence Clem approached me outside Gilbert's cell. "You wonder what he is thinking, don't you?" Clem said. "Whatever it is, he's sure not on this planet."

For two weeks, the only way officers could get Gilbert to obey their commands was by offering him food, as if he were a trained animal being rewarded with treats.

"What's frustrating about this," Dr. Poitier said one day, "is that we all know this man can be helped by medication. There is no doubt about it. He's been in this jail before, and we all know he responds well to medication. The last time he was in here, we got him into treatment, and he thanked us later because the medication made him better. But now the law is forcing us to stand back and do nothing while he continues to get worse. If this man's arm was fractured, we'd be accused of negligence and cruelty if we didn't help him. But because he's mentally ill, we're not supposed to interfere until he asks us. It's tragic. This man is a human being and deserves better."

I had found my first inmate to shadow.

D uring Dr. Poitier's morning rounds, I watched for other inmates whose cases I could track. One morning, we happened upon Ted Jackson on the ninth floor's B wing, which is where mentally ill inmates accused of misdemeanor crimes were kept. According to Judge Leifman's misdemeanor diversion program, the prisoners in B wing were only supposed to be housed in jail for a maximum of forty-eight hours. They were supposed to be transferred into one of Miami's seven mental health community crisis centers as quickly as possible for treatment.

Ted Jackson had been arrested on a Wednesday afternoon and hadn't been wearing a shirt when the police had brought him in. I was surprised by how physically fit he was. Most inmates on the ninth floor were homeless and in poor health. But Jackson, who was forty-two years old and white, had a "six-pack" and the muscular arms of a bodybuilder. He was wearing blue denim jeans that had been ironed and cherry-colored Nike running shoes that looked brand-new.

"I need my medication," Jackson announced.

"What do you take?" Dr. Poitier asked.

"Lithium, clozapine, and Risperdal," he replied. "But I've got to take lithium in its pill form. It's got to be coated, otherwise it gives me diarrhea."

Dr. Poitier said the jail didn't have tablets, just liquid, causing Jackson to frown. "Oh that's just great," he said sarcastically. "You're telling me I'm going to be getting the runs while I'm stuck in here?"

Dr. Poitier asked Jackson how he'd bruised his face, because both his cheeks were swollen and red, and his chest was badly scraped as if he'd been dragged across a floor.

Jackson glanced at the correctional officer standing nearby and then said, "Ah, I fell down a few days ago."

Dr. Poitier continued his rounds, but I returned ten minutes later and asked Jackson if he would agree to be interviewed. When he said yes, the officer on duty unlocked his cell and motioned the prisoner to step forward. Jackson, who had a gray blanket draped around his shoulders, started to come out, but he was stopped by the officer.

"You've got to leave the blanket in the cell," she ordered.

Jackson glanced back at a black inmate who was standing near the commode. There was only one blanket in the cell and Jackson had it. As soon as he tossed it onto one of the steel bunks, the inmate snatched it.

"You can use it for now," Jackson declared, "but I want it when I get back here from talking to this guy."

I noticed there was only one mattress in the two-man cell, too, and Jackson had been using it. As soon as the officer locked the door, the other inmate scrambled onto the mattress.

We were taken to a tiny cubicle used by attorneys when they spoke to their clients. The officer in the control booth in the lobby could see us through the room's windows but couldn't hear what we were saying. Jackson signed a privacy release for the jail that the officer handed him, and the officer left us.

Jackson said he had been diagnosed with bipolar disorder while serving in the military. But he immediately changed the subject.

"I'm really glad I met you," he gushed, "because I've got a story to tell that's going to change the entire world. Do you know where the oil from the Alaska pipeline goes? Japan. They've been stealing our technology since 1950. It's Eisenhower's fault. I wrote a letter to President Bush and told him about the Book of Daniel. The Vietnam War wasn't in the Bible and it wasn't supposed to happen. That was man's stupidity. Bush's decision to go to war with Iraq was made because of me and my letter. It's all linked to Isaiah. There's too much to explain in one sitting. Whew! Where to begin? It will take hours of us talking. I don't know if you can ever really grasp it all. It has to do with a computer being built in Belgium. I met the maker on an airplane when I was flying to Miami. I asked him to slow down its construction. Read the Book of Daniel and you'll see why. You should be in this world, but not of it. The American public is retarded, man. They don't know what's going on. I'm trying to warn people. I met James Brown in South Beach. He and his family were in a car and stopped at the corner. I said, 'James Brown, the greatest running back who ever lived.' He said, 'I won't go that far.' I said, 'I would.' I told him I wouldn't disturb his privacy because he was with his family, but we both understood. We shared a moment. Now I know what he's doing in California and he knows what I'm doing here. I don't want to take credit for the war in Iraq, but I don't think Bush would have started it if he hadn't got my letter. I told him about the computer and those identifying chips. They're putting them in children. They put them in every house they build and they're all linked to this computer in Belgium. President Bush was saved at a Billy Graham prayer meeting. He and I sometimes communicate telepathically. Only you can't tell anyone, because the Iraqis will come and get me if they know. There are really eleven commandments in Exodus. Bush knows. I told him. I dance every day for exercise. Dancing is great exercise. Wanna see?"

Jackson popped from his chair and began shuffling his feet. The officer from the control booth walked over, opened the door, and said, "You need to sit down!"

"I'm just demonstrating my dancing."

"I don't care what you're doing. Sit down now!"

Jackson slumped back into his plastic chair.

"I didn't want to tell the doctor about my face," he said, touching one of the angry bruises. "Because them cops beat me up over in Miami Beach. I didn't want to say nothing because the guards here might be in cahoots with them other cops and I don't want them beating me up too."

"Why did they beat you up?"

"Because of graffiti I wrote. I told them right off I was the one doing it, but they said they were going to teach me a lesson and they hit me hard while I was handcuffed."

I asked him about his military service.

"I liked it. The other day, I was in the VA hospital and I met a man who told me three times he'd died during an operation. He was absolutely dead. Stone cold. And he saw this white light and he heard a voice that said, 'Not your time yet.' I never met anyone like him. It gave me the biggest boost because it shows it's true. White people don't understand, but black people do. They're more in touch with their spiritual feelings. The Army sent me to Grenada. I had two hundred and seventy-five people under my command. But they started coming after me. They started picking on me. For seven months I took it. Then they forced me out. But that's not important. I got to get out of here so I can tell the president about the computer and the stuff that got me in trouble with the police in the first place—about Jesus coming back."

Jackson leaned in close and whispered that God had given him a revelation. He wasn't certain why God had chosen him, but it didn't matter. "He told me Jesus will be returning in 2007. That's the graffiti that I been writing—Jesus 2007. The cops don't like it. Do you think the cops in Miami Beach are all Jews?"

Jackson said that he'd taken notes about what God had said to him. He'd gone to a local Kinko's and made copies of them. He called his notes from God "Puppet Master." The manager of the copying store had given him enough credit to duplicate several thousand copies. In fact, Jackson owed the store $4,000. He had a copy of a Puppet Master sheet in the back pocket of his pants and he handed it to me after glancing out the window to see if the officer was watching us. Here is some of what God told him:

> Chew gum, tell yourself in the blood of Jesus—scat, flee, stay away. Lucifer hates to hear or be near someone chanting to themselves in the blood of Jesus. Sooner or later you will be set free. Don't let the turkeys pull you down. Now you are soaring like an eagle.

The officer rapped on the glass and yelled, "Five more minutes."

Jackson said, "You can keep my notes. I hope I get that blanket back in my cell. It's cold in here but I don't want to have to fight that guy for it. I had the mattress and the blanket when they brought him in this morning, so I should get to keep them."

I followed Jackson. Once inside his cell, he asked the other inmate to surrender the blanket, but he refused. Jackson called out to the correctional officer on duty.

"Hey, I need a blanket."

"There ain't any more," she replied. "Just be quiet and don't be causing me no trouble."

I spent the next hour watching Jackson from the center hallway. He couldn't see me, but I had a good view of him. He paced for a while and then began dancing. When the ninth-floor nurse came by pushing her medicine cart, Jackson asked if she had brought his medication. She checked her clipboard and said she didn't have any pills for him.

"But I need my medicine," he complained.

She said there was nothing on his chart about him getting any. She then shooed him away from the cell door and called his cellmate. As soon as the other prisoner climbed off the bunk with the mattress, Jackson scooted onto it, claiming the prize for himself. But the other man clung tight to the blanket.

That afternoon, I drove to the Miami Beach Police Department's South Beach station and paid for a copy of Jackson's arrest report.

Miami Beach Police Department
Offense Incident Report

Incident location: *900–1400 Blk. of the Seawall.* **Businessname:** *Lummis Park.* **Description:** *Criminal Mischief.* **Suspect:** *Ted Jackson.* **Height** *6′* **Weight** *165* **Eye Color** *Brn* **Hair Color** *Brn* **Complexion** *Light* **Facial Hair** *None* **Teeth** *Good*

Narrative:

On the above date, suspect was observed by this officer writing graffiti with a red ink indelible marker on the top of the public seawall at the above described location. Suspect used a large red permanent marker to damage this city property. When I approached the suspect and ordered him to cease this unlawful activity, he looked at me and ran away toward the beach despite my loud verbal command to stop. I immediately advised Htq. I saw the suspect running along the beach and ordered him to stop and lay down on the sand. He looked back at me—I was in a police uniform—and then he continued to run away. At this point, Officer Jones joined me and we caught up with Jackson and informed him he was under arrest and to lay on the sand. He refused and began to run away again. Loud verbal commands were given, but Jackson failed to comply with my orders. Jackson was advised that he would be sprayed with AOS if he didn't comply. He again attempted to run away and was sprayed in the face by me with a one-second burst to the face. Jackson was placed on the sand and secured. It is believed Jackson is responsible for 50–100 painting incidents in South Beach alone. Post Miranda, he admitted to the graffiti, along with the other graffiti documented between the 900 block through the 1400 block of the seawall, along Ocean Drive. He said he wrote: "Jesus 2007." Suspect was transported to the Miami-Dade jail.

The next morning, I went to see Jackson again, but he had been taken to the Bayview Center for Mental Health, a community crisis center in North Miami that had a contract with the county to treat psychotic inmates from the jail accused of misdemeanors. Two days later, I drove there on a Sunday afternoon. Bayview is a one-story building painted light green with dark-green trim. It is located in a poor neighborhood near Interstate 95. I was afraid Bayview wouldn't let me inside if its director found out I was a reporter, so I planned my arrival during regular weekend visiting hours and joined about a dozen others who had come to see patients. I signed in at the desk and wrote down Ted Jackson's name as the patient whom I had come to visit. I'd brought along a Subway sandwich, potato chips, and a soda for Jackson. The lone staff member on duty in the visitors' room was preoccupied with the kickoff of a Miami Dolphins football game and didn't ask me any questions. Instead, he nodded toward an overstuffed chair near a corner and then pointed toward me when Jackson came into the room. I waved the sandwich at Jackson and reminded him who I was.

"Mr. Writerman," he said, sticking out his hand. "Hey, there's something I need to tell you. It's about Jesus."

I cut him off and asked if he had ever gotten any antipsychotic medicine while he was being held in the jail.

"No, they never gave me a darn thing. And I never got a blanket either and it was cold there. But I did get to sleep on the mattress."

He asked if I would mention in my book that there had been profanity written on the ninth-floor walls inside his cell. "It was hard to think clearly with all that filth around."

He was wearing a red T-shirt and I asked him where he'd gotten it. He'd been told to choose a shirt to wear from a box of donated clothing when he'd first arrived at Bayview.

"I asked if it was clean because I didn't want anything from someone with AIDS," he explained, "but the guy just told me to take the shirt and shut up. That's how they are. They don't like you to bother them."

"What happened after you were brought here?" I asked.

"They gave me medicine to help me sleep. I went to bed on Friday afternoon, and today is the first day I've been up for more than an hour. They like to keep you drugged up in these places. They said I'd see a doctor tomorrow, since this was a weekend."

I asked if he'd always lived in Miami, and he laughed and said, "No way, I'm an Ohio boy." He'd moved to South Beach seven years ago to escape Midwest winters. He lived in an apartment close to the beach. He didn't have a job. He received $1,000 a month from a trust fund that his father had created just before he'd died. His mother was now eighty-two years old and still lived in Ohio. He called her every night on a cell phone. "They took my phone away from me when I went to jail." They'd also taken his wallet and a gold necklace with a big cross on it that he claimed was worth $250. He hadn't known anyone when he'd arrived in Florida, and he still didn't have any friends here. The owner of a bicycle shop near his apartment kept a spare apartment key for him in case he locked himself out.

"That bike man sold me handlebars for my bike. That's how I know him. I don't have a car. Them bars were just sitting in his store's attic. They're banana bars. I painted my bike fluorescent orange and it's one-of-a-kind. I got it rigged up so I can put my fishing equipment on it."

Jackson said the Army discharged him in 1983 after his mental illness was diagnosed. "I see a doctor once a month at the VA."

"Does the Veterans Administration doctor know that you've been arrested?"

"I'll tell him when I see him next time. I don't think what them cops did was right, the beating, you know? I didn't deserve to get hit like that. I was only trying to tell people about Jesus."

Jackson told me that a few weeks before he was arrested, he had been standing on a street corner handing out copies of his Puppet Master flyer when a teenager had stopped to speak to him.

"Come to find out, this young man was a prostitute. He sure enough was. He was a runaway living on the street, and I was surprised because he was just a kid. I asked him if he'd ever gone fishing and he hadn't, and that just about made me cry."

Jackson invited the youth to go fishing with him.

"This kid says to me, 'When?' I said to him, 'Well, why not right now? I got an extra pole and two bikes in my apartment.'"

They rode the bikes to the southern tip of Miami Beach, where they caught five mackerel, which Jackson cleaned and cooked for their dinner that night.

"You should've seen this kid. Why, his whole face was lit up when he caught his first fish. It was beautiful, man."

Jackson invited the teenager to spend the night, but began having second thoughts after the prostitute asked him if he wanted to have sex. The next morning, they went fishing again but they didn't catch anything. The boy asked if he could spend the night again and Jackson said he could. When Jackson got up the next morning, his houseguest was gone and so were Jackson's cash and credit card.

"I was trying to help him and he stole from me."

I asked Jackson if a lot of people took advantage of him, and he said,

"Well, sometimes it's hard to know who is really your friend and who just wants something from you."

When visiting hours ended, I left, and Jackson was given some pills and went back to bed. Four days later, he was driven back to the jail. Because he had undergone "treatment" at Bayview, all the charges filed against him were dismissed. But he was told that he owed $649 in court costs that had to be paid within thirty days, otherwise a bench warrant would be issued for his arrest. The jail returned his cell phone and bill-fold, but his gold cross necklace wasn't in his property bag. The officer insisted that Jackson hadn't been wearing a necklace when the Miami Beach police first booked him into jail, and Jackson couldn't remember if he had been.

From the jail's exit, he walked a half block to a bus stop, where he caught the city bus going to South Beach. But during the trip, he began thinking about fishing, and that got him thinking about how the creeks and streams in America were becoming polluted and how fish were dying, and he became so preoccupied that he missed the next stop, where he was supposed to transfer.

He used his cell phone to call me, and when I didn't answer, he left me a long message about how something needed to be done to save the fish and streams. Because he'd missed his connection, it took him another hour to retrace his steps and get on the right bus. By the time he finally reached his apartment, the trip had taken him four hours rather than an hour.

He telephoned his mother, because he knew she'd be worried about him. She already had heard that he had been in jail, because Dr. Poitier had called her. She asked Jackson if he'd been taking his antipsychotic medicine, and he said he had but that maybe he needed to increase the dose. After he hung up, Jackson decided to go fishing even though it was almost midnight. He was gathering his gear when he noticed a pile of

Puppet Master flyers on the floor next to his bike. They got him think-ing about Jesus and how He was coming back in 2007, so Jackson put his fishing pole aside and scooped up a handful of his papers and went out to distribute them.

I 'd found a second inmate to shadow. After I listened to his telephone message to me, I made a note. Even though Jackson had been arrested, put in jail, sent to the Bayview Center, given drugs, and released through Judge Leifman's diversion program, he sounded about the same as when we'd first spoken in jail.

As far as I could tell, Ted Jackson was still not thinking clearly.

I decided to branch outside the jail so I could meet other parents who, like me, had mentally ill children. How did their experiences compare with mine? I contacted the National Alliance for the Mentally Ill, which is known by its acronym NAMI (pronounced nam-me) and bills itself as "the nation's voice on mental illness." It's generally the first group that parents contact when mental illness strikes. If you call the Miami chapter, you'll end up speaking to either Rachel Diaz or Judy Robinson. They are the driving force behind the chapter, and as one longtime NAMI member would later tell me, "You have to decide rather quickly here if you're a Rachel person or a Judy person." The two women had been friends once, but now they rarely spoke or had much nice to say about the other. Their personalities were as different as their opinions.

I was surprised when I met Rachel Diaz and she told me she was eighty. She certainly didn't look or seem her age. A petite and modest woman with short salt-and-pepper hair cut in a no-nonsense pageboy, Diaz helped found the NAMI chapter in Miami in 1980 after her husband became a recluse. Although they were still married, they hadn't lived together for years. Diaz told me that he suffered from anosognosia—a term she and others in NAMI used to describe a "lack of insight," which they insist occurs when someone becomes mentally ill.

"Our loved ones are not in denial of their mental illness," she said. "They are unable to recognize that the feelings, voices, delusions, or irrational thoughts they are experiencing are due to malfunctions in their brain's frontal lobes." Put simply, their brains don't tell them they are sick. In fact, they tell them just the opposite—that everything is fine.

Some doctors have questioned whether anosognosia is a valid medical condition. But advocates, such as Diaz, insist it explains why psychotic individuals can't decide on their own when they need to be medicated. As I listened to her describe anosognosia, I thought about Mike and how confident he had been when we were in the Inova Fairfax Hospital emergency room that there was nothing odd about his thinking.

I asked Diaz if I could attend the monthly NAMI support group meeting that she hosted. "Of course." She beamed. "A representative from the Bristol-Myers Squibb company is coming to talk to us about Abilify."

Abilify, or aripiprazole, was a new antipsychotic drug that was being prescribed to treat schizophrenia, schizoaffective disorder, and bipolar disorder. It was being promoted as a new wonder drug, just as Thorazine once had been. A few nights later, I arrived at the meeting early enough to help set up folding chairs in a classroom inside a church. Even though Diaz expected only seventeen to attend, the drug company's representative had assured her that he'd stay as long as necessary to answer questions. Bristol-Myers Squibb was hoping to turn Abilify into the most prescribed antipsychotic drug on the market, and he wasn't going to miss any chance that he had to sell it. The number-one spot was currently being held by Zyprexa, which was made by Eli Lilly and Company. A check of Lilly's annual report in 2003 revealed why Bristol-Myers Squibb was so eager to promote Abilify. Eli Lilly had sold more than $4.3 billion worth of Zyprexa that year alone—about one-third of the company's *entire* medical sales. Bristol-Myers Squibb had set a target of $1 billion in Abilify sales in 2004 and appeared to have launched a grassroots campaign aimed at NAMI groups such as Diaz's. It wasn't the only drug maker trying to claim a piece of the mental illness profit pie. Pfizer was also pushing its drug: Geodon (ziprasidone hydrochloride) and Janssen Pharmaceutica, a part of Johnson & Johnson, was pitching Risperdal (risperidone).

Usually, Spanish was spoken in Diaz's group, but out of courtesy to the drug salesman, tonight's session was to be conducted in English.

"Mental illness," Diaz began, "is a brain disorder caused by a chemical imbalance." It was not a sickness that its victims brought on themselves, nor was it caused by poor parenting, excessive drinking, or deviant behavior, she declared. There was no reason for anyone in the group to be embarrassed because he or she loved someone who was mentally ill. "Would you be ashamed if your spouse was stricken with cancer?" she asked rhetorically. Diaz liked to begin her meetings with this opening message, because she thought both the mentally ill and their relatives frequently felt guilty and embarrassed because of what they were going through. She then introduced the drug salesman.

"Perhaps you should begin by explaining the dopamine theory," Diaz told him. Although no one knows what actually causes mental illness, "the dopamine theory" is the most widely accepted hypothesis and the one endorsed by the federal government's National Institute of Mental Health (NIMH), Diaz explained.

Following Diaz's prodding, the salesman quickly gave the group a biology lesson. Human brains contain approximately one hundred billion cells called neurons. They are the gray matter that actually performs the brain's work—controlling a person's thoughts, senses, and actions. Neurons are connected to other neurons, as many as one thousand to ten thousand. The connecting points between them are called synapses. Messages race across the synapses at a rate of 600 per second. Chemicals known as neurotransmitters carry these messages from one neuron to the next. While there are many different chemicals that can act as neuro-transmitters, the one that is most commonly associated with mental ill-ness is dopamine. During a psychotic episode, the brains of schizophrenics have an excess of dopamine flooding their neurons. The first medicine that had successfully "blocked" this excess dopamine was Thorazine. As soon as the extra dopamine swimming inside a schizophrenic's head had been brought under control, the voices and hallucinations had either decreased or stopped. This led NIMH to conclude that excess dopamine is one of the reasons people's brains malfunction.

The salesman punched several keys on his portable computer, and a projector flashed two large blue circles onto the church's wall. There were smaller yellow beads floating between the two blue dots. He explained that the blue circles represented neurons and the yellow beads were dopamine. The next slide was identical to the first, except that nearly all of the yellow beads—the dopamine—were now being blocked by red X's. The X's represented Abilify.

"Abilify corrects the dopamine supply so the brain gets the exact amount that it needs to function correctly," he proudly declared.

The next slide that flashed on the wall contained a list of antipsy-chotic medicines ranked by the year when they were introduced. The first was Thorazine (chlorpromazine), which was marketed in 1952. Dur-ing the 1960s, several other dopamine blockers had been manufactured, including Haldol (haloperidol), Prolixin (fluphenazine hydrochloride), Mellaril (thioridazine hydrochloride), Loxitane (loxapine), and Trilafon (perphenazine). But no new antipsychotic medications had been made in the 1970s and 1980s. This was because of the antipsychiatry move-ment and a shift in the mood of the country. Although antipsychotic drugs had started out being heralded, they had lost their luster after doctors in state mental hospitals began abusing them to keep their pa-tients docile.

In the 1990s, a new generation of antipsychotic drugs had been invented. They were called "atypical antipsychotics," because their manufacturers wanted to distance them from the older ones. Instead of blocking *all* the dopamine that passed between the brain's neurons, these drugs targeted specific "neuron receptors" and allowed some dopamine to pass, but only a necessary amount.

This refinement was a major breakthrough, the salesman announced, because the older medications had caused a number of dreadful side effects by indiscriminately blocking *all* dopamine. The most common was a condition that caused patients to develop Parkinson-like symptoms, including jerky movements. The salesman said the new medications didn't cause side effects that were as harmful or severe as those caused by the earlier drugs.

The first of the atypical drugs was Clozaril (clozapine), followed by Risperdal (risperidone), Zyprexa (olanzapine), and Seroquel (quetiapine fumarate). In 2000, Geodon (ziprasidone hydrochloride) was introduced, and in 2003—Abilify.

The salesman spent the rest of his pitch bragging about how Abilify was a more effective and less expensive drug than Zyprexa, which costs an average of $500 per month compared with $250 to $350 a month for Abilify, depending on the dosage.

One of Diaz's group members raised her hand. "My daughter became violent and mean when she was given Abilify," she said. "We had to get her off it—immediately."

Before the flustered salesman could respond, another member volunteered that Abilify had helped her husband stop hearing voices, something no other drug had achieved. Thumbing through a heavy satchel that she had brought with her, Diaz plucked an NIMH bulletin from a file folder. Holding it up for everyone to see, she told her group that a government study had found that 70 percent of patients with schizophrenia had improved after they were given antipsychotic medication. But 25 percent improved only minimally or not at all, and 5 percent actually became worse when they were given drugs that blocked excess dopamine. "Every mentally ill person is different. Their brains are unique," she explained. "Some can be helped and some cannot be helped."

Continuing, Diaz said that while antipsychotic medications were able to reduce delusions, hallucinations, aggressive behavior, thinking disorders, and other symptoms of mental illness, they were certainly not a cure. "Taking these drugs is not like swallowing an aspirin," she said. "Mental illness is not going to disappear because you take a pill. You do *not* become well. The sickness will always be there because the chemistry in your brain is not correctly balanced. This is why it is important to educate yourself about these drugs and what they do. Always remember that this is a big business and there is a big industry dedicated to trying to keep our mentally ill loved ones exactly where they are today. Doctors, hospitals, and drug companies—each has a vested interest in the mentally ill because they are making money off of their suffering."

Her comments seemed to surprise the Bristol-Myers Squibb salesman, but she wasn't finished. While Abilify and other medications might be able to make the "positive symptoms" of mental disorders disappear, she said, they did not alleviate the "negative symptoms," such as feelings of apathy and ambivalence and a flattening of emotions.

"There is no magical pill out," she warned. "The most important thing for all of us to remember is that our loved ones are sick. They did not ask for these diseases any more than we ask to get the flu. Remember, too, that *we* are not the victims. We suffer because we *care*, but the mentally ill are the real victims."

A week later, I hurried up two flights of steps at a different church in a different Miami neighborhood, where Judy Robinson was holding her monthly NAMI meeting. In her mid-seventies, Robinson was a former New Yorker, a onetime child actor, an accomplished vocalist, Jewish, divorced, attractive, and stylishly dressed. Like Rachel Diaz, Judy Robinson had gotten involved in NAMI after someone she loved had become ill. It was her son Jeffrey.

I quickly discovered that the two women ran their support meetings completely differently. Diaz disliked offering members advice about their personal problems. She preferred focusing on the latest scientific studies and spent much of her time behind the scenes, writing letters to newspapers and politicians. Judy Robinson was the Miami mental health community's Dr. Phil. She was a dynamic public speaker, was frequently quoted in *The Miami Herald*, served on a half dozen boards and committees, and didn't mind telling her group members exactly what they needed to do. She had a reputation for being hard-nosed, hard-charging, and highly opinionated. Some called her pushy and she didn't deny it. If stepping on toes got things done, she put down both feet—hard.

Robinson always brought two placards to her class and put them up for everyone to read. About a dozen rules were written on them: *Be respectful. Don't interrupt. Don't dwell on the past. Be concise: don't take more than three minutes to discuss your story.* A dozen group members took their seats around a U-shaped table for the evening's meeting. Robinson started by telling them about Alison, a regular who had been absent recently. She said Alison had telephoned her in a panic about three months earlier because her daughter had been jailed.

"As many of you know, Alison's daughter has a long history of going off her medicine, getting into trouble, and then manipulating her mother into saving her," Robinson explained. "Only this time, things worked out differently and I'm going to tell you why."

Robinson said she'd been blunt with Alison when she'd called for advice. "I said, 'Listen, I have the experience to help you, but you aren't going to like what I'm going to say.'" She then advised Alison not to rescue her daughter. Instead, Robinson called a social worker at the women's jail and made certain Alison's daughter had been put in a cell on the psych floor so she'd be safe. Robinson then told Alison that she needed to apply for legal guardianship over her daughter—a move that would enable her to control her daughter's treatment regimen. Next, Robinson instructed Alison to contact the county judge who'd been assigned to hear her daughter's criminal case. "I told her *not* to call him directly but to fax him a letter that explained her daughter's mental problems."

Robinson said Alison had had a tough time accepting her advice. Alison's first instinct had been to rush to the jail. But Robinson warned her not to give in to those emotions. "I told her, 'Listen, I know how hard it is because I have been through this many, many times with my own son. I had my son's therapist tell me not to visit him in jail, not to be at his beck and call, not to allow him to manipulate me, because it doesn't serve any therapeutic purpose.' What I was telling her was tough love, but little by little, if you take the right steps, it will make a difference."

With Robinson's help, Alison arranged for her daughter to be transferred from the jail directly into a hospital. Because Alison was now her daughter's legal guardian, she could force her ward to take antipsychotic medicine, Robinson claimed. And her daughter had slowly gotten better. At that point, Robinson had given Alison permission to finally visit her daughter. "I told her that when she saw her daughter, she needed to pick her words carefully. Her daughter didn't need to hear her mother's anger. She didn't need to hear how frustrated she was. I said, 'What you need to tell your daughter is this: I'm sorry this has happened. We all make choices and these are yours. This is not what I had hoped for you. But you've got to take some responsibility for your actions and you've got to stay on your medication.'"

Robinson told the group that she'd gotten a call from Alison a few hours before tonight's meeting. "Her daughter is about to be released from the hospital, and the two of them are getting along better now than they ever have. Her daughter is taking her medicine. No one is kidding themselves. This is still an uphill battle, but both mother and daughter are moving forward because their relationship has changed."

Several of the members in Robinson's group began to applaud, but Robinson cut them short. "We've got a lot to get through tonight, so let's get moving," she declared. Turning to her left, she asked the woman sitting next to her to tell the group about her week.

"I've good news to share," the woman said, smiling. Her thirty-two-year-old son had moved back into her house after being homeless. The woman's eyes filled with tears as she described how she used to drive by him on her way to work each morning. "He was living on the street, and I'd see him searching through garbage cans for food," she recalled, her voice cracking with emotion. But Robinson had urged her to practice tough love. And she had told her son that he couldn't come home until he agreed to take his antipsychotic medication. It had been terrible, she said, but after *nine years* of her watching her son live on the street, he had finally agreed to take his medicine and had gotten well enough to move home. Nine years.

"He didn't want to go with me to my sister's house on Sunday for dinner," the woman continued. "I told him, 'That's fine, honey.' But I didn't fix him anything special for dinner. I let him get something out of the refrigerator, and then later when I brought home lots of really great food, he saw what he had missed. I think next weekend, he'll want to go." She laughed, and the others began clapping.

An older man spoke next about problems he had been having with his adult son who lived with him. A former high school music teacher, his son had been stricken with bipolar disorder, had lost his job, and had been forced to move home. "Lately, he's started playing with a band and is staying up late at night and sleeping during the day," explained the father, who was in his eighties. "I know erratic schedules are disastrous for persons who have bipolar disorder. But my son is not a boy. He's in his fifties. Can I set a curfew for him at his age?"

Robinson jotted down a note. "We'll get back to you after everyone is finished," she explained. "For right now, let's keep moving."

"I've made real progress with my bipolar son," the next speaker said. One night when she got home from her job, she discovered her son had spent the day rearranging all the furniture in their house. He'd even rehung the paintings. "I was furious, but instead of yelling at him, I did what Judy has taught us to do. I used the 'I' word. I said 'I'm happy you've taken an interest in how our living room is arranged, but I would've liked you discussing it with me first.' I talked about *my* feelings rather than attacking him. And it worked! We didn't get into a huge fight, and no one ran out of the house angry."

The next member said she was worried about her twenty-year-old schizophrenic son. "He doesn't have any friends. He sits in his room all day," she said. "My husband and I wonder if he'll always be like this."

Robinson made another note.

"My husband and I have been arguing all week," another speaker said. "We've been invited to a bar mitzvah, and my husband doesn't want our son to go because he's afraid he'll embarrass us. But I say he's our son and should go."

Once again, Robinson scribbled on her notepad.

The last parent to speak said her mentally ill son had moved into a car parked in the driveway. "He only comes inside to use the toilet. The last time he acted like this, he got violent and ended up in jail. I don't know what to do."

Robinson scanned her notes and then moved down the list in reverse order. To the woman whose son was sleeping in the family car, she said, "You need to get him professional help *now*, and if he won't go in with you voluntarily, then go to court to force him into the hospital."

To the mother fussing about the bar mitzvah, she said, "This really isn't about that invitation. It's about you always stepping in and rescuing your son from his own actions. Draw some boundaries, set some rules, and then don't back down. My son Jeff was arrested more than forty times. Don't you think that was embarrassing to me? If your son wants to go to the bar mitzvah, tell him he'll have to stay on his medicines and act right."

To the mother whose boy was lonely, Robinson wrote out an address. It was a county-run drop-in center in Miami where the mentally ill could socialize. "They can talk, play pool, watch television there." For a moment, Robinson allowed other members of her group to suggest ways to get the woman's son out of his bedroom. She then mentioned that her son Jeff was a volunteer worker at the VA hospital. But she candidly admitted that it was tough even for him to make friends. "Loneliness and isolation is a huge, huge problem for our mentally ill loved ones."

Robinson then told the elderly father that he could set a curfew for his adult son because he was living in his father's house. "He needs to respect you."

Having dispensed her advice, Robinson turned to Carol, the only group member who had not talked about her week. "I've asked Carol to wait until now, because what she has to share is especially important," Robinson explained.

Looking a bit nervous, Carol said that her thirty-four-year-old son had begun acting oddly one afternoon. "His psychiatrist had changed his medication for bipolar disorder."

"These doctors are always playing with medicines," Robinson interjected. "And a lot of the time they don't have any clue what's going to happen. It's disgraceful."

Returning to her story, Carol said her son had gone out for a walk. An hour later, the FBI called and told her that he was standing outside its office, "trying to commune with its computers." She telephoned her husband, who left his job to pick up their son. When they got home, their son got angry and pushed his father. Carol called 911. "I told the dispatcher my son was mentally ill and needed to be taken to the hospital. There was something wrong with his medication." But when the police arrived, they arrested him. "This cop told us he was charging my son with domestic violence. My husband said, 'Look, I'm not going to press charges. He's sick. He needs help. His medicine got screwed up.' I said, 'This is only going to make things worse for us.' I started begging this cop, but he took my son to jail. That's when I called Judy."

"At one-thirty in the morning," Robinson chimed in.

"Yes, I woke her up. I didn't know who else to call."

Robinson had made certain that Carol's son was put on the ninth floor and not in the jail's general inmate population. The next morning, Robinson phoned the public defender's office for Carol. "They got my son released from jail on his own recognizance," Carol said, "which was great, but what was I supposed to do with him? He was still unstable."

Because her son had been charged with domestic violence, he wasn't allowed to return to his parents' house. "Here I was, standing on the sidewalk outside the jail with my son who's psychotic, and we've got no place to go. I called Robinson on my cell phone."

Robinson told her to walk to Cedars Medical Center, which was one block away from the jail. But her son didn't want to go. "I called Judy back and said, 'What can I do now?' And Judy said, 'Tell him it's either the hospital or the jail.' I said to her, 'Is that true?' And Judy said, 'He won't know if it is or isn't.' So I closed my cell phone and I told him that he was going back to jail, and then he agreed to go into the hospital voluntarily."

Robinson waited a moment and then asked, "What can we learn from this incident?" No one said anything. "Folks," Robinson snapped, "this system is broken! It doesn't work! The doctor shouldn't have fooled with her son's medication. The cops shouldn't have arrested him. You've got to become your own advocate here and fight for your loved ones. Otherwise, without you, they're going to end up in a real mess."

I watched the faces of the parents sitting around the table and wondered how they did it: the mother who had watched her son living homeless on the street for *nine* years, the father in his eighties who was still
taking care of his adult son, and Judy Robinson herself. She had said that
Jeff had been arrested more than forty times by the police. *Forty times.*
I remembered what Rachel Diaz had said during her meeting—how
mental illness is a chemical imbalance, how no one chooses to be mentally ill. And how drugs don't always help alleviate everyone's symptoms.

I began to sweat. A feeling of dread washed over me. After Mike had
begun taking his medication and was discharged from the hospital psych
ward, I had felt a sense of hope. Surely, the worst was behind us when
it came to getting him medical treatment. But sitting at this table now
with these other parents, I was starting to realize that there were no
guarantees when it came to mental illness, and as simpleminded as it
might seem, I was beginning to understand that bipolar disorder was not
like a cold that would go away if Mike took his medicine.

Mike was mentally ill. That was a lifetime illness. And like it or not,
what happened to him was going to affect me too, for the rest of our
lives.

J udy Robinson wanted me to meet someone, so on a Saturday morning we met at her house and started what would be a two-hour drive. During it, I asked her to tell me about her son Jeff.

She said he had been eighteen the first time he'd been arrested in 1969. Jeff had been with friends inside a Royal Castle hamburger stand when a plainclothes police officer had come inside. The boys were noisy, so the cop ordered them to quiet down. Jeff had argued with him, and their dispute ended with Jeff being booked into the Miami jail. A furious Judy hired an attorney, and a judge dismissed the charges.

But that incident had proven prologue.

Jeff's mental illness, which was later diagnosed as schizoaffective disorder, grew worse as he aged. (Schizoaffective disorder bridges the gap between bipolar disorder and schizophrenia. Bipolar disorder causes mood shifts. Schizophrenia is a thought disorder that makes its victims hallucinate. Schizoaffective is both a mood disorder and a thought disorder.) Jeff soon developed a habit of seeking out the police to argue with them whenever he became manic. During the next three decades, he would be jailed thirty-nine times in Miami and a couple more times during trips outside the state. Often when Robinson visited him in jail, he would have bruises on his face from fistfights. Robinson was afraid that Jeff would eventually be shot during a confrontation with the police.

In the 1990s, she read that the police in Memphis had started a training program to help its officers handle mentally ill suspects. She called the Memphis Police Department and spoke to Lieutenant Sam Cochran. At Robinson's urging, I would later telephone Cochran, and during our interview he would repeat much of what Robinson had told me on our Saturday-morning drive.

Like other American cities, Memphis hadn't been prepared when the Tennessee legislature began deinstitutionalization. Hundreds of psychotic patients had been tossed out into the streets. By the fall of 1987, the Memphis Police Department was averaging ten emergency calls per day associated with psychotic suspects. One of them involved a twenty-six-year-old black man with a history of psychiatric problems who appeared one morning outside an apartment building waving a butcher knife in the air. By the time the police arrived, a crowd had gathered and the deranged man had slashed his own arm and was bleeding. The officers, who were white, ordered him to drop the weapon. Instead, he raised it above his head and stepped forward. The two officers drew their service revolvers and shot him eight times in the chest, killing him.

Relations between the predominantly white police and the black community already were strained, and the shooting set off a firestorm. To appease black leaders, the mayor appointed a panel of mental health experts to investigate. It decided that the police needed more training. But the Memphis police chief said his officers were already getting nine hours of instruction specifically about the mentally ill and that was enough. The real problem, he claimed, was a failed mental health system.

After much finger-pointing, the panel and the police agreed to sit down and talk. Lieutenant Cochran was on the police department's side, and what he heard surprised him. He discovered that the families of mentally ill suspects didn't trust the Memphis police. Neither did the doctors, mental health workers, and hospital staffs. They all thought the police caused more harm than good, because their Rambo-style tactics simply fueled a mentally unbalanced person's paranoia rather than helping to calm the situation. Meanwhile, the police didn't understand why doctors refused to treat mentally ill people and were discharging them before they were stable.

The first thing both sides agreed on was that the police needed to continue responding to emergencies rather than having the city form a specially trained unit of psychiatrists to answer 911 calls. This led them to discussing what sort of officer should be dispatched. They agreed it should be someone who wanted to help a deranged suspect rather than arrest him. The two sides then decided these officers needed to be members of a highly trained squad, just like SWAT, which most departments had. They decided to call it a Crisis Intervention Team (CIT).

Cochran helped pick thirty-two officers for CIT training. As part of their instruction, they were taken inside a psychiatric ward in a Memphis hospital. On the streets, the police saw the mentally ill as dangerous, unpredictable lunatics. In the hospital, they saw those same people on medication and realized they were someone's brother, sister, child, or parent. The police then took the doctors on patrol with them so they could see what the cops faced on the streets.

In addition to those "cultural exchanges," the officers participated in spontaneous role-playing with the doctors, showing the recruits "verbal tricks" that psychiatrists used in hospitals to calm psychotic suspects. The police were told that their priority was getting a disturbed suspect into a hospital, not rushing him to jail. During the eighty-hour training session, they also learned that mental illness was a disease, not a crime.

The first CIT class graduated on May 9, 1988, and while Cochran was hopeful, he wasn't certain the program was going to work. Less than twenty-four hours later, a CIT officer prevented a suicide. It was the start of a series of dramatic success stories. A disturbed man who believed his neighbors were trying to kill him was disarmed without anyone's being harmed; a woman waving a knife at "dead people" who she insisted were trying to rape her was talked into dropping her weapon; a man who had climbed a 200-foot-tall radio tower was persuaded by a CIT officer to come down after thirteen hours of negotiations. By the end of its first year, the Memphis CIT had transported 1,533 people to local mental health facilities—instead of jail. Even better, they had not killed a single suspect.

Judy Robinson had been so impressed by the Memphis CIT program that she had begun lobbying the police jurisdictions in Miami to start CIT training. But none of the chiefs would listen to her. Still, Robinson didn't give up. During the next *six years*, she kept pushing them. Unfortunately, they weren't convinced until the Miami police ran into Richard Beatty.

A Vietnam War veteran who had been mentally ill for thirty-three years, Beatty often thought he was still fighting the North Vietnamese. On June 6, 2001, Beatty walked into Cuatro Caminos, an all-night cafeteria, at 4:30 A.M. The night manager ordered him to leave. In the past, the fifty-six-year-old Beatty always had gone peacefully, but this time he pulled out a pocketknife and waved its three-inch-long blade at the manager. Beatty then fled, and the angry supervisor chased him and flagged down a Miami police cruiser.

During the next several minutes, Beatty led a parade of Miami officers on a twelve-block chase. Twice, the police shot him in the face with pepper spray. Each time, he kept running. At one point, the police tried to pin him between a fence and a police car. But he smashed the cruiser's side mirror and slipped away.

Beatty eventually was surrounded by a dozen officers. He was still holding his pocketknife. One of the policemen slid behind him and swung a telescoping club at the weapon, hoping to knock it free. But the officer's swing missed, and Beatty spun around.

"Drop the knife!" one of the officers yelled.

Beatty didn't. He began to move forward, and the officers opened fire with their semiautomatic handguns. Beatty was hit fourteen times and killed.

Mental health advocates in Miami were outraged. "He was executed in the street," an ACLU lawyer declared. "Beatty would still be alive today if the Miami Police Department were serious about training their force to deal with mentally ill people."

When Judy Robinson read about Beatty's death, she—once again—urged the Miami police to begin CIT training. This time, the department relented. Robinson was asked to be one of the CIT instructors. She told officers what it was like to be the parent of a mentally disturbed son and to be afraid of the police. The first Miami CIT took to the streets in 2002. During its first six months, the team answered 2,026 calls, including several that involved armed deranged suspects. No one was killed and no officers were injured.

The Miami police's decision to create a CIT prompted other local police departments to jump on board. But the biggest force in the area—the Miami-Dade County Police Department—dug in its heels. Its director, Carlos Alvarez, insisted that his three thousand officers received sufficient training on their own and didn't need Memphis cops to tell them how to do their jobs.

Alvarez simply didn't get it, Robinson said. Over the next several months, other mentally ill suspects would lose their lives.

On May 28, 2002, officers killed John Santella Jr., after the twenty-two-year-old stabbed himself in the chest nearly a dozen times with an ice pick and then lunged with it at the police.

On January 30, 2003, officers cut down Arnold Clark after he plunged a knife into his stomach, then pulled it out and approached them. Clark suffered from chronic schizophrenia.

Then on February 8, 2003, another incident occurred that enraged Judy Robinson. Robert Steven Mills III had become the next psychotic suspect to tangle with Alvarez's officers. His mother was the woman whom Robinson wanted me to interview. "I want you to hear directly from her what happened. Remember, it all could have been avoided if Miami-Dade County had CIT-trained officers," Robinson said as we pulled into the driveway of a two-story house.

R enee Sherman, a striking woman in her early forties, told me that her son Robbie had always been a difficult child. "Even in the womb. He used to kick me so hard I would be in tears. It was like I had a tornado in my belly."

He didn't socialize well with other children in preschool. In kindergarten, when other kids drew pictures of stick houses, pets, and smiling yellow suns, Robbie sketched a person burning in flames.

"It's Mommy," he told the teacher.

In second grade, he was put in a class for emotionally disturbed children. Doctors prescribed Ritalin. By his tenth birthday, he'd been hospitalized eight times because of uncontrollable outbursts. Psychiatrists at Jackson Memorial Hospital said he had bipolar disorder.

"A parent never forgets the moment when a doctor says your child is mentally ill," Sherman said. "He told me real casual, 'Oh, your son is bipolar and he'll never get any better,' like it didn't mean anything. But I was crushed. I said, 'He *will* get better. My God, he's just a small boy!'"

But Robbie didn't.

By this point, she was divorced from Robbie's father, and when she fell in love with Dennis Sherman, she warned him. "Something is wrong with my son, seriously wrong, and you need to think about whether or not you want to spend your future with me. He might never get any better, and I love my son and I'll always need to be there for him."

"I love you," Dennis assured her. But later he admitted that he had no idea just how difficult life with his stepson would be.

Unable to control Robbie's flare-ups, the Shermans sent him to a private boarding school that specialized in helping children with behavior and mental disorders. The doctors there took him off Ritalin and began treating him with Seroquel. Overnight, his mood swings leveled off, and after two years he was stable enough to return home and celebrate his bar mitzvah. For a brief period, Robbie attended public school and participated in the Boy Scouts and the family was happy. But then he began showing side effects from Seroquel that alarmed his doctors. They began experimenting with other drugs. None worked. By now Robbie was a teenager and bigger than his mother and stepfather. They slept with their bedroom door locked.

Robbie dropped out of high school during his senior year. His mood swings became extreme. Just before his eighteenth birthday, he and his mother got into a loud argument. Dennis stepped between them. Robbie shoved him. Renee called the police. They arrested Robbie even though neither Dennis nor Renee wanted him charged. They followed the police to the station and bailed Robbie out of jail.

Still angry, Robbie left home. For six months, he wandered across Florida. He'd call his mom from pay phones, depressed and sobbing. She'd send him cash, but rather than using it to come home, he'd spend it at strip clubs.

Robinson chastised Sherman at their NAMI support group meetings for "enabling" Robbie by giving him money. But she couldn't help herself. She hated that he was homeless. Behind her husband's back, she sneaked cash from their accounts and went through $20,000 before he stopped her.

When the money ran out, Robbie came home. His mother found him a cheap apartment in Miami, and he promised to try a new antipsychotic medicine. But he didn't. One night, Sherman called Robinson for advice because Robbie was manic. Robinson told her to use a Florida law called the Baker Act to force him into a hospital for treatment. During the next six months, Sherman tried four separate times to force her son into treatment. But her attempts were blocked by a judge, who ac-

knowledged in court that Robbie was clearly "out of his mind" but refused to hospitalize him because the deranged youth did not appear to
be in any imminent danger to either himself or anyone else. (It was the
same story I'd heard from other parents. The same civil rights laws that
I'd encountered with Mike.)

Sherman said Robbie was so angry that he began hiding from her.
Still, she kept trying to force her son to get help. On a Friday night, she
called Robbie's apartment and left a tearful message on his answering machine: "You're sick. Please, please, let me take you to the hospital. I love
you. Please call me!"

To her surprise, he called back, but most of what he said didn't make
any sense. Still, she knew where he was, and the Shermans raced to his
apartment. When they got there, he was gone. Robbie had left her a hate-
ful note taped to the door.

The next day, a Saturday, was their wedding anniversary, but neither
of them felt like celebrating. That same afternoon, Robbie put on his
Rollerblades and skated three miles from a friend's apartment—where
he'd been hiding from his parents—to his ex-girlfriend's house. By the
time he reached it, he was sweaty, exhausted, disheveled, and psychotic.
He began screaming when the girl refused to come outside. Someone
called the Miami-Dade County police.

Robbie had taken off his skates and lain down on the lawn to rest
when the first two officers arrived. They told him that he was trespassing and ordered him to leave. Robbie began arguing with them. Without warning, he grabbed one of his Rollerblades and threw it at a window
of his ex-girlfriend's house. The skate crashed through the glass. Robbie
grabbed a jagged seven-inch-long shard. The police drew their guns and
fired. Robbie was hit three times and died on the front lawn.

Renee Sherman didn't learn about her son's death until Sunday
morning, when two detectives came to her house. Devastated, she called
Judy Robinson.

"They killed him!" she kept repeating. "They killed my son!"

A few days later, Jim DeFede, a popular columnist at *The Miami Herald*, phoned Robinson to ask her about the CIT training program. She lashed out at Director Alvarez for refusing to enroll his officers in it.

DeFede quoted her in his column and also revealed an incredible irony. At about the same time Robbie was being gunned down by the Miami-Dade County police, a CIT-trained officer from the Miami police force had disarmed a mentally ill man swinging a butcher knife without anyone's being hurt.

Because of DeFede's column, several television stations sent news crews to Robbie's funeral. The Shermans asked Robinson to speak to reporters. She talked about how a CIT officer would have been trained to defuse the situation without Robbie's being killed. "This young man had a chance to live," she said into the cameras, her voice rising in anger, "and the police took it away."

R enee Sherman was crying by the time she finished telling me about her son's death. "Would you like to see Robbie's photograph?" she asked. She disappeared into a bedroom and then returned with a 5-by-7-inch print.

"I was a good mother," she said, her hands shaking and her voice cracking. "I loved my son. Why did this have to happen? Why did they have to shoot him? Why wouldn't anyone listen to me when I told them he was sick? Why did they have to shoot him? I loved my Robbie! Why did they have to shoot him?"

Her husband put his arm around her and she buried her face in his shoulder and sobbed. I looked at the photograph of Robbie in the gold frame. The teenager smiling back at me could have been anyone's son. He could have been Judy Robinson's son Jeff.

And he could have been Mike.

needed a break. I needed to go home. I booked a flight and closed my eyes as the jet roared down the Miami International Airport runway. As the aircraft lifted into the air, I fell asleep and dreamt I was back on the ninth floor, walking with Dr. Poitier on his morning rounds. We were moving from cell to cell when we suddenly came up to one that was crowded with inmates. I noticed a prisoner duck under a steel bunk, and I bent down and peered through the smudged glass cell front at the figure lurking there. He was in the fetal position, chewing on discarded orange peels, and when he moved his head, I got a clear look at his face.

It was me.

I jerked awake. I thought about the dream and how I had had almost the exact same dream during my first night in Miami. Only this time, I had seen myself inside the cell instead of Mike. *Was it really that odd?* Since Mike's breakdown and arrest, I had not thought about much else except mental illness. And after spending several weeks watching events on the ninth floor, I didn't find it peculiar that the images of that hellhole had invaded my sleep. Still, I wondered, why was *I* under the steel bunk? And then it came to me and it seemed obvious.

We lock up the mentally ill because they terrify us. We are afraid of them and even more frightened of what they symbolize. We want to believe they did something that caused their insanity. That is why we can justify housing them in inhumane conditions and punishing rather than treating them. The federal government says mental illness is a chemical imbalance, and because of that it's a sickness and not something, as Rachel Diaz said, that anyone seeks or wants or deserves to get any more than he seeks, wants, or deserves to get a cold.

But deep down, we really don't want to believe that's true. Because if we did, we would have to admit: *It could happen to us. It could happen to me.* I could become the sniveling, deranged creature hiding under the steel bunk nibbling on day-old orange peels. And that is such a frightening thought that we quietly search for explanations to prove that the mentally ill really aren't like us and they somehow deserve the torment they suffer.

PART
TWO

SMOKE IN THE AIR

Deinstitutionalization has become a cruel embarrassment, a reform gone terribly wrong, threatening not only the former mental inmates but also the quality of life for all New Yorkers.

—New York Times *editorial,*
June 5, 1981

A friend recommended that we hire Andrew Kersey to defend Mike in court. Kersey had recently started his own legal practice after working for several years as a prosecutor. "If you want to know how the other side thinks," my friend quipped, "then hire someone who was once part of that team."

Mike, his mother, and I met Kersey in his cramped law office. In his thirties, he had a Southern drawl and an aw-shucks modest manner. He told us that he was confident he could get the two felony charges filed against Mike reduced to two misdemeanors, because this was his first arrest, because he'd clearly not been thinking clearly, and because he was enrolled in a day treatment program.

When we left Kersey's office, I felt relieved. Having Mike plead guilty to two misdemeanors would not prevent him from pursuing his career or permanently stain his record. A few days later, Kersey called to tell us that he'd talked to the Fairfax assistant commonwealth's attorney, who was prosecuting Mike, and he'd agreed on a plea bargain. In return for Mike's giving up his right to a trial, the two felony charges would be reduced to two misdemeanors. Mike would plead guilty and the prosecutor would then recommend that the judge sentence Mike to a year of probation. He'd also be *required to complete Penny Hinkle's treatment program. It was exactly what Kersey had said he could deliver.*

On the morning of his arraignment, I asked Mike if he understood what was going to happen in court. He didn't. His antipsychotic medication was still making it difficult for him to concentrate and understand things. But he said he was excited about going there.

"Why?" I asked.

"Because I get to wear my new suit!"

Before he'd become manic, he'd bought a suit for when he went on job interviews in New York. He'd never gotten to wear it.

When we arrived at the Fairfax County Courthouse, I noticed that the owners of the house that Mike had broken into were sitting in the courtroom. I walked over and greeted them. The husband nodded, but his wife refused to make eye contact. I decided it didn't matter. All of this would soon be over. They could get on with their lives and Mike could get on with his.

I was on my way back to where Mike was seated when Kersey entered the chamber and hurried over to us. "There's a problem," he whispered. Mike and I followed him into the hallway.

"The deal's off," he announced.

"What?"

Kersey said that he'd just spent a half hour arguing with the prosecutor. From what he'd been able to learn, the prosecutor had failed to clear our plea-bargain deal with the homeowners, and when they were told about it earlier this morning, the wife had gotten angry.

"She wants your son put in jail or an institution," Kersey said.

"But we already had a deal," I complained. "The prosecutor already said yes."

"Well, now he's saying no," Kersey replied. "The victims are demanding that your son plead guilty to at least one felony charge."

"But that will ruin his future," I protested.

Kersey gave us a sympathetic look and said, "What's odd about all this is that the judge will still give Mike the exact same sentence. He'd get a year of probation and no jail time—the same thing that he would have gotten if he'd pleaded guilty to two misdemeanors. So the victims aren't really gaining anything."

"Then what's the point?" I asked, becoming exasperated. "All this is going to do is make it tougher for Mike to live a normal life. Why would she want that?"

Kersey said, "I don't know. I'll ask her. Maybe she doesn't understand that he's going to get the same sentence." Kersey disappeared into the courtroom, leaving us in the hallway. I checked my watch. Six minutes to go before court started. A few moments later, Kersey reappeared and explained that the husband didn't care if Mike pleaded guilty to two misdemeanors or to a single felony.

"But his wife wants him punished. She's saying he did sixty thousand dollars' worth of damage to their house."

"Sixty thousand!" I exclaimed. That was more than twice what she'd originally said. "That's ridiculous!"

Kersey said she was afraid Mike might come back. "What she really wants is for him to be put in prison, but that's just not going to happen."

"I was in their house," I said. "I saw the damage. She's making this much worse than it is!"

Kersey shrugged. "She is the victim."

I didn't feel that way. As far as I was concerned, Mike was the victim. He'd not asked to become mentally ill. He'd thought he was dreaming when he broke into their house.

I asked Kersey if we could negotiate a new plea bargain with the prosecutor or force him to stick to our original deal.

"No," Kersey replied. In Virginia, victims wielded tremendous clout, especially when the prosecutor is an elected official. No politician wants to be accused of being soft on criminals.

"But this is Mike's future," I snapped. "For godsakes, he is mentally ill.

Doesn't she get that? Doesn't the prosecutor understand that? He broke into their house to take a bubble bath!"

But I was wasting time preaching to the converted. We had four minutes until court began.

"What are our options?" I asked.

Kersey explained that Mike could plead guilty to a felony. If he did, this would all be over. Or he could plead not guilty and the judge would set a trial date. But, he added, a jury would probably find Mike guilty, since he'd been arrested inside the house. Then Kersey offered us another option. Mike could plead not guilty by reason of insanity, known in court lingo as NGI.

"I think we could win. I feel we could put on a strong case and the jury would acquit him," Kersey explained. But then, just as quickly, he said that he'd be reluctant to recommend the NGI defense. If we won, Mike would not walk away free. He would be taken from the courtroom to a state forensic hospital for evaluation. Mike could spend weeks in jail waiting for a vacancy in Virginia's overcrowded forensic facility, and there would be no way to predict how long he might end up being held there. Even worse, he'd be identified in the court records forever as having been found innocent but insane.

"We'd win," Kersey said, "but your son would lose."

I checked my watch. Three minutes and ticking. Three minutes to decide which was the lesser of three punishments that, as Mike's father, I believed were all unfair.

"Offer them money," I said. "If they let Mike plead to misdemeanors, we'll pay them."

Kersey frowned. He didn't think it was smart to open that door. Besides, he wasn't certain the wife was after cash. She seemed to be legitimately afraid of Mike, plus she was angry that the prosecutor hadn't consulted her in advance. Up to this point, all of the focus had been on Mike and getting him help. What about her? What about her family? Apparently, no one had consulted them.

Two minutes.

"What do you want to do?" he asked me.

I didn't know. Just then, Kersey had another idea. Often, victims bond with the police. They trust each other. Maybe Detective Armel could help us, he said. Maybe she could explain to the woman that Mike's punishment was going to be the same regardless of whether he pleaded to a felony or to two misdemeanors. He scooted back inside the courtroom.

This time, I followed him. I wanted to watch, but I stayed across the room. Kersey spoke first to Detective Armel, and then they walked over together to where the couple was sitting. When Armel bent down to whisper to them, the husband turned his head and spotted me. I retreated back into the hallway. I didn't want to irritate him.

There was a minute left.

Mike and I stood by the door, waiting. He didn't have any idea what was happening. He was watching people walking down the hallway and entering other courtrooms. Kersey rejoined us and shook his head, indicating that nothing had changed. The wife was still demanding that Mike plead guilty to a felony. Detective Armel had told her that the punishment would be the same, but it hadn't mattered.

"She's really angry that he's not being put in jail."

I looked at Mike dressed in his new suit and thought, Why couldn't you have chosen a house that was owned by someone more sympathetic?

"How do you want to handle this?" Kersey asked.

We had run out of time. Mike and I followed Kersey back into the courtroom. I noticed that Detective Armel was still hovering over the victims. I didn't know what to tell Kersey. Which was better? Pleading guilty to a felony and having Mike marked for life? Or risking a trial and having him found guilty? Or fighting the charges by pleading NGI? I'd been given less than ten minutes to make a decision that was going to forever alter my son's future.

Kersey was waiting. The judge came into the courtroom. Everyone rose.

The clerk began reading the calendar of cases. Mike's name was third on the list. This was supposed to be routine, I thought. It was supposed to have already been resolved. For the first time in my life, I was literally frozen with indecision. Again, I looked at Mike. Then I looked at Kersey. He needed an answer.

At that moment, I saw Detective Armel walk down the aisle to the prosecutor's table. She leaned across the divider that separated court officials from the audience and whispered something. I glanced over at the husband and wife. She was crying. But I felt no sympathy for her, only contempt.

Detective Armel nodded toward Kersey, and he walked down to them. As soon as they finished talking, the clerk called Mike's criminal case number. The prosecutor said, "Judge, we'd like to continue this case."

A temporary reprieve. The judge agreed to a three-month delay.

Kersey hustled us out into the hallway. The wife was still insisting that Mike plead guilty to a felony, he explained, but Detective Armel had gotten us more time by telling them that Kersey might be able to come up with an offer that would guarantee their security.

"Like what?" I asked.

"I'm not sure," he replied. "Maybe a restraining order, a longer probation than usual, a promise of ongoing mental treatment—something that we could use to pacify her so your son doesn't have to become a felon.

"Detective Armel just did us a really big favor," Kersey said.

The homeowners and Detective Armel exited the courtroom. None of them looked at us.

"Mike," I said, "do you see those people walking there?"

He glanced at them and said he vaguely remembered Detective Armel, but he had no idea who the couple was.

I turned to Kersey: "He doesn't even know her. He selected their house by chance. Why is she doing this?"

Kersey shrugged. "Maybe because she can. But that really doesn't matter, does it? What matters is that we have three months to work on them."

A gaggle of smokers was clustered outside the automatic glass doors at the courthouse exit. I noticed when Mike and I walked by them that one of the smokers was blowing rings. He reached out and snatched one of them in his hand. Then he opened his fingers and there was nothing there.

Mike was mentally ill. His illness had chosen him. While he had been psychotic, he had broken into a house to take a bubble bath. And now a complete stranger, who didn't know anything about him, was dictating his future. At that moment, I felt like a man trying to grab smoke in the air.

Chapter   1 0

I was raining when I returned to Miami. The cloudiness matched my mood. Judge Steven Leifman had arranged for me to go on a "ride-along" with a member of the Miami Police Department's Crisis Intervention Team so I could see firsthand how CIT officers handled mentally ill suspects. The rain had stopped by the time Officer Mario Garcia and I left a substation in the Little Havana neighborhood for the start of the three-P.M.-to-midnight shift. But the streets were still slick, and water splashed in tiny waves onto the sidewalks as it backed up behind deluged drains. As Garcia drove his squad car along Northwest Seventeenth Avenue, he plucked an unlit cigar from his lips and, using it as a pointer, jabbed at the passenger window next to me.

"Look over there!" he said.

An anemic-looking, soaked older man was bent down on the sidewalk, dipping a paper cup from McDonald's into the gutter. He raised it to his lips and gulped down its cloudy brown contents.

Garcia fumbled through a stack of forms on the console, keeping one eye on traffic, the other on the documents. Finally, his fingers found a pink paper, which he tugged out. It contained the department's guidelines for dealing with the homeless.

"You aren't supposed to arrest someone just because they're living on the street," he explained, "even if they are drinking water out of the gutter and are crazy."

In 1988, the American Civil Liberties Union of Florida accused the Miami police of harassing homeless persons as part of a campaign to drive them off the streets. When the class-action lawsuit finally came to trial four years later, a federal judge ruled that the police had been intimidating them. The city appealed, and another five years passed. In the end, the city had been forced to cough up $600,000 in damages, which was distributed to some five thousand homeless people. The police also had been ordered to back off. The colored sheet that Garcia was now holding spelled out the new rules. Even though a homeless suspect might be violating a law, he was to be left alone as long as he was engaged in a "life-sustaining activity." The paper listed eleven of them:

1. Being in a public park after hours
2. Being nude in public while carrying out daily necessities (such as urination and defecation)
3. Lighting a fire in a park
4. Obstructing passage on sidewalks
5. Living or sleeping in vehicles
6. Loitering in public restrooms
7. Littering
8. Camping in city parks
9. Using facilities for other than their intended purposes (such as sleeping on a park bench)
10. Constructing temporary structures in public parks
11. Trespassing on public property

Obviously, everyone who is homeless is not mentally ill. The homeless epidemic in our nation started in major cities in the 1980s largely because of cutbacks that then President Ronald Reagan made in federal housing subsidies. But a major study undertaken by the City of Miami in 2003 found that "chronically homeless" individuals were, in fact, mentally ill. In a population of 2 million, at any given time, there were 1,700 individuals living in cars, public shelters, or on the street, the study found. Most were able to move rather quickly into some form of public housing. There was, however, a group of 507 individuals who were permanent street dwellers. These 507 were not indigent, down-on-their-luck families. They were single people and *every one of them* was mentally ill. Several had "co-occurring disorders," such as alcohol and/or drug addictions. The study found that 71 percent of the 507 "chronically homeless" refused to live in shelters. It further discovered that *every one of them* had been arrested and jailed at some point. The old man slurping rainwater from the gutter was one of Miami's 507 chronically homeless who had an obvious mental disorder.

Returning the sheet of rules to the stack, Garcia said that it seemed odd to him that instead of finding ways to help the mentally ill move off the streets, the city had been forced to adopt stringent guidelines to protect their rights to live on them and to remain crazy.

"Seeing another human being living like an animal in America," Garcia said, "it just shouldn't be like that. It gets frustrating not being able to do anything legally to help."

Garcia had volunteered for CIT training as soon as the Miami police offered it. He wanted the extra 2.5 percent increase in salary. He was one of seventy CIT-trained officers under the supervision of Sergeant Joe Seiglie. Another thirty were scheduled to begin CIT training in a few weeks. During an average month, CIT officers responded to 189 calls.

The dispatcher's voice crackled on Garcia's car radio and directed him to an old motel that had been converted into one-bedroom units. Two other patrolmen were already there, but neither had CIT training. A woman had slashed her wrist with a paring knife. Her husband, who was waiting for Garcia at the door, explained that his wife had cut herself because today was her fiftieth birthday. She had gotten homesick for Cuba and had called her ex-husband there. Although they had been divorced twenty years, whenever she stopped taking her antipsychotic medication she became confused and thought they were still together.

Garcia went inside, to where a paramedic was bandaging the woman's arm. She was sitting at a kitchen table, dressed in a tired housecoat and ratty slippers. She wasn't wearing makeup. Her face was badly lined, and her figure was pudgy and looked worn-out. Garcia asked her if she still wanted to kill herself.

"*Sí, sí,*" she replied.

Garcia asked to see the woman's prescription. The husband handed him an empty medicine bottle. Garcia recognized the drug. It was for patients who had bipolar disorder. Garcia asked if she had tried to kill herself before.

"*Sí, sí.*" She sobbed.

Her husband held up four fingers.

"She's got lots of cut marks on her wrists," the paramedic treating her volunteered.

As soon as the bandage was in place, Garcia explained that he was taking the woman to Miami's Jackson Memorial Hospital. Her husband wiped several tears from his face and nodded. Garcia led her to his squad car. During the fifteen-minute ride to the hospital, she mumbled incoherently in the back seat.

"Getting her admitted will be simple," Garcia said. "Her husband has insurance through his job. Everyone will tell you it doesn't matter if you have insurance, but—" Garcia didn't finish his sentence. Instead, he stuck his still-unlit cigar back into his mouth and winked.

The next CIT call came while Garcia was still inside the emergency room filling out paperwork. A manager at an assisted-living facility, known as an ALF, had requested help because one of his mentally ill residents had allegedly threatened another patient. During the ride there, Garcia explained that ALFs were private boarding homes that had sprung up in Miami after deinstitutionalization. The state paid ALF operators to provide room and board to mental patients who had been dumped from state institutions.

There were no identifying signs posted outside the bright-pink, two-story, Spanish-style house whose manager had called. The ALF looked no different from any other stucco home in the working-class neighborhood.

"His name is Sid and he's dangerous," the manager declared as soon as Garcia stepped from his squad car. Sid suffered from paranoid schizophrenia, had stopped taking his medicine, and had started smacking the palm of his hand against his head to silence the voices that he had started hearing.

"He needs to go to a crisis center or a hospital," the manager explained.

Garcia strolled to the back of the house, where Sid and five other ALF residents were sitting under a grape arbor in cheap plastic chairs. All of them were smoking.

"Please don't take me to jail!" Sid exclaimed as soon as he saw Garcia.

"I'm not here to take you to jail," Garcia replied.

Garcia asked Sid if he was hearing voices in his head.

"I'm okay," Sid answered. "I hit them out." He slapped his temple hard with his open hand.

Garcia asked Sid if he was feeling suicidal or if he wanted to hurt anyone.

"No, I've never done nothing like that."

Garcia returned to the front of the house, where the manager was waiting.

"You need to call an ambulance to take him to a crisis center," Garcia said.

"Why can't you do it?" the manager replied in an indignant tone.

"Other officers have done this for me before. You can just transport him in your car."

Garcia shook his head. "I'll wait here while you make the call."

An ambulance arrived moments later, and Garcia escorted the paramedics to where Sid was still sitting.

"These men are going to take you to the hospital so you can feel better," Garcia explained. Sid went with them without complaint. As the ambulance was pulling away, the ALF manger complained, "I don't know why you couldn't have taken him."

Back inside the car, Garcia explained that ALFs were supposed to hire an ambulance to transport psychotic clients to a treatment center, a precaution in case they needed medical help en route. But calling an ambulance cost the ALF $200 to $350 per trip. Getting the police to drive a patient there was free. "The managers always claim a resident has threatened someone," Garcia said. "That way they can save money. But we're not a taxi service."

Continuing, Garcia said, "I wouldn't leave a dog in most of these ALFs. A lot of these owners are simply trying to make as much money off these people as they can. They don't do anything to really help them. Then, as soon as one of them acts buggy, they call us and want them removed."

An hour passed before another CIT call came in. A schizophrenic man had wandered away from another ALF. This facility was near the famous Orange Bowl in a depressed neighborhood. Garcia had been there several times because of similar problems in the past. "You're about to see one of the worst ALFs in Little Havana," he promised. Moments later, he stopped at the curb of what looked like an abandoned house. The sidewalk was missing jagged chunks of concrete. Broken glass bottles, crushed beer cans, and yellowed newspapers had collected at the bottom of the chain-link fence that surrounded a front yard of burnt grass. Two men, both elderly, were sitting on what used to be the bench seat from a car but had now been pressed into service as porch furniture. There was a rusty metal TV tray covered with ashes and extinguished cigarettes next to them. The one-story fifties-era house didn't have a front screen door, and the door was wide open because there was no air conditioning. Garcia walked into a living room illuminated by a lone lightbulb dangling from a ceiling wire. An ancient color television was playing, but no one was watching it.

Garcia called out and a manager came down a hallway. He led Garcia to the entrance of what had once been a single bedroom but now was split into two separate quarters by a gray sheetrock wall. The only window, which was open, was also halved by the improvised divider so that air could flow into both sides of the cramped spaces. Each cubicle was about four feet wide and ten feet long. One of the house's residents was sitting on the edge of a bunk bed fashioned from two-by-fours, his bare feet planted on filthy linoleum riddled with quarter-sized holes that exposed old plank flooring. The house's only bathroom was across the hall and reeked of unflushed feces and urine.

"He doesn't know when his roommate left," the manager said, with no embarrassment at either his tenant's disappearance or the crackhouse conditions of his place.

Garcia noticed a pencil drawing that was thumbtacked to the wall. It was of a flower in a pot under a giant sun. The flower had eyes and a big smile. The manager said, "Julio, the resident who's missing, drew that. He's a *real* artist." He laughed, mocking the drawing.

Garcia filled out a missing person's report and then returned to the porch and asked the two men sitting there if they had seen Julio leave.

"No. I don't know Julio," one of the men said.

"Yes, you do. He lives here with us," the other explained. "I was in the state hospital with him."

"Oh," the first answered. "Yes, I saw him today, but now he's gone."

For about five minutes, Garcia cruised the neighborhood, but he didn't spot Julio. The dispatcher interrupted his search. A two-car accident had happened a few blocks away. In addition to CIT calls, Garcia was expected to do his other police chores.

An hour later, another CIT call came in. This time, the dispatcher sent Garcia to a residence in Little Havana where an elderly Cuban couple lived. They were both in their eighties and the woman had Alzheimer's disease. The husband explained that most days, his wife was fine, but she had gotten confused after she'd taken a nap. When she woke up, she accused him of selling her sewing machine and had started to scream. A neighbor called the police.

"She gave that sewing machine away four years ago to our niece," he said. "Please don't arrest her."

The woman mistook Garcia for one of their grandchildren and opened her arms to give him a hug. For the next twenty minutes, Garcia tried to console the husband. When Garcia started to leave, the old man began to sob.

"*Gracias, gracias,*" he muttered. "My wife was once a beautiful woman. Now I don't know what to do. I can't afford a nursing home, but we can't keep living like this."

Back in the squad car, Garcia said, "Sometimes there's not much we can do but listen."

An alarm sounded at a nearby gas station and Garcia served as backup for another squad car. It was a false alarm caused when the rain, which had started to fall again, short-circuited the station's electrical system. The police officer, who had gotten there first, said, "You couldn't pay me enough to take CIT training. If I see someone is psycho, I call CIT and say, 'Hello, boys, this one's all yours.'"

It was quiet for the remainder of Garcia's shift. On his drive back to the substation, he rode along Northwest Seventeenth Avenue, the same route that he'd followed earlier. As he neared a corner, he slowed and shone his car's spotlight on a storefront. Burrowed next to the business's glass door was the homeless psychotic who had earlier been slurping water from the gutter. He was sleeping on a pillow made from a garbage bag, his body wrapped in a tattered blanket.

The next afternoon, Garcia had been at work for less than ten minutes on the three-o'clock shift when he got a "code three" call. That meant Garcia had permission to use his squad car's red-and-blue lights and siren to race to an incident. The radio dispatcher explained that a woman had called asking for help because her mentally ill son had attacked her in their home. He'd hit her with his fists and pressed a knife against her throat, but she'd managed to break free and was now locked in a bathroom, talking to the police on a cell phone.

The mother warned them that her son was schizophrenic and had stopped taking his antipsychotic medication. He had spent much of the morning drinking beer and had armed himself with two kitchen knives.

By the time Garcia reached the house, another CIT-trained officer was already trying to talk the armed attacker—a forty-six-year-old man standing on the front porch—into surrendering. The suspect was wearing a jogging suit and had tucked a knife up each of its loose sleeves. Their wooden handles were jutting out and he was holding his hands together in front of him so that he could whip out the weapons in a hurry.

Garcia sprang from his cruiser and slipped from his holster a black pistol that looked like a semiautomatic. It was an M26 Taser, an electric stun gun issued to CIT officers. He began weaving his way along the side of the house's property line out of the deranged man's eyesight.

"What's your name?" the first CIT officer asked the suspect. The patrolman was standing about fifteen feet directly in front of the porch.

"Sanchez," the man yelled back.

Miami police officers are trained to project a "commanding and authoritative presence" whenever they respond to an emergency. But when they are confronted by a mentally ill suspect, CIT officers always try to appear nonthreatening and helpful.

"Why don't you put down the knives," the officer said, "so we can talk without having to worry about anyone getting cut?"

"No!" Sanchez replied. "I'll kill you if you come closer!"

"No one is going to come closer," the officer calmly answered. "We want to help you."

By this point, Garcia had crept up next to the side of the house and was quietly moving into a position where he would be behind the suspect. He was worried that the suspect might be trying to commit "suicide by proxy." That was the term the Miami police used to describe someone who wanted the police to kill him.

Now that Garcia was in position behind the suspect, the other CIT officer began to reach for his Taser. Sanchez reacted by curling his fingers around the handles on the two knives, apparently preparing for a fight. "Come on!" he hollered.

The M26 Taser that both officers were carrying had a range of twenty-one feet. Garcia aimed his at the center of Sanchez's back and fired. Two needle-shaped prongs shot out, easily piercing Sanchez's thin nylon running jacket. The Taser emitted a 50,000-volt charge and maintained it for five seconds. But Sanchez didn't crumble. He turned and glared at Garcia.

The CIT officer standing in front of Sanchez fired his Taser next, hitting Sanchez with an equal 50,000-volt impact. For a moment, Sanchez seemed bewildered, and then he collapsed. Worried that Sanchez still might draw his knives, Garcia jumped onto the porch and jammed his Taser's barrel against Sanchez's neck, striking him with a third jolt. Sanchez tried to knock the gun away just as the first CIT officer poked his Taser into him. It was this fourth shock that caused Sanchez to surrender. The police carefully withdrew the knives from his sleeves. One was ten inches long, the other, six. Sanchez was handcuffed and examined by paramedics. He hadn't been injured. He was driven to jail and taken directly to the ninth floor.

"I can tell you right now," Sergeant Seiglie said afterward, "if it weren't for CIT training and the issuing of Tasers, that man would be dead. There's no question. In the past we would have shot and killed him."

Chapter 1 1

Dr. Poitier had encouraging news when I returned to the ninth floor.

An involuntary-commitment hearing was going to be held later in the morning for Freddie Gilbert. The last time that I had seen Gilbert, the inmate had been so mentally incapacitated that he couldn't speak. After several frustrating weeks of watching Gilbert's condition worsen, Dr. Poitier had arranged for the hulking figure to be sent from the jail to Jackson Memorial Hospital, where he'd been examined by two psychiatrists. They had signed a commitment petition asking a judge to force Gilbert into a six-month treatment program.

Dr. Poitier was excited, because he felt Gilbert was finally going to get the intensive care that he needed. He also believed the case would be "precedent-setting," because Gilbert had been charged with misdemeanors, not felonies. He explained that inmates accused of minor crimes were usually released from jail through Judge Leifman's diversion program. But Gilbert already had been down that path nearly a dozen times and had always ended up homeless and psychotic. It was going to take more than a few days in a community crisis center to help him think more clearly. The courts, however, had always been reluctant to force someone into long-term care if he was charged with crimes that weren't considered too weighty.

"If you commit a serious crime," Dr. Poitier said, "the system will be forced to deal with you. You will be sent to a state forensic hospital. But if you are arrested for a misdemeanor and you are *chronically* mentally ill, then you never get the intensive help you need. You get stuck in a revolving door."

Judge Leifman had let it be known that he was monitoring Gilbert's case. The inmate was one of Miami's 507 chronically mentally ill, and the judge was especially interested in finding ways to help them move off the streets. That was why the two psychiatrists had gotten involved. They had filed their petition in a civil—not a criminal—court under Florida's Baker Act, a 1972 law that spelled out when a person could be forced into a mental hospital.

"None of this would be happening if it weren't for Judge Leifman," Dr. Poitier said, "and I think it is what we should be doing more of."

Not everyone was as pleased as Dr. Poitier. Gilbert was automatically being represented by a public defender, who complained that his client was being railroaded. Today's session would be typical of commitment hearings held every day across America and similar to the one that I had sat through when Mike had been hospitalized. This was because Florida's Baker Act, like commitment laws in most other states, had been patterned after a model 1967 California law. The commitment procedures had become standardized. The first step was persuading a judge that a defendant was ill. The police then took the defendant to a hospital. During the next seventy-two hours, he would be examined by two doctors, and if they agreed he was impaired, a formal Baker Act hearing would be scheduled. It had to take place within five days. The defendant could hire a private attorney, but most relied on public defenders.

At this morning's hearing, it would be up to the Miami-Dade state's attorney's office to present "clear and convincing evidence" that showed that Gilbert needed to be forcibly hospitalized. To prove this, the prosecutor had to meet four criteria. But most judges across the nation boiled those rules down into a single test: Was a defendant in "imminent danger" of "inflicting serious harm" to himself or someone else? If he was, he was committed. If he wasn't, he was released.

In Miami, the state's attorney's office had not paid much attention to Baker Act cases in the past. They had never been a priority. But the public defender's office had vigorously fought to keep its clients from being forcibly hospitalized. Because of this lopsided attitude, hundreds of people thought to be mentally ill had been freed.

"If this inmate is committed today," Dr. Poitier said, "it will send a strong message to the mental health community. It will show we are serious about getting these chronic, homeless, mentally ill patients off the street and into treatment."

Dr. Poitier believed the Baker Act was too restrictive and badly in need of an overhaul. "We know more about mental illness now than we did thirty years ago. We know mental illness is not a choice. It is an organic brain disorder, and we have developed drugs that we know can help most people who have it live normal lives. But we have misguided civil rights laws stopping us from intervening."

As a doctor, Dr. Poitier was disgusted when he saw homeless psychotics on the street. "If our society says that barely surviving, that living on the street like an animal is acceptable for people who are mentally sick, then I say, 'No! No! No!'"

"What about their civil rights?" I asked. "Their right to be crazy?"

"I've never had one person whom I've helped say, 'Doc, I wish you would have left me crazy on the streets.'"

Dr. Poitier checked his wristwatch. He didn't want to be late for Gilbert's hearing, which was being held in a special courtroom inside a hospital about four blocks away. "What I really dislike about all of this," he explained as he walked to the ninth-floor elevator, "is that—as a doctor—my first concern is restoring this man's mental health. But that is not the first concern of the lawyers, or of the judge who will be making this decision. This should be a medical matter, not a legal issue."

Reporters are not allowed in commitment hearings. But I knew what usually happened in them, because I'd sat through Mike's. When Dr. Poitier returned two hours later, he felt good about his testimony. There had been one exchange, however, that irked him. Dr. Poitier testified that Gilbert was dangerous. At which point the public defender had demanded proof. He asked Dr. Poitier to produce "incident reports" to back up his statement. Correctional officers are required to file an incident report whenever a prisoner gets into a fight or scuffle.

Dr. Poitier's testimony was critical because the prosecutor needed it to prove that Gilbert's mental condition put him in "imminent danger." Dr. Poitier told the judge that he hadn't been instructed to bring any incident reports with him to the hearing. But that wasn't good enough for the public defender. He suspected that Dr. Poitier was exaggerating because he wanted to get Gilbert help. Gilbert had a reputation for being passive in jail. The public defender had asked the judge to strike Dr. Poitier's testimony because it couldn't be substantiated. The judge had refused, but Dr. Poitier felt offended just the same, because his honesty had been questioned.

"Adversarial proceedings may work well in criminal cases," Dr. Poitier complained, "but they are a poor way to proceed when you're trying to help someone who has a medical problem. I always find testifying to be a frustrating experience because we should be focused on what is best for a mentally ill person, not what the mentally ill person wants—especially if he is not thinking clearly. Yet that is exactly what the public defender focuses on."

Continuing, he said, "I don't think any of us, including attorneys, should let our jobs keep us from doing what is morally right. I understand all of us think what we are doing is morally right. But when we can't agree on what is morally right, then we should do what is reasonable, and as a doctor, I have trouble letting an obviously mentally ill person go back on the streets untreated. We need to have some compassion here and understand that this person is suffering, truly suffering, from a serious brain disorder. A person who is a chronic schizophrenic doesn't have full control over his thoughts. He can't make rational decisions. If you release him untreated back into the community, you aren't protecting his civil rights. You're condemning him to staying sick and a horrible life of suffering on the streets."

I wanted to hear the other side of this argument, so I interviewed a public defender who specialized in commitment hearings. He said he had been berated hundreds of times by parents, police officers, and even psychiatrists after he successfully helped a psychotic defendant go free. He asked not to be named in this book, so he could speak candidly, and then he told me that he often urges his clients before a hearing to take antipsychotic medication and enter a hospital treatment program *voluntarily*. But if they are adamant in saying no and they insist they are not mentally ill, he feels morally obligated to protect their civil rights.

There are two ways public defenders can represent the mentally ill, he explained. The attorney can decide that he is going to do what *he* thinks is in the best interest of his client, and if he decides that a defendant needs to be hospitalized, then that is what he tells a judge. The second approach is to act as the *client's lawyer*, not as his guardian, or his parent, or his doctor. And as his lawyer, he does whatever the accused wishes, regardless of how preposterous it might seem. This is the route that he personally follows, because he believes his clients have a constitutional right to due process and to have their feelings, even if they are crazy, presented to a judge.

During our interview, he insisted that his actions in commitment hearings are no different from what a public defender does in a criminal courtroom. A lawyer might suspect that his client is guilty of murder, rape, burglary, or another crime, but he is still ethically bound to put on a vigorous defense that would force the state to prove beyond a reasonable doubt that his client is guilty.

Privately, the public defender said he did not feel any pleasure from seeing an obviously mentally ill client avoid hospitalization. But whenever someone began to hassle him for his role in freeing them, he suggested they complain to the state's attorney for not presenting sufficient evidence. Or lobby the state legislature to change the commitment criteria. Without due process, he declared, anyone could be involuntarily committed.

I would later interview other public defenders and civil rights attorneys, and every one of them would make this same argument. All of them felt passionately about protecting "the constitutional rights of the mentally ill."

During interviews, I would tell them about Mike and how I had tried to get a doctor to forcibly treat him. And while they would sympathize with me, each of them said they would have fought my attempts to force my son to take antipsychotic medicine. At that point, I always asked if they had anyone in their families who was seriously mentally ill. Not one of them had. Not one.

O n the day of Gilbert's commitment hearing, Dr. Poitier got a telephone call from his supervisor around 3 P.M. at the jail. He was told that the public defender's office had filed a formal complaint against him because of his testimony. Its attorneys claimed that he shouldn't have been allowed to testify about Gilbert because of the recently implemented federal HIPAA law. That statute prohibited doctors from discussing their clients' medical conditions without first getting written permission from them. Because Dr. Poitier had treated Gilbert on the ninth floor, he had served as the inmate's de facto doctor and therefore was bound by HIPAA to keep silent about his mental condition, the attorneys argued. Their complaint had been turned over to the state's attorney's office to answer, but until it was resolved, Dr. Poitier was told that he should no longer testify in Baker Act hearings. Dr. Poitier saw it as another step by public defenders to keep doctors out of hearings.

No sooner had Dr. Poitier ended that call than his phone rang again. This time it was a state prosecutor. The Baker Act judge had ruled in their favor. Gilbert had been involuntarily committed to a treatment program for six months.

Dr. Poitier broke into a huge grin. "This call makes this a good day," he said wearily, "a very good day. We now have a chance to save this man."

O ne of the reasons I decided to write this book was that I didn't understand why civil rights laws had prevented me from getting Mike help even though he was clearly delusional. After listening to Dr. Poitier describe his frustration with the Baker Act commitment process, I decided to contact Dr. Morton Birnbaum. Most historians credit him with being the father of the civil rights movement for the mentally ill. I wanted to ask why he had advocated laws that were now being used to keep patients from being treated.

Both a general practitioner and a psychiatrist, Dr. Birnbaum took my telephone call at a medical clinic that he had founded in a poor Brooklyn neighborhood. He was still working there daily, even though he was in his seventies and had recently suffered a stroke.

I told Dr. Birnbaum about Mike and the anger I'd felt as his father when an emergency room doctor turned us away. I expected Dr. Birnbaum to bristle and give me the same legal rationale as the public defenders whom I'd interviewed. But he didn't. Instead, he said he had never intended for the civil rights campaign that he helped launch to cause the results that it had. When I asked him to explain, he took me back into the past.

———————

D r. Birnbaum was studying public policy and mental illness in 1959 at Harvard University in a postdoctorate program when he came up with an idea that he thought would help the mentally ill. Later it became known as Birnbaum's "right to treatment" theory. He spelled it out in an article that he mailed off to the *New England Journal of Medicine*. But that magazine rejected it. Undeterred, he sent his paper to the *Journal of the American Medical Association*. But *JAMA* also returned it. During the coming year, he submitted his thesis to fifty different publications, and every one of them refused to print it. Finally, the *American Bar Association Journal* published Birnbaum's theory in May 1960.

Birnbaum's premise was that mental patients in state hospitals had a *constitutional* "right to treatment." At first glance, this sounds like common sense. But it actually was a revolutionary idea, because it gave the mentally ill a *legal* right to demand adequate health care.

At the time, most mental patients had been locked in state hospitals against their will. They were placed there by relatives or judges. Once committed, they were told they would not be discharged until they showed improvement. But there were no treatment programs in most state hospitals. Instead, they were operated as giant warehouses. The patients were trapped in a Catch-22. They couldn't be released until they got better. But without treatment, they couldn't get better.

Birnbaum wrote that this predicament meant patients were being condemned to the equivalent of sentences of life imprisonment. Yet most of them had never committed a crime or been given an opportunity to defend themselves in court.

Continuing with his argument, Birnbaum said the patients' no-win situation violated their constitutional rights, as defined by the Fifth Amendment, which states that no citizen can be deprived of his liberty without due process. This caused Birnbaum to conclude that state mental hospitals either had to immediately begin treating patients or had to set them free regardless of their mental conditions.

"My goal was to force the states to begin treating these patients' illnesses," he told me.

The doctor had expected his theory to set off a firestorm, especially after *The New York Times* published a news story about it. But there were no angry rebuttals or endorsements. No one in the medical or the legal profession seemed to notice.

Several weeks later, however, Dr. Birnbaum received a letter from Kenneth Donaldson, a patient being held in the Florida State Hospital in Chattahoochee. He had read the *New York Times* story and he asked Birnbaum if he would test his right-to-treatment argument by defending him. Curious, Birnbaum investigated Donaldson's background.

Donaldson had suffered his first breakdown in 1943, when he was thirty-four, married, and working in a defense plant. He'd been forced into a state hospital and given twenty-three electric shock treatments—against his will—before he'd been ruled well enough to be discharged. In 1956, he'd begun acting paranoid again. He was taken before the bench and committed to Chattahoochee even though he had not broken any laws or hurt anyone. The judge said, "You go up there to Chattahoochee for a few weeks and take some of that new medication—what's the name of it?—and you'll be right back." This was when Thorazine was first being touted as a wonder drug.

But Donaldson discovered that getting out of Chattahoochee was not so easy. By the time he contacted Dr. Birnbaum, Donaldson had been in the hospital for five years. He was being punished by its doctors, he claimed, because he refused to admit that he was psychotic. In their opinion, that alone was prima facie evidence that he was.

Although Dr. Birnbaum had a family of five to support and a medical practice to run, he agreed to represent Donaldson for free. He filed a lawsuit, arguing that Donaldson's constitutional "right to treatment" was being violated. At first, Florida officials didn't take the suit seriously. They asked a judge to dismiss it. And that might have happened if fate had not intervened.

It turned out that Donaldson wasn't the only person who had read about Dr. Birnbaum's novel theory. David L. Bazelon, a federal judge in Washington, D.C., also had studied it, and the jurist decided to test it in a case that had been brought before him. It involved Charles Rouse, who had been forcibly institutionalized after he had been arrested on a minor charge and declared insane. A public defender had stumbled upon Rouse in St. Elizabeths Hospital, the federal government's sprawling mental facility outside Washington, D.C., and had asked a lower court to free him. The judge had refused, and the case had been sent to Judge Bazelon on an appeal. Bazelon was both an activist judge and ardent civil rights advocate. He ordered the lower court to reconsider its ruling based on Dr. Birnbaum's right-to-treatment theory.

Sensing that an important legal precedent was about to be set, the public defender's office recruited Charles Halpern, a rising star in the Washington firm of Arnold & Porter, to defend Rouse. In the end, the lower court ordered Rouse freed—but on a technicality, not because of Birnbaum's theory. Still, the fact that a nationally known and prominent judge had cited Birnbaum's argument in a legal brief gave it immediate credibility.

It also helped set the stage for a landmark civil rights ruling. That came about because of a third lawsuit.

In 1970, Alabama fired more than a hundred employees at a state mental hospital in Tuscaloosa to save money. The workers wanted their jobs back, but they didn't have any legal grounds to fight their terminations—until a clever attorney named George Dean suggested a backdoor approach. Rather than sue the state for the workers, Dean filed a class-action lawsuit on behalf of the mental patients. In it, he argued that the job cuts had deprived the patients of their constitutional right to treatment as defined by Dr. Birnbaum.

Alabama officials laughed at the suit, but an Alabama judge, who had heard about Judge Bazelon's ruling, scheduled the case for trial. Almost overnight, *Wyatt v. Stickney* mushroomed into the country's first major civil rights battle for the mentally ill. The American Civil Liberties Union and a half dozen other national organizations filed "friend of the court" briefs supporting the patients' demand for better treatment. Attorney Dean also invited Dr. Birnbaum and Charles Halpern to join his legal team. Halpern brought along two other energetic lawyers: Paul Friedman, a fellow Yale Law School graduate and close personal friend, and Bruce Ennis, who worked for the New York Civil Liberties Union.

Dean proved to be a master at getting media attention, and in Alabama, he found plenty of horror stories to expose. In a series of stomach-churning court sessions, Dean described how a young girl had been locked inside a wooden cage for months at a state hospital and how employees had used electric cattle prods to torture patients. The judge was so disgusted that he ordered the state to overhaul its entire state hospital system. Alabama officials accused him of overstepping his bounds. The state legislature then cried poor. It said the state couldn't afford to fix all the problems that the judge wanted repaired. But Dean outsmarted them. He released financial records that showed the Heart of Dixie state was spending more each year hosting the Alabama Junior Miss pageant and swine shows at county fairs than it spent caring for its mentally ill. Badly humiliated, the legislators begrudgingly approved additional funding and the rehiring of all the fired workers, plus two hundred more.

It was a huge victory, especially for Dr. Birnbaum, whose legal thesis was crucial to the suit. But a rift had developed inside the legal team. Dr. Birnbaum was happy the state had been forced to begin providing patients with care. Attorney Dean was thrilled because he had gotten the fired workers their jobs back. But Halpern, Friedman, and Ennis suspected that conditions at the hospitals would deteriorate after the lawsuit was settled. They wanted Alabama to permanently close all its hospitals.

The arguing between the lawyers became so bitter that Dr. Birnbaum resigned from the team. Halpern, Friedman, and Ennis, meanwhile, returned to Washington, where they founded the Mental Health Law Project, a firm that they created specifically to file suits against states and challenge mental health laws.

The timing of the three Washington, D.C., lawyers couldn't have been better. The nation was in the midst of the antiasylum *One Flew Over the Cuckoo's Nest* movement. By the end of the firm's first year, it had filed class-action suits against hospitals in Nebraska, Tennessee, Maine, Florida, South Carolina, North Carolina, and Virginia. The firm's tactics were simple yet effective. It would argue that Birnbaum's right-to-treatment theory required states to provide patients with adequate treatment. It would then demand that the state legislatures spend millions of dollars to renovate their hospitals. Rather than cough up those extra funds, most legislatures voted to shut down their aged institutions. It made perfect sense. After all, the federal government was also pressuring the states to deinstitutionalize.

In addition to filing lawsuits, the Mental Health Law Project branched out into other areas. It seized control of the Donaldson case that Dr. Birnbaum had initiated in Florida and took it all the way to the U.S. Supreme Court. In a majority opinion, Chief Justice Warren Burger sided with the activists:

A finding of "mental illness" alone cannot justify a State's locking a person up against his will and keeping him indefinitely in simple custodial confinement. . . . In short, a state cannot constitutionally confine a non dangerous individual who is capable of surviving safely in freedom by himself or with the help of willing and responsible family members or friends.

It was this landmark ruling that opened up a Pandora's box. *If a state couldn't lock up a person because he was mentally ill, then at what point could it intervene?*

Most states tried to answer that question by copying a California commitment law called the Lanterman-Petris-Short Act, named after the three politicians who'd introduced it. Passed in 1967, it was the first law to say that a mentally ill person had to be "a danger to himself or to others" before he could be committed.

The Mental Health Law Project and the ACLU began pushing judges in dozens of other lawsuits to define what constituted "danger." In a Mississippi case, a judge said having a family member or a friend claim they'd been threatened wasn't sufficient to force a mentally ill person into a hospital. There had to be an "overt act or threat to prove a substantial likelihood of danger." In another state, a judge decided the danger had to be "imminent." In a Wisconsin case, a mentally disturbed man was freed after his court-appointed attorney got a psychiatrist to acknowledge that the defendant's eating of his own feces did not put him in any "imminent danger." In yet another case, it was decided the parents—who were concerned about their daughter's repeated threats of suicide—had to wait until she had actually attempted to kill herself before she met the "imminent danger" criteria.

In Wisconsin, Halpern, Friedman, and Ennis came to the defense of Alberta Lessard, and her case led to another important federal court ruling. This time, the justices decided that mentally ill people were entitled to the same legal protections during commitment hearings as suspects were in criminal cases. Before *Lessard v. Schmidt*, commitment hearings had been informal affairs. Now they became stricter and adversarial.

The Mental Health Law Project continued to push its civil rights agenda. It filed suits to stop doctors from conducting lobotomies, administering electroshock, and forcing patients to undergo other unwanted procedures, including involuntary sterilization. This led to another critical ruling. In it, the Supreme Court decided that mentally ill persons had the right to refuse medical treatment, including the taking of antipsychotic drugs, which were being overprescribed in state mental hospitals to sedate and control patients. Halpern, Friedman, and Ennis continued racking up impressive victories. They won the right for mental patients to be confined in the least restrictive manner possible. And in another controversial decision, the courts limited a parent's ability to compel their adult child to undergo treatment. The test case involved Richard Roe III (a court-imposed pseudonym), who developed schizophrenia but refused to take medication even though it had always helped him recover. His father had stepped in as his son's legal guardian—a maneuver parents often take when they want to intervene. But civil rights lawyers leaped in and challenged the father's authority. A judge sided with them. He said Roe's father was not "impartial" and therefore he shouldn't be allowed to interfere. Instead, the judge appointed a guardian *ad litem* to decide what was in Roe's best interest. That decision further outraged parents, because it removed them completely from the decision-making process.

The public got a dramatic glimpse of just how effective the Mental Health Law Project and the ACLU had been in protecting the rights of the mentally ill when New York mayor Ed Koch tangled with Joyce Brown in 1987. Worried that the homeless might freeze during a particularly bitter winter, Mayor Koch sent city workers to forcibly remove them from the streets and house them in shelters. Brown, who was then forty years old, happened to be the first to be picked up, and a television camera crew recorded her furious reaction as she was dragged into a van.

The case became a media sensation. Brown, who had schizophrenia, had been living on the sidewalk in front of a restaurant's hot-air vent for more than a year. She used the street as her latrine, frequently spat insults at passersby, and ripped up and urinated on money that she was given. She would sometimes dash into traffic, bringing it to a halt, and she was notorious for lifting up her skirt and exposing her bare buttocks to black men while screaming, "Kiss my black ass!" City officials had tried to hospitalize her at least five times, but doctors had released her because they said she did not meet the "imminent danger" criteria.

The New York chapter for the ACLU accused Mayor Koch of violating Brown's civil rights by snatching her off the streets. It filed a suit, demanding that Brown be discharged from Bellevue Hospital, which was where she'd been taken. Brown, meanwhile, told reporters that she was a "political prisoner."

In court, Brown's attorney admitted that his client's decision to live on a sidewalk was not something most people would do or understand, but he emphasized that Brown wasn't posing a threat to herself or anyone else. He added that it was her choice to be homeless and argued that she should be allowed to live as she wished.

When Mayor Koch's attorneys pointed out that Brown was severely mentally ill, ate out of garbage cans, and often was so delusional that she defecated in her own clothes, her attorney insisted that nutritional food could be found in discarded trash bins and admitted that the smell of feces might be unpleasant, but claimed it was not a serious threat to Brown's physical health. He also reminded the judge that being mentally ill was not illegal.

The judge ruled in Brown's favor and ordered the city to release her. But Mayor Koch refused. At a press conference, he declared that the "best way to actually honor the rights of the acutely mentally ill" was by getting them help, not by abandoning them to die on the streets. Before an appellate court could rule, hospital officials freed Brown on their own.

For a short time, Brown was a cause célèbre. Harvard Law School invited her to give a lecture; the ACLU had her operate its seventy-two-button telephone switchboard for a *New York Times* photographer, to demonstrate how smart she was. But her stability didn't last. In 1989, a local television station showed footage of her on the same corner where she'd been picked up originally. She was screaming, cursing, and slapping her behind in front of the camera.

The Joyce Brown case proved prophetic. By the 1990s, frustrated parents were repeating a new term, coined by Wisconsin psychiatrist Darold Treffert. The mentally ill were being allowed to "die with their rights on."

D uring our interview, Dr. Birnbaum said he had never intended for his right-to-treatment theory to be used by the Mental Health Law Project to shut down state mental hospitals or to make it nearly impossible for parents to force their children into treatment programs. I thought about Mike and realized that the roadblocks I'd encountered were not unique to Virginia or even new. They dated back to court decisions issued twenty years earlier. As much as I hated to admit it, the doctor at Inova Fairfax Hospital had been following the law when he'd refused to treat Mike.

But I also noticed something else. All the civil rights protections that the Mental Health Law Project had pushed through had been enacted before the federal government had determined that mental illness is caused by a chemical imbalance in the brain—a fact confirmed by MRI (magnetic resonance imaging). Acting crazy is not a *choice*, as some civil rights lawyers had vehemently argued in their lawsuits. Newer antipsychotic medications also had been developed that were effective in alleviating the symptoms of many psychoses without making a patient suffer through a lobotomy or other dangerous procedure.

Were the civil rights safeguards passed two decades before still needed? Or, as Dr. Poitier had told me, was it time for them to be reexamined?

After talking to Dr. Birnbaum, I contacted Robert Bernstein, the director of the Mental Health Law Project in our nation's capital. By this point, it had renamed itself: the Judge David L. Bazelon Center for Mental Health Law, in honor of the famous civil rights jurist.

Bernstein insisted that the rights that his organization had spent decades championing were just as necessary today as they had ever been. Rather than attacking them, the public needed to focus on fixing a national mental health care system that was in complete shambles. The mentally ill needed better-funded community mental health centers and affordable housing, plus access to jobs and educational programs.

I agreed, but told him that we seemed to be discussing two different issues. I didn't see how any of those laudable projects—better-funded centers, affordable housing, access to jobs, and educational programs— were going to help someone such as Joyce Brown, who was convinced that she wasn't sick and therefore that she didn't need treatment or any other mental health intervention.

Bernstein disagreed, so I asked him how he, as a trained psychologist, would convince someone such as Brown to voluntarily take advantage of a treatment program. He began by telling me what he *wouldn't* do. He wouldn't grab a chronically ill, homeless patient off the street, force her into a hospital, and make her take antipsychotic drugs.

"Okay, how would you help her, then?" I asked.

Bernstein again replied that he would begin by improving the national mental health care system. But I pushed him for specifics and continued to prod him. Eventually, he said that he would help a person such as Brown by giving her individual attention. He would assign a social worker to monitor and befriend her. He would tell that social worker to offer her a friendly cup of coffee each morning, offer her a meal, offer her a change of clothing and a safe place to sleep. He would encourage the social worker to develop a personal relationship with her that would lead, he hoped, to her entering a treatment program voluntarily.

It sounded wonderful.

But then I thought about the first time that I'd met Freddie Gilbert, standing naked in a C-wing cell on the ninth floor, so crazy that he couldn't even speak. I thought about how Gilbert was one of Miami's *507* chronically mentally ill street dwellers, and that was just in a single city. I thought about how the federal government had said mental illness was a chemical brain disorder that caused a person to not think rationally. Finally, I thought about Mike.

So I asked Bernstein what he would have done if Mike had been his son. How would he have reacted if he had driven his psychotic child to a hospital emergency room and had been turned away because of a civil rights law?

Bernstein refused to bite. Instead, he repeated what he had already said. He talked about how the government needed to improve the mental health care system. And he again recited how he did not believe in forcing anyone to accept medical treatment unless that person was in "imminent danger."

Deep down, I wondered, Would he have been willing to watch his son or daughter become more and more delusional, knowing that the law would not allow him to intervene until his child hurt either himself or someone else?

Would he?

What parent could?

T he day began badly for Dr. Poitier. And it was only 7 A.M. A water pipe had burst above his office. His medical charts had been safely locked in a cabinet, but the soppy deluge had turned the papers on his desk to mush and made the tile floor glisten. Worse, a rank sewage smell now permeated the room. A trustee was sent in with a mop. Luckily, Dr. Poitier was scheduled to spend much of his morning in the courthouse.

I stayed behind in C wing. I'd wanted to observe an average day on the ninth floor. An hour into the morning shift, a correctional officer yelled, "Fight! Fight!" and bolted toward cell number six. Two officers hurried to help, while the fourth began asking the nurses, social workers, and me to leave. All of us started toward the lobby except Evelyn Johnson, the chief nurse on duty. She defiantly positioned herself so she could watch what was going on inside cell six.

The officers removed an inmate with a bloody nose from the cell. But the other combatant refused to come forward to be handcuffed. Instead, he backed into a corner and raised his fists. The officers were about to enter the cell and physically remove him when Johnson spoke up. She offered to call Dr. Poitier. "He can give him a sedative," she said.

Johnson's interference visibly irritated them. But the officers didn't want the nurse to cause a scene. An officer told me later that Johnson had lodged complaints about their tactics in the past. He also admitted they were nervous because I was a witness to all this.

The officers begrudgingly agreed to leave the inmate alone while Johnson paged Dr. Poitier. He returned to C wing and gave the inmate a shot. Within minutes, the prisoner was sleeping peacefully in his cell and Dr. Poitier had returned to the courthouse.

When I asked Johnson why she had refused to exit C wing, she selected her words carefully. When she had first started working in the jail in 1982, the only time she had been asked to leave was when the correctional officers planned on "fooling" with an inmate. The jail now had strict procedures that spelled out when they could use physical force, but Johnson was still nervous whenever she or other noncorrectional staff were asked to walk out of a cell block.

One of the officers, who was peeved at Johnson, was not so guarded when I asked him about her. "She didn't want to go because she thought we were going to kick that inmate's ass," he said. "And we probably would have."

The incident was an example of the natural friction that existed on the ninth floor each day between the officers and medical personnel. The nurses, social workers, and Dr. Poitier saw the inmates as *patients*. The officers saw them as *prisoners*. "Our job," an officer explained, "is custody, care, and control. These inmates are here because they broke the law. They're criminals first, mentally ill second."

But Nurse Johnson felt otherwise. "Nurses are nurturers. These officers approach problems differently from us. Bridging the gap sometimes takes creativity—to make certain people don't do the wrong thing."

Johnson had worked with mentally ill prisoners in the jail longer than any other nurse on C wing and longer than most officers there, too. She was well aware of the dangers she faced. Inmates had screamed at her, threatened her, and tried to humiliate her. One morning, an inmate had called her over to his cell. When she went to see what he wanted, he tossed a cup of feces and urine at her. This was before the vents in the cells were sealed, and the concoction splashed on her hair and face. She ran into a bathroom to wash, but couldn't get it all out. She drove home, spent a long time in the shower, and then took a half-hour walk around the block to calm down. When she returned to work, a corrections officer said the inmate was going to be "taught a lesson." Johnson got upset. She didn't want the inmate harmed. But the officer insisted that the prisoner had to be punished, otherwise he'd pull the same disgusting stunt on someone else. When Johnson threatened to report anyone who touched the inmate, the officer backed off.

Later, she confronted the prisoner. "I've tried to help you," she said. "Why did you do that ugly thing to me?"

"Because you were the first person I saw," he replied.

That exchange had reminded Johnson that she couldn't take anything personally on the ninth floor. "These inmates aren't themselves when they're sick," she explained. "They might yell horrible curse words at you one day and tell you they love you the next. All of us who work here understand that—or we should."

When Dr. Poitier returned to C wing from the courthouse, he asked if I wanted to attend a private luncheon with him on the jail's seventh floor. Plates of deli sandwiches and chilled soft drinks were spread out in a classroom there. The food had been brought in by a salesman from Janssen Pharmaceutica. He was hosting the spread because he'd learned that a competing salesman from Eli Lilly and Company had been trying to lure Dr. Poitier into using his company's products.

The Miami jail spent about $2.5 million per year on medication, and the lion's share went to Janssen for its antipsychotic drug Risperdal (risperidone). This was because the jail operated under a "fail first" system. Dr. Poitier was required to prescribe Risperdal to inmates even if they had been taking a different medication before they were arrested. The prisoners had to "fail first" on Risperdal before they could be given Zyprexa, Abilify, or other medications.

The reason was money.

Risperdal cost about one-third as much as the other drugs. It also could be used by nearly anyone. This made it a favorite not only in jails, but with other governmental agencies as well. Five states, including Florida, had recently removed Zyprexa from their "preferred drug" list—a step taken to force Medicaid patients either to switch to Risperdal or to pay the difference for Zyprexa out of their own pockets.

The makers of Zyprexa had reacted to this attack by sending their sales reps into the trenches to win support from doctors for their antipsychotic drug. An Eli Lilly salesman had told Dr. Poitier that Zyprexa actually was more cost-effective than Risperdal because it reduced the number of fights in a jail, especially between inmates and officers. This saved money by cutting down on employee injury/sick days, disability payments, and lawsuits. The Lilly associate also claimed Zyprexa was faster-acting, so jails could release prisoners sooner, thus further reducing costs. He had offered to fly a psychiatrist from a New York jail to Miami to talk personally with Dr. Poitier about Zyprexa's virtues.

Dr. Poitier had told his bosses at the Miami-Dade County Health Care Trust about that offer, but they had ordered him not to accept it. Instead, they had contacted Janssen, and it had hurriedly dispatched its representative to host today's luncheon and explain why Risperdal was still a superior choice for the jail.

After everyone had eaten, the Janssen rep began touting Risperdal and attacking its rivals. He also hinted that Janssen would soon be releasing a new form of Risperdal that could be given once a month instead of daily. He knew Dr. Poitier would find that interesting, because the chance of getting a mentally ill person to take twelve doses per year was much higher than the chance of getting him to take daily pills.

After we returned to the ninth floor, Dr. Poitier told me that he really hadn't learned much new during the lunch. He understood the reasoning behind the fail-first policy. Still, he would have preferred to keep inmates on the same prescriptions that they were taking on the streets. *Why risk a possible breakdown?*

Dr. Poitier was keenly interested in antipsychotic medications because he believed they were the mentally ill's best hope. He also found them fascinating because his wife was a pharmacist and his father had been one, too.

"I grew up in a medical family," he explained. "My parents expected me to become a doctor and I never thought of becoming anything else." Just the same, they had been disappointed when he chose forensic psychiatry instead of becoming a general practitioner. "Even in my profession today, there is a prejudice against those of us who work in prisons and jails. There's a feeling we have to work in these environments because we can't get jobs anywhere else."

That might have been true about the two other psychiatrists who worked inside the jail. Both of them were foreign born and foreign trained. But Dr. Poitier was a native of Miami.

Born in 1954, he had grown up in two black neighborhoods that today are slums but during segregated times had been middle- and upper-class areas. In 1972, he'd entered Morehouse College in Atlanta, Georgia, an all-male African-American school, which counted among its graduates Martin Luther King Jr. Poitier's professors had urged him to select a profession that he could use to help the black community. Later, at the University of Miami Medical School, Poitier had been encouraged by Dr. Sanford Jacobson, the white head of the forensic psychiatry department, to work with criminals.

"People who are arrested have one strike against them," Dr. Poitier explained. "Being arrested and being black is even worse. But being arrested, being a minority, and being mentally ill puts you in the worst of the worst situation. The inmates I see every day on the ninth floor are among society's most marginalized citizens. Early on, I thought, If I can help them, then I'm doing my job as a doctor and I'm also giving something back to my community."

Dr. Poitier spent ten years at South Florida Evaluation & Treatment Center, a maximum-security psychiatric hospital only a few blocks from the main jail. Later, Dr. Jacobson recruited him to become the jail's chief psychiatrist. At first, he didn't think the switch from the state-run forensic center to the ninth floor would be that different. He was wrong. Although both held dangerous inmates, the center had been run like a hospital. Not the jail. A correctional officer told Dr. Poitier on his first day, "You're a guest here and don't you ever forget it. This is *our* jail."

Dr. Poitier needed to spend the afternoon completing paperwork after the luncheon, so I left him alone and returned to C wing. I watched Nurse Johnson tell one of the correctional officers that she needed an inmate removed from his cell so she could speak to him in private. The officer said he was busy. She asked another, but that officer also was busy. Johnson waited and waited. But none of them made any attempt to help her. She had to wait until a fresh crew of correctional officers came on board. No one had to explain why. Johnson knew she was being shunned for interfering earlier that morning.

Dr. Poitier was still at work after the shift change. His cramped quarters smelled antiseptic. Even by government standards, the space was second-rate. Its furnishings were minimal: a gunmetal-gray desk, a squeaky swivel chair, a wooden chair, mismatched file cabinets, and a well-used coffeepot perched precariously on an overloaded shelf. There was no carpet, no window, no view, no photographs of his wife and children, or any professional certificates displayed on the walls. The room was at the lip of C wing, a location that guaranteed Dr. Poitier would have no privacy, because people were constantly passing back and forth in front of his open door. There was a toilet and a sink in a cubicle at the rear of his office. It was the only private facility on the ninth floor, and during the day, female correctional officers, nurses, and social workers slipped in and out every few minutes to use it. Dr. Poitier could have barred them, but he was too polite. Instead, he silently endured the steady stream of women brushing by his desk and the sounds of the constant toilet-flushing.

Near 5 P.M., his phone rang. The jail's administrative director called to tell him that the fail-first policy with Risperdal wasn't going to be modified. There was no money in the budget for a switch to Zyprexa or other, newer drugs.

Outside Dr. Poitier's office, an officer yelled, "Fight!" This was followed by the sounds of running. Another scuffle had broken out in a cell. There was a loud scream, and then another. Dr. Poitier looked weary. "This environment can wear on you," he said.

"Then why do you still work here?" I asked.

He thought for a moment and then answered: "The inmates who end up here have been given up on. But *some* can and do get better. And that's the driving force that keeps me coming to work each day—knowing I can make a difference. Knowing I *do* make a difference.

"Besides," he added with a toothy smile, "if I didn't do this, who would?"

Chapter 14

I was curious about what had happened to Ted Jackson, the mentally ill prisoner whom I'd met in jail during my first trip to Miami. He had just been released from the Bayview Center when I'd last checked on him. I decided to call his South Beach apartment, and when he didn't answer, I assumed he either was out fishing or was standing on a street corner, handing out his Puppet Master flyers that predicted Jesus would return in 2007.

But I began to worry when I still wasn't able to reach him after several days. I became even more anxious when I bumped into the jail's chief social worker, Theodore Thomas, and he told me that Jackson had been arrested for a second time and booked into jail shortly after I had returned home after my first Miami visit.

"They brought him in while you were gone, and he was in pretty rough shape," Thomas explained. Jackson's face had been so badly bruised and swollen that Dr. Poitier had transferred him directly to Jackson Memorial Hospital.

"When did all this happen?" I asked.

"About three weeks ago," Thomas said.

I decided to try calling Jackson again that night. If he didn't answer,

I was going to drive to his apartment to investigate. I dialed his number, and after several rings a groggy voice said, "Hello." It was him.

"Did I wake you?" I asked.

"Yeah," he said sleepily.

I reminded him who I was and then said, "I heard you got arrested again—right after I left town. What happened?"

Jackson said he had been distributing leaflets when two Miami Beach police officers accused him of painting "Jesus 2007" graffiti on a nearby building. He was handcuffed and taken to the South Beach police station, where a third officer was waiting. That policeman told Jackson the city was tired of him writing graffiti everywhere.

"I said, 'I'm not going to write any more graffiti, but I'm still going to pass out my literature.' That's when that policeman punched me. He hit me several times in the face. Hard. When I fell down on my knees, one of them put his nightstick under my throat and started choking me, and the other bent one of my arms back so hard I heard the bone crack."

Jackson said the officer who struck him warned him that if he didn't "get it this time," they would have to teach him "another lesson." Jackson was told that he was being charged with thirty-two separate counts of writing graffiti and was driven to jail.

An X-ray at the hospital confirmed that Jackson's arm was fractured. He was also found to have head lice, which he insisted he'd gotten from the wool blanket that he had used at the jail the first time he'd been arrested. "That blanket wasn't washed. It was just passed around by inmates."

After doctors at the hospital patched him up, Jackson was told that all the charges filed against him had been dismissed and he could leave.

While I was shocked to hear that Jackson had allegedly been beaten, I wasn't surprised that he'd been arrested again after I'd last seen him. Because of the disjointed telephone messages that he had left on my cell phone hours after he'd been discharged, it had been obvious he had still not been thinking clearly. A case manager from Bayview was supposed to have kept track of Jackson after he was released to make certain he didn't have a relapse.

"I never heard from nobody from that place," he said. "They just give you drugs and send you on your way."

I asked what sort of medication he was now taking. He had been prescribed lithium, clozapine, and Risperdal before his double arrests. His psychiatrist at the VA medical center had replaced the Risperdal with Seroquel, he said, which was more potent and known to work well at controlling mood swings. The doctor also had increased his doses of clozapine. Often called the "drug of last resort," it was used when patients did not respond well to other medicines.

While there are no standard doses for any of these medications, the VA psychiatrist had prescribed amounts near the maximum recommendation for Jackson. According to its maker, Seroquel was most effective in the 400-to-500-milligrams-per-day range. The maximum was 750 milligrams. Jackson was taking 600 milligrams. Clozapine topped out at 900 milligrams per day. Jackson was told to take 800. Jackson said the combination of lithium, Seroquel, and clozapine made him so tired that he was now sleeping nearly twenty-four hours a day, which was good, because he was frightened to go outside his apartment for fear he'd run into the Miami Beach police. "I know they're watching me."

I asked Jackson if he had been charged any additional court fees because of his second arrest. I knew he still owed $649 from his first case. Jackson said he hadn't been assessed any more. But he had run up a new debt.

Before this second arrest, he had met a man in South Beach named Charlie. "He acted like he wanted to be my friend," Jackson explained. Charlie had asked Jackson to help him pick out some stereo equipment. They met at a South Beach electronics store one morning, and Charlie persuaded Jackson to charge $500 on his credit card for various items. "He promised he'd pay me back," Jackson said. But of course Charlie hadn't.

Jackson had found out where Charlie lived and had begun leaving telephone messages on his answering machine, demanding repayment. But then Jackson had been arrested for a second time and sent to jail. Somehow, Charlie had learned about the arrest, and when Jackson was freed, there was a message on his answering machine from Charlie. "He said he was going to tell the Miami Beach police I was threatening him," Jackson said. "He told me to leave him alone or he'd have me arrested. He said everyone knew I was crazy and no one would believe anything I said." Not wanting to risk getting into trouble again, Jackson had decided to give up getting repaid.

"Now I got the credit card company sending me a bill and the court sending me a letter telling me I still owe $649 in court costs. Plus I got Kinko's calling me about the money I owe them. I also got a fractured arm and my face all bruised up by the cops and I got lice."

Jackson had left his apartment only once in nearly a month. He'd kept his appointment with his VA doctor. That was it. "My psychiatrist told me I'm being paranoid hiding like this, and them cops should be afraid of me," he said. "The doctor says I should contact a lawyer and sue them. But I don't want to do that. But I'm telling you, man, I've already taken two ass-whuppings without fighting back from these cops and I'm not going to take another. If they come for me again, I'm going to fight back, and someone is going to end up dead. *I mean it!* I'm not going to let them beat on me like that anymore."

Jackson said he was afraid to leave his apartment to meet with me, so I ended the call. The next morning, I drove to the Miami Beach Police Department and asked a records clerk there to give me a copy of Jackson's second arrest report. She said there wasn't anything in the file that showed he'd ever been brought into the station on the night that Jackson had said he'd been beaten. That was odd, because I'd already checked the jail's records, and they showed that Jackson had been booked into the rear lobby by two Miami Beach police officers and had subsequently been transferred to a hospital.

I put in a call to a spokesman for the Miami Beach police, and I was told that someone would get in touch with me about Jackson's case. (No one ever did.)

The next evening, my cell phone rang. It was Jackson. "I'm sorry for not meeting you yesterday. I don't want to disappoint you, but it's best for me just to lay low right now and stay in my apartment. Them cops hurt me bad. But you can call me the next time you're in Miami, okay? I like having you as a friend. Besides, I want you to put in your book about how Jesus is coming back. That's important."

"What are you going to do if the Miami police knock on your door?" I asked.

There was a long pause. "I just hope they don't, 'cause I already told you, I'm not taking another ass-whupping."

Chapter 15

I wanted to find other inmates—in addition to Ted Jackson and Freddie Gilbert—to shadow. So I went to the jail's booking area on a Thursday night. This was when the bus from the state forensic hospital in Chatta- hoochee was scheduled to arrive each week, returning inmates to Miami who had been deemed "mentally competent" to stand trial. I got there early, curious to see what sort of mental condition the riders would be in. I would then select one to watch and interview.

Everyone brought to the jail entered through a cavernous rectangle of about sixty by forty feet known simply as "the rear lobby." Drunks, drug dealers, petty hustlers, hookers, thieves, reckless drivers, burglars, child abusers, murderers, white-collar criminals—prisoners of every sort, size, and description—were hustled inside without ceremony at all times of the day and night for processing.

Regardless of the criminal charges filed against them, or whether they were drunk or sober, mousy or itching to fight, sane or psychotic, the procedure was much the same. They were photographed, searched, and fingerprinted. At one point during the booking process, inmates were led to a steel table where they were ordered to empty the contents of their pockets and told to lean forward and place both palms on the smooth surface so they could be frisked. Although only men are housed in the main jail, women are also booked through its rear lobby. They are then held in a secure area until they can be driven to the women's jail a few blocks away. Male correctional officers are not permitted to search female inmates, but women officers can search both sexes.

At 10:30 P.M., word spread through the lobby that "the bus" had pulled into the jail's enclosed courtyard. It carried a small cargo: one woman and three men. They were ordered to join a half dozen other prisoners waiting to be processed. There was another woman already in that line, and when she stepped through the double gates into the lobby, she nearly brought work to a standstill.

She was clearly not from "the bus," nor was she the sort of prisoner that correctional officers usually saw. In her early thirties, she was dressed in Dorinha jeans that had been bleached nearly white, cut low in the back, and worn so tight they appeared to have been spray-painted onto her well-shaped legs and buttocks. Her midriff was exposed, revealing tanned, firm abs and a pierced belly button decorated with three rhinestones dangling from a silver chain. A blue tube top stretched around her Dolly Parton–sized chest. She had cascading bleached-blond hair. Her makeup had been meticulously applied, accenting her high cheekbones and baby-smooth complexion. She stared straight ahead with the practiced indifference of a woman used to being gawked at by both men and women. She had been arrested for selling knockoff designer purses in an exclusive South Beach accessories shop that she owned.

The difference between her mouth-dropping entrance and the arrival of the dumpy woman from "the bus" walking behind her couldn't have been more dramatic. The latter shuffled forward, her eyes locked on the concrete floor. There was no makeup on her face, which was lined with crevices and pockmarked. She seemed much older than forty-eight, which was the age listed on her arrest sheet. Her clothing was a combination of castoffs. The dark-blue sweater she was wearing had a gaping hole in its left shoulder. A faded yellow T-shirt peeked through the ragged opening. At one time, her baggy pants had been fire-alarm red. Now they were a faded pink and two sizes too large. Someone had cinched them together at the waist with zigzag stitches made of heavy white thread. Sweat socks and navy-blue canvas Keds with holes in their toes finished her ensemble. Her plain brown hair was stringy and unwashed. There was a bald patch above her right ear where she had jerked out several fistfuls of hair. The only time she'd lifted her eyes was when she'd been told to glance at the ceiling camera so her mug shot could be taken. Strangely, she had smiled, revealing badly yellowed teeth.

While the mentally ill inmate waited, the stunning model strutted to the steel search table, removed her jewelry, spread her legs seductively, and leaned forward. Before this moment, there had been only two correctional officers posted there. But they were joined by seven police officers, who had brought prisoners into the rear lobby to be booked, and now clustered around the table to watch. As a hefty female correctional officer roughly patted down the blonde, one of the cops whispered something vulgar that caused the other leering officers to chuckle.

The show ended as soon as the inmate was taken away. Now it was the crazed woman's turn. The crowd immediately dispersed. No one wanted to watch her. An officer asked if she knew where she was. It took her a moment and then she said, "My name is Alice Ann Collyer and I'm in the Miami jail."

A ccording to Alice Ann Collyer's thick file at the Gerstein courthouse, she'd been arrested for the first time in Miami in 1985 at age thirty-one for disorderly conduct. Between 1986 and 2000, she'd been jailed nine more times for various crimes related to her mental illness. In nearly every one of those instances, she'd been released within a few days. There was nothing in her file that showed she had ever received any meaningful treatment for her schizophrenia. In November 2000, she had been arrested for assaulting an elderly person. She was still waiting to be tried on that charge.

Florida takes attacks against its senior citizens seriously. They are felonies, regardless of whether or not a victim is injured. According to eyewitness statements in Collyer's court file, she had been loitering at a city bus stop in South Beach when she noticed an elderly woman staring at her. Collyer screamed, "Stop looking at me, old lady! Stop stealing my thoughts." She then sprang from the bench and shoved the seventy-five-year-old woman in her chest. The push caused her to step backward, but she hadn't lost her balance or fallen. Collyer, meanwhile, had run away. A witness hurried outside from a nearby bagel shop to help the elderly victim.

"That woman's crazy," he told her. "Someone needs to do something to get her off the streets." Another man rushed forward and said, "If you get her locked up, she might get some help." But the woman told them that she didn't want to cause anyone any trouble.

By chance, a Miami Beach police officer arrived. She was on her way to buy a bagel, but the witnesses called her over and explained what had just happened.

"I'm not hurt," the elderly woman protested. "It's not a big deal."

But the policewoman sided with the two witnesses. "If I arrest her, she'll be put in jail and then sent to a hospital," the cop volunteered.

As soon as the woman heard that, she agreed to sign a complaint, and the officer arrested Collyer in a nearby alley.

The state's attorney's office, which prosecuted criminal cases in Miami, noticed that Collyer had been arrested twice before for pushing elderly women in surprise attacks. Afraid that she might eventually harm someone, a prosecutor charged Collyer as a "habitual offender." That made the penalty that she now faced even more serious. A year earlier, Florida legislators had passed a habitual offender act—sometimes called a three-strikes law—to get violent felons off the streets. Because the bus-stop shoving was Collyer's "third strike," she now faced a mandatory sentence of at least five years in prison—all because she was severely mentally ill and had shoved an elderly woman at a bus stop. A judge sent her to Chattahoochee to be made mentally competent.

I wanted to learn more about Alice Ann Collyer, so I asked Dr. Poitier to arrange for me to visit the Women's Detention Center, a nondescript building within walking distance. He introduced me to Alida Renoso, a cheerful woman in her seventies, who was the psychiatrist there. On an average day, about sixty of the 350 women in the detention center had serious mental disorders.

Dr. Renoso had been trained as a surgeon in her native Cuba but had fled the island in the 1960s and had switched to psychiatry after settling in Miami. She worked a full day on Mondays, but came in on Wednesdays and Fridays only long enough to handle emergencies and write prescriptions. Marie Fleurmont, the jail's social worker, watched the "psych inmates" whenever Dr. Renoso wasn't available. Born in Haiti, Fleurmont had worked as a hospital nurse in New York City before moving to Florida. Her former coworkers had called her the "pencil lady" because her English was so heavily accented that she had to write everything down for them to read. After moving to Miami, she earned a master's degree in social work and perfected her English, although many prisoners still complained that both she and Dr. Renoso were difficult to understand.

Dr. Renoso invited me to go with her and Fleurmont on their morning rounds. There were thirty mentally ill women living in group cells and another thirty-four locked in individual cells under close supervision. We began by entering a pentagon-shaped pod that contained five "safety cells" reserved for women under suicide watch. The cells resembled pieces of a sliced pie. They joined together in the center of the pod and then extended backward in a V-shape. There were no glass cell fronts as in the men's jail. Each cell's solid steel door had a small square window. Painted cinder blocks separated the doors.

Dr. Renoso and Fleurmont skipped the first cell even though there was a naked woman inside it curled in the fetal position on a thin blue pad on the floor. She was sleeping. "She's not one of ours," Dr. Renoso explained. The prisoner was an illegal alien who had been arrested by federal immigration agents. Immigration was paying the Miami jail a monthly fee to house her until its lawyers could decide what to do with the psychotic inmate. Because of the woman's illegal status, Dr. Renoso was not allowed to treat her.

A pale white face was peering through the smudged window in the next cell. I didn't recognize Alice Ann Collyer at first, because she had torn more hair from her forehead. As soon as she spotted Dr. Renoso, Collyer smacked the door and demanded that she open its food slot. A female correctional officer unbolted the opening, and Collyer handed a folded piece of white paper through it.

"This is important," she said. "You need to do something about it right away."

Dr. Renoso asked her how she was feeling, but Collyer walked away, turning her back to us. Dr. Renoso skimmed the message and slipped it into the pocket of her coat. As we stepped away, Collyer yelled, "This is bullshit!"

The next cell was vacant. Its inhabitant had been sent to Chatta-hoochee on the returning bus that morning. But another occupant was waiting when we reached the fourth room.

"I keep hearing a voice saying I'm bad because I've been rude to my mother," the woman said.

"Stop listening to that voice," Dr. Renoso replied in a firm tone. "Your mother visited you yesterday and she's fine."

The woman had been hearing voices since she was eight years old.

Now she was thirty-five and had been diagnosed as being both mentally retarded and schizophrenic. She had been charged with attempted murder after she had attacked her mother with a knife. She had been in jail two months.

"Okay, thank you, Doctor," she replied, childlike.

The prisoner in the pod's final cell was sobbing and moaning loudly. Rapping on the door, Dr. Renoso asked, "Why are you crying? Stop that!"

"It's the medicine," the inmate groaned. "It makes me sad! Why are you torturing me?"

"That medicine is helping you," Dr. Renoso replied. "Stop acting like that. Stop crying."

It took Dr. Renoso an hour to make her way through another safety pod and then through the group cells. When she returned to her office, she remembered Collyer's note. She plucked it from her pocket and handed it to me:

A woman needs sex. Please let me out so I can have sex. I will fuck the first man who wants to have sex. I am woman and woman must need sex.

She tucked the note into Collyer's file.

"This is a very sad case," Dr. Renoso said, referring to Collyer. "The first time she came back to us from Chattahoochee, she was doing wonderfully. But the lawyers waited so long, she decompensated and had to be sent back to the hospital."

"So," I said, "this is the second time that she has come back from the hospital since she was arrested?"

Dr. Renoso nodded. "She just got back, but I'm afraid that she is not in as good a shape mentally as she should be. I'm afraid that by the time her trial is held, she will have to be sent to the hospital again."

"For a third time?"

Dr. Renoso nodded.

Collyer's court records showed that she had been traveling between the jail and Chattahoochee for *three years* and still had not been put on trial or found guilty of any crime.

"There was a time," Dr. Renoso continued, "when a patient like this would have spent her entire life locked in a state mental hospital, because she is such a sick woman. I worked in a state hospital and I know how horrible the conditions in them were. But is her life any better today? Have we really helped her? At least there, she might have had access to some programs or some art therapy. Now she's in a cell all day."

Dr. Renoso went on: "We've closed nearly all of these state hospitals, so there is nowhere for someone like her to live. If we turn her loose, she will roam the streets, where women like her are abused, raped, and beaten. If they are not living on the streets, they are in jails and prisons. Either way, we are not helping them. All we are doing in this jail is babysitting."

I went to see Collyer later in the safety pod and explained who I was and what I was doing. I asked her if she wanted to talk to me about her life.

"No!" she snapped.

I waited several days and tried again. But Collyer was even more mentally confused when we talked. She mistook me for a doctor, so I decided that I couldn't, in good conscience, continue to ask her questions. The third time that I went to the women's center to check on Collyer, Dr. Renoso told me that she was gone.

A judge had sent three psychiatrists to examine her, and all of them had decided that she was not competent to be put on trial. She had been sent back to Chattahoochee on the bus. It was her *third* trip, the *third* time doctors at the forensic hospital had been asked to make her competent enough for trial. Dr. Renoso wasn't sure when Collyer might be coming back.

I counted the days on a calendar between the morning when Collyer had been arrested in South Beach for shoving an elderly woman and today. It was 1,151 days. That was how long she had been in jail, in the state forensic hospital, and riding on the bus.

1,151 days.

H ow could Dr. Renoso make such an outlandish statement?
How could she suggest that Alice Ann Collyer was no
better off today than she would have been living in the
old state asylum system? What about deinstitutionaliza-
tion, the civil rights reforms of the 1980s, the class-action lawsuits filed
by the Mental Health Law Project?

I decided to put her remarks to a test. The landmark civil rights case
in Florida that had challenged conditions in state hospitals was *Sanbourne v. Chiles*. The Chiles was then Governor Lawton Chiles, and the
Sanbourne was Deidra Sanbourne, a patient who had spent nearly
twenty years locked in a state mental hospital.

Sanbourne v. Chiles had been filed in 1988 and had turned Sanbourne
into a poster child for patients. She had become their face in the Florida
media. She had been portrayed as being "representative." So how had
her life been changed by the lawsuit? Was she now living comfortably
in an ALF, homeless on the streets, or, much like Alice Ann Collyer,
riding on round-trip bus rides between a jail and Chattahoochee? Was
she better off?

I set out to find Deidra Sanbourne.

I called the lawyers who had filed *Sanbourne v. Chiles*. They referred me to a social worker named Susan Curran, and she proved eager to tell me how that landmark lawsuit had come about and what she knew about Sanbourne.

T ired of hearing about abuses in state mental hospitals, Congress passed a law in 1986 that required every state to monitor how patients were being treated in state institutions. For two years, Florida dragged its feet, but it finally created a watchdog office called the Advocacy Center for Persons with Disabilities. Its director decided his first official act would be to send an inspection team into South Florida State Hospital to evaluate how its patients were being treated. That hospital was selected because it was located just north of Miami and was easy to get to. The other three state-run hospitals were in remote areas.

The director knew state inspectors had done periodic reviews. But he assumed most of them had been rubber-stamped affairs. He wanted something much more thorough, so he hired a private firm, Therapeutic Concepts, to suggest ways his team could discover what really was taking place in the facility. The consulting firm came up with a unique approach. It selected eighteen patients at random and then assigned inspectors to shadow them for three days. At four predetermined times each day, the team members would write down everything they saw happening during a five-minute interval. They would note whom the patient was talking to, what kind of mood the patient was in, what the patient was wearing, and what the hospital staff was doing. These notes would then be compiled so the director could get an accurate snapshot of everyday life.

Susan Curran had been in charge of the inspection. Clutching her notebook, she pounded on the locked door of an all-male ward just before 6:30 A.M. in August 1988 on the first day of the hospital visit. After several moments, a nurse finally opened the door and hurried Curran across an open ward into a glass-enclosed nurses' station.

"You need to stay locked in here," she warned. "Otherwise, you will get hurt."

Curran peered through the windows. Thirty men were milling around on the outside and all of them were naked. Their clothing wasn't brought to them until 8 A.M. No one had been issued pajamas. Curran saw a patient pull a cigarette from a hiding spot and raise it to his lips. But before he could light it, another tried to snatch it. The two men began fighting, and a third jumped in. Then a fourth. The nurse ignored the brawl. A fifth made a grab. After several more seconds, the strongest emerged with his broken trophy. He smoked it while standing with his fists clenched.

Curran saw the patient whom she'd been assigned to monitor, crawling across the floor. "George" was easy to spot because he was a double amputee.

"Where's his wheelchair?" she asked.

"He don't got one."

A pounding noise on the ward's door announced the arrival of clothes. An orderly pushed a laundry cart inside and dumped its contents on the floor. The naked men scrambled to pick through the shirts, pants, underwear, socks. First come, first wear. Curran watched as George fought through the throng to collect leftovers.

George did nothing the remainder of that morning, because there was nothing for him to do. No recreation, no therapy. Nothing.

Around noon, Curran needed to use a bathroom, but there were no safe facilities for her inside the men's ward. She walked to a nearby women's unit. The first patient she saw there was a gray-haired woman, completely naked, tied in a chair with a pool of urine underneath her.

Curran fought the urge to vomit. That night, she couldn't sleep. By the end of the three-day inspection, she was outraged. "I met with the hospital administrators and they were shocked by *our* shock," Curran told me. "They kept saying: 'What do you expect? *These people are men-*

tally ill.' It was clear they didn't see their patients as human beings. I learned you can never underestimate how much people will stigmatize and devalue the mentally ill."

An angry Curran held a press conference and described what her team had found. She told how nude patients could be seen by people driving by the hospital because there were no curtains on any of the windows. She explained how patients were not allowed to own anything, even toothbrushes. These were kept in a communal bucket and rinsed out with a hose between uses. There was no toilet paper because the staff claimed patients would use it to clog the commodes. None of the women was issued underwear, because, the staff said, they'd lose it. Leather restraints were used to immobilize and to punish patients. The hospital was overrun with stray cats. Because of repeated budget cuts, skeletal nursing crews were expected to control hundreds of inmates. Fistfights broke out daily, not only between patients but between patients and staff members as well. To help maintain order, doctors were overdrugging patients so they'd spend their days asleep in chairs, drooling.

Curran gave the media copies of her team's notes.

The lack of underwear for the women means that a female having her monthly period has no way to secure a pad in place except to shuffle slowly with her legs together.

Another team member wrote:

Not only did patients lack underwear, there was no toothpaste or even toothbrushes the days I observed. No one had bothered to wash the supply. There was one dirty comb and one brush for thirty women. . . . The young woman I followed had attempted suicide and been institutionalized. She is quite bright and intelligent, but there is nothing for this resident or any other to do.

Curran's news conference infuriated the public. The hospital's director was fired and state officials promised to make immediate changes. But Curran remained skeptical. Almost from the day it had opened in 1957, the hospital had been underfunded, overcrowded, and poorly administered. Located in an area called Pembroke Pines, it had been built to house 484 patients. It soon held 1,700. When rumors surfaced in 1970 that patients were being tortured, the federal government threatened to seize control. Afraid the Justice Department would force the state to spend millions on repairs, the Florida legislature leaped onto the deinstitutionalization bandwagon. Overnight, it began emptying its wards. The daily census in the state's four asylums plunged from 9,812 patients to 2,838 in a five-year period. Most were simply tossed out the front gates.

The sudden appearance of ranting patients on street corners did not go unnoticed. In what was a typical exposé at the time, *Miami Herald* reporter Paul Shannon wrote:

Florida's policy of emptying its mental institutions [has caused] hundreds of patients . . . to be packed into aging hotels and houses that are little better than slums. . . . The worst buildings contain the stuff of nightmares. Piles of trash and feces litter the floors. Half-naked men wander purposelessly through hallways, and doors swing open into hot and fetid rooms where others, gazing vacantly at the ceiling, lie neglected on dirty cots.

By the time Susan Curran began her 1988 inspection, the hospital had trimmed its population to 573 patients. They were still being held there because they were so chronically disturbed that even the most callous staff members could not justify pushing them out.

A civil rights lawyer named Alice Nelson decided to visit the hospital after Curran's news conference. She worked at Southern Legal Counsel, a public interest firm. "The hospital was truly medieval," she told me later. At one point during her hospital tour, Nelson asked what had been done to prevent naked patients from being spied on by people traveling past the hospital.

"We fixed that," a staff member reported.

Nelson assumed curtains had been hung. But she was wrong. "The staff had spray-painted all of the windows black: That was their solution— black spray paint."

Nelson contacted Deborah Whisnant, a lawyer who worked with Curran at the Advocacy Center, and together they decided to sue Florida. They asked the Mental Health Law Project for advice, and its lawyers told them to use Dr. Morton Birnbaum's "right to treatment" argument to file a class-action lawsuit. Nelson and Whisnant began scouring the patient rolls to find a lead plaintiff. They came up with nine possibilities. But when Nelson met individually with them, she decided that seven were simply too unreliable. She was worried they would bail out if they were offered a pack of cigarettes or threatened. Of the two remaining names, Deidra Sanbourne stuck out. Before she became ill, Sanbourne had worked as a legal secretary in a Miami law firm. Despite her mental failings, she understood what Nelson was proposing.

Nelson and Whisnant filed *Sanbourne v. Chiles*. It was the first class-action lawsuit filed against Florida that demanded patients in state hospitals either be given adequate treatment or be released. Nelson would later remember that Sanbourne had been enthusiastic. "She was proud of what we were doing and she really believed it would make a difference. All of us did."

But as the lawsuit began to drag through the court system, Sanbourne became discouraged. The reason for the snail's pace was politics. Governor Chiles had not been surprised when Nelson sued the state. After Curran's press conference, Chiles expected it. Besides, other states also were coming under attack by civil rights lawyers. What worried Chiles was that an activist federal judge might take control of the suit. Chiles had seen how federal judges had forced other states to pay millions in repairs. So Chiles had instructed Howard Talenfeld, a private attorney who specialized in mental health lawsuits, to do whatever he could to avoid having the case move forward. In turn, Talenfeld offered to negotiate an out-of-court settlement with Nelson. He promised to make fixes at the hospital.

The Mental Health Law Project's lawyers recognized what Chiles and Talenfeld were trying to do. They objected. They wanted the hospital shut down permanently, so they began pressuring Nelson not to negotiate. Nelson felt trapped in the middle.

Based on the state's shoddy track record, she wasn't sure she could trust it to make changes at the hospital. But as a former social worker, Nelson had seen what had happened during deinstitutionalization. "There were no community services out there for people like Deidra," she explained. "What good was it going to do to shut down the hospital if the patients were going to be sent untreated into the streets?"

When Talenfeld offered to bring in a team of outside experts to monitor the state's progress, Nelson agreed to hold the suit in abeyance. She then began recruiting some of the best and brightest mental health experts in the nation to come to Florida. Martha Knisley, who'd run Ohio's mental health department, later recalled how excited everyone had felt. "We saw this as an opportunity to really bring about dynamic changes in a state that needed desperately to move forward," she said.

By this point, a new hospital administrator, David Sofferin, had been hired. At a press conference, he symbolically removed his jacket and rolled up his sleeves to show that he was ready to make changes. One of his first was issuing "hygiene kits" to all the patients. They contained toiletries, including toothbrushes. He put toilet paper in the bathrooms, removed locks that had prevented patients from coming into the administration's offices, and issued the women underwear. "We all wanted to do the right thing," Sofferin said later.

Deidra Sanbourne, who went by the name DeeDee, met with every outside expert Nelson brought to the hospital. "She was a real inspiration to us," Knisley recalled. "She was determined to be treated respectfully, and she believed the lawsuit would lead to real changes for her and the other patients. This lawsuit really became an important part of her life."

So much so that Nelson and the outside experts began to worry that Sanbourne was setting herself up for disappointment. Martha Hodge, who was flown in to set up treatment programs, later remembered that Sanbourne "absolutely believed" the lawsuit was going to get her discharged. "She thought it could help her get a nice home and possibly a job or maybe a life partner. And that's what she really wanted the lawsuit to do—*to get her a new life.*"

Attorney Nelson spent hours talking to Sanbourne about her expectations. "We all cared about her and we didn't want her to feel let down," said Hodge. But privately all of them questioned whether she was someone who could ever be safely released. Hodge later described her as an example of an "iatrogenic" patient—a term used to describe the negative effects brought on by living inside an institution for decades. "I didn't see much in her future except continued institutionalization. Sadly, Deidra just got iller and iller and worser and worser as time went on."

Two years after the lawsuit was filed, an exasperated Nelson told Talenfeld that the state wasn't doing enough. She moved forward with the case in court. But by then the public's interest in the hospital had waned. Susan Curran's shocking revelations had been forgotten. A judge ordered the two sides to reach an out-of-court settlement. Negotiations took months. Finally, in 1993, five years after the suit had been filed, Nelson signed a settlement. The state promised to make more improvements at the hospital and agreed to set aside $3 million to open three drop-in centers for the mentally ill in area communities. The centers would provide them with a gathering spot to socialize. The money was called "the Sanbourne funds."

"The conditions at the hospital went from being barbaric to being human," recalled Knisley, "but the settlement fell short of what we had all wanted. Florida just didn't have the stomach for making real social progress. . . . It was satisfied being in the backwater of social commitment, and the hospital got a Band-Aid instead of what it needed."

If the outside experts felt disappointed, Sanbourne felt betrayed.

"She lost faith in us," Knisley said. She refused to meet with Nelson and her advisers. When Hodges bumped into her one day at the hospital, Sanbourne spit in her face.

"Even if people are very, very ill, they know when you've given up on them," Knisley said. "If we, somehow, could have gotten to her before she'd spent so many years in the hospital, she might have had a chance. But by the time we met her, no rehabilitation was really going to work. She'd been ravaged by shock treatments and the older drugs. We were simply too late."

The panel of experts went home. Alice Nelson filed another class-action suit, this time about Florida's juvenile facilities. The hospital's administrator, David Sofferin, moved to a better-paying job in Kansas. Everyone left but Sanbourne.

Two years later, the hospital was rocked by scandal. A patient with schizophrenia was found dead after he was given the wrong medicine. A state investigator called conditions in the hospital "shameful." The patient had lost thirty pounds in thirty days without *anyone*'s noticing.

Despite all the state's promises, the hospital had, once again, become a horrific asylum. In 1997, the Florida legislature voted to wash its hands of the place. The institution became the first psychiatric hospital in the nation to be turned over by a state to a for-profit corporation. The legislature agreed to pay $32 million per year to Atlantic Shores Health-care, a subsidiary of the Wackenhut Security Corporation, to run it.

Changes came quickly. The new owners razed many of the compound's old buildings and erected a new 350-bed facility with dormitories clustered around a clock tower and picturesque gazebo. Within ten months, the hospital had been accredited, something the state had never been able to achieve. Atlantic Shores Healthcare's doctors also began discharging patients who had been locked up nearly all of their lives.

And that included Deidra Sanbourne.

Although the outside experts had thought she was too sick to ever be released, Atlantic Shores Healthcare said otherwise. A judge had committed her to the state hospital in February 1982. Nearly two decades later, in December 2001, she was put in a van and driven to an ALF in Miami Beach. She had been officially discharged. What happened next?

For that answer, I needed to find her family.

S usan Wagner was blunt.

"We didn't have the best relationship," she said, when I asked her about her older sister, Deidra "DeeDee" Sanbourne. "My sister was not an easy person to be around after she got sick. There were times when I hated being with her. But she was my sister and I loved her just the same."

From the beginning, life had been difficult for both girls. Sanbourne's January 5, 1946, birth certificate identified her father as Donald Michael Sanbourne, but that was a lie. Their mother, Frances March, had a penchant for falling in love with married men. Not wanting to reveal the identity of Sanbourne's actual father, Frances conjured up the last name Sanbourne simply because she liked how it sounded. Born seven years later, Susan Wagner also was the product of her mother's failed relationship with a married man. She, too, would never be told her father's name.

As a single mother, Frances had little time for her two daughters. Their upbringing fell on their grandparents, who lived with them. Their grandmother was a closet alcoholic. Their grandfather suffered from a case of self-diagnosed "bad nerves." It was up to Frances to support the five-member household on her meager salary as a clerk in a Miami department store. Of them all, DeeDee seemed to have the best shot. Her mother would later brag about how an elementary school teacher had once called her to school for a parent conference. Frances had been afraid her daughter had gotten into trouble, but the teacher said he simply "wanted to meet the mother of such a perfect child."

In high school, Sanbourne earned good marks and dated a star base-ball player. She later went to work as a legal secretary, a job that intro-duced her to a much grander social set. By this point, Frances had moved out, leaving her older daughter to support the others. Sanbourne didn't complain. At age twenty-two, she had fallen in love with an up-and-coming lawyer. They spent their weekends at the beach and their nights in glitzy restaurants.

And then her life crashed.

It started when she became pregnant and miscarried. That incident set off an unseen current that began tugging her backward. She became depressed and afraid to leave the house. Her boyfriend broke off their romance. She was fired from her job. One morning, she started pulling out clumps of her hair.

"My sister realized something wasn't right with her mentally," Wag-ner recalled, "so she went to see a psychiatrist. Then she started reading everything she could about mental illness and drugs. She wanted to do whatever she could to stop her mental illness."

But knowledge couldn't prevent what was happening. Sanbourne began hallucinating. "We'd take DeeDee to the hospital and they'd keep her a few days until she got better," said Wagner. "Then they'd release her and she'd slip again."

During her rational periods, Sanbourne talked about how her own mind was deceiving her. Her grandmother spent hours trying to help her differentiate between what was real and what wasn't. By her twenty-eighth birthday, she had been hospitalized nearly a half dozen times. Her diagnosis: "schizoaffective disorder, bipolar type, with a dependent personality disorder and arterial hypertension." The doctors told her family there was no known cure.

"DeeDee kept our entire family in turmoil," Wagner said. In 1979, the girls' grandmother died. Wagner would later blame her ill sister for "killing" her. "She didn't physically murder her," she said. "She simply wore her out. My grandmother had been the main person who'd watched over her."

After the funeral, Wagner couldn't take it any longer. She moved into an apartment, leaving Sanbourne alone with their grandfather. One morning in 1982, Sanbourne chased him out of the house waving a butcher knife. A judge committed her to South Florida State Hospital.

Sanbourne proved to be a troublesome patient. She yelled racial slurs at black employees and refused to take her antipsychotic medicine. When she began having sex with male patients, doctors gave her injections of Thorazine that made her so groggy she could barely speak. Despite her mental problems, Sanbourne got the message. She became compliant to avoid being intentionally overmedicated.

At about this time, her mother resurfaced in her life. Frances visited her faithfully every weekend. During her lucid periods, Sanbourne took up drawing and earned a reputation in the hospital for her skills. Whenever she drew a portrait, she painted her subject smoking a cigarette whether he or she was a smoker or not. She thought it was funny.

"My mother and I were visiting one weekend when we saw a sheet posted on a bulletin board with the words 'Sanbourne versus Chiles Lawsuit' written in big capital letters," Wagner said. "It was the first me and Mom had heard anything about it. We asked DeeDee and she got a big smile on her face."

Her sister and her mother weren't so thrilled. "No one had ever asked us if we wanted her involved in a lawsuit, and my mom was her legal guardian."

Sanbourne told them that her attorneys were going to get her discharged. That scared Wagner. "I kept thinking, 'Who's going to take care of her?' These doctors had tried everything possible to help her and nothing had worked. They'd told us she was one of those patients who just couldn't be helped. My mother wasn't going to be able to handle her if she was turned loose, and I wouldn't, either."

When the lawsuit was settled and Sanbourne was still locked up, Wagner and her mother felt relieved. In 1997, after Atlantic Shores Healthcare took charge of the facility, Sanbourne began to show signs of improvement. "My sister was getting better care, more individual attention, and it showed. She was taking better care of herself. We were so happy."

And then one morning in November 2001, Susan Wagner arrived at the hospital to visit her sister and was surprised when an employee said, "I guess this is one of the last times we'll be seeing you here."

"Why's that?" she asked.

"Because your sister is being discharged next month."

Wagner was flabbergasted. She went to see the hospital administrator.

"You can't do this!" she exclaimed. "My sister was sent here by a judge. You don't have a legal right to just let her go!"

But the Atlantic Shores Healthcare administrator said federal civil rights laws required patients to be housed in the "least restrictive" environments possible, and her treatment team had decided Deidra Sanbourne no longer needed to be hospitalized.

"Bullshit!" Wagner snapped. "She's been locked up too long to be put out on the street. You can't do this to her!"

Atlantic Shores Heathcare felt otherwise. It had gone forward with the discharge despite Wagner's protests.

I spoke to officials at Atlantic Shores Healthcare several times while preparing this book. They refused to answer any questions about the company's decision to discharge Deidra Sanbourne. A spokesman said the company was prohibited by federal HIPAA laws from discussing individual patients. At that point, I asked Susan Wagner to send Atlantic Shores Healthcare a written request for her sister's discharge records. At the time, Wagner was her sister's legal guardian and her sister had signed a release that entitled Wagner to see all her medical records. Despite repeated written and verbal requests, Atlantic Shores Healthcare still declined to provide Wagner with any documents.

Wagner and her husband, Robert, later told me that they believed Atlantic Shores Healthcare had discharged Sanbourne prematurely to save money. The cost of caring for a chronically mentally ill patient in a Florida hospital when she was released was $86,000 per year. The Wagners were not the first to criticize the hospital for its discharge policies. The state was paying Atlantic Shores Healthcare a set fee each year regardless of how many of its 350 beds were occupied. In newspaper stories about the company's contract with the state, critics suggested Atlantic Shores Healthcare was attempting to maximize its profits by keeping as many beds empty as possible. The company steadfastly denied that charge. Public records showed the average hospital stay for a patient at the hospital was 8.2 years when the state ran it. The average patient stay under Atlantic Shores Healthcare was 185 days.

"I told 'em, 'You're throwing her out,' " Susan Wagner said.

Her husband added, "I said, 'You're abandoning the weakest of the weak, the frailest of the frail to the streets.' "

On the day Sanbourne was released, Robert Wagner told his wife, "There's no way she's going to make it. She is too sick. I'll give her a year before she's dead."

Although Atlantic Shores Healthcare refused to release any documents, I was able to obtain some copies of Deidra Sanbourne's medical records. Susan Wagner and I scoured them for details that would justify why, after nearly twenty years, Atlantic Shores Healthcare had decided Sanbourne was well enough to be released.

The company's internal memos showed that her medical condition had been automatically evaluated every six months. For more than three years, her medical team noted that she had not shown signs of any significant improvement. But in the fall of 2001, the members of the team changed their minds and concluded she was ready to be discharged. There were no details in the leaked files that explained why.

Before a patient could be freed, Atlantic Shores Healthcare was required to prepare a discharge plan. The one that the company designed for Sanbourne was extremely optimistic. Dated December 7, 2001, the plan said that after her release, she would be "trained" to ride the local bus system. She would be taught how to budget her $608 monthly federal disability payment and how to cook for herself. The medical team said Sanbourne "possessed some employable skills" and had expressed an interest in finding a job in the community. It mentioned there was even a chance that she might attend college.

While that glowing analysis might have impressed someone who hadn't known Sanbourne or her psychiatric condition, Susan Wagner laughed when she read it. And then she turned teary-eyed.

But even the rosy tenor of the Atlantic Shores Healthcare discharge report couldn't hide several red flags. The doctors said Sanbourne would not be attending day treatment programs because "of her unsuccessful response to traditional mental health services." To an experienced eye that was a clear warning that this person was either chronically mentally ill, uncooperative, or both. The report further noted that its patient needed to be monitored by a Florida Assertive Community Treatment (FACT) team, which meant a case worker would be assigned to check on her after she was discharged, daily if necessary. The state approved only a limited number of patients for monitoring, because it cost $10,000 per year for every client on a FACT team roster. It was another warning sign.

Sanbourne herself began expressing mixed feelings as her release date came closer. A month before her discharge, she was taken to a McDonald's outside the hospital to see how she handled being in public. A hospital worker wrote that Sanbourne was "hyperactive" but didn't act inappropriately. Five days later, that same worker noted that the patient had become "ambivalent" about leaving the hospital and was afraid. Despite this, Sanbourne was driven from the hospital to Delta House, an assisted-living facility in South Beach, shortly before Christmas.

How had she adjusted to her new life? The answer to that question would be found in yet another stack of medical files.

A FACT team monitor helped Deidra Sanbourne move into her room at Delta House, a two-story ALF in South Beach licensed to hold ninety residents. Eighty-two of its tenants were mentally ill; the other eight were drug abusers. The rectangular boardinghouse backed up to a stagnant canal and was bordered by a trash-strewn vacant lot. Its lobby was jammed with folding chairs that had been positioned in front of a television. The facility's manager sat behind a glass window, similar to those found at drive-in banks. A dark hallway led to motel-like rooms. Two residents lived in each. The lobby's television was the house's only form of recreation and entertainment. Sanbourne's days were unstructured. She could come and go as she pleased and do whatever she wished.

The FACT team monitor was being paid by the state to keep tabs on her, and one of his duties was to maintain a patient log. In his first entry, he noted that she appeared "delusional" and was having "racing thoughts" when she arrived. The next day, he wrote that she had become "very sad and depressed" during their fifteen-minute session. She "showed a flat affect."

Sanbourne told him that she wanted to move back to the state hospital, but he assured her that those homesick feelings would pass. He dropped by two days later, but she refused to speak to him. She hid behind her bedroom door and wouldn't open it. He decided to check on her the following day, but she wasn't in the building and no one knew where she had gone.

Susan Wagner had telephoned her sister several times, but Sanbourne refused to accept calls from her. Wagner wasn't sure why. All she knew was that her sister was upset.

According to the patient log, Sanbourne stopped taking her medicine. Within days, she became so "psychotic, delusional and bizarre in her thinking" that the FACT team monitor drove her to a Miami Beach hospital and admitted her into its psychiatric wing.

She had lasted two weeks before she'd been rehospitalized.

Wagner had warned Atlantic Shores Healthcare that her sister couldn't make it on her own. "I thought, 'Well, at least now they'll move her back into the state hospital, where she'll be safe,'" she recalled. But Wagner was wrong. Atlantic Shores Healthcare did not take her back.

Wagner learned that her sister was supposed to be taking twelve medications every day. "I thought, 'How can these doctors let a person who's taking *twelve* different drugs run loose on the streets twenty-four/seven?'"

After four days in the hospital, Sanbourne was driven back to Delta House. Her FACT team monitor noted that she had appeared heavily sedated during the ride and had been wearing inappropriate makeup that made her look clownish. He later discovered that she had used a permanent marker as an eyebrow pencil. Incredibly, the FACT team monitor dropped Sanbourne off and then left to see another client. An hour later, he was called back because Sanbourne had gotten into a fistfight with her roommate. He arranged for her to move into a different room. He also called a psychiatrist, who agreed to increase the amount of medication that she was on. She was being increasingly sedated.

"I was worried," Wagner later told me. "I'd telephone and she wouldn't be there. I'd stop in to see her and no one would know where she was. I'd say, 'How can you *not* know where she is?' And they'd say, 'Well, she's not a prisoner here. There's nothing we can do about where she goes.' I can't tell you how upsetting that was. My sister was a very, very sick woman, yet they were letting her come and go. I will never believe this was about what was best for Deidra. It was about saving money. Delta House was cheaper than a state hospital."

Sanbourne had some good days, but not many. When the FACT team monitor stopped in to see her, she frequently refused to meet with him. He often found her "delusional in her thinking," according to his log. In one entry, he noted that she had asked him more than forty times during a twenty-minute period when she could "go home" to New York City, a place she'd never visited.

By the end of her first month at Delta House, Sanbourne had "regressed," her monitor wrote. She'd begun wearing mismatched clothing, had stopped taking baths, and had become a bed wetter.

During a visit, Wagner became alarmed when her sister announced that she would soon be leaving for Manhattan.

"DeeDee, we've never lived in New York City," Wagner said.

"My sister lives there," Sanbourne replied.

"I'm your sister."

"No you're not!"

When Wagner complained that her sister smelled of urine during the visit, the FACT team monitor arranged for a nurse to talk to Sanbourne about hygiene. By the end of her second full month in Delta House, Sanbourne had again stopped taking her daily medication. The FACT team worker offered her an incentive: $2 for every day she took her pills. She began taking them and spent the money on cigarettes.

By week nine, Sanbourne was so psychotic that she had to be hospitalized again in a psychiatric ward.

And that is how her life continued. Consider these log entries:

* *June 9th, 2002: Client admits stealing clothing . . . she continues to be very disorganized in her speech. Staff suspects client has been "cheeking" medication and later spitting it out.*
* *July 16th: Client not seen. Out for walk. ALF staff says she continues to steal clothing . . . has been taking medication 80–90 percent of time.*
* *August 6th: Client was not home. Out walking.*
* *August 20th: Client didn't want to meet.*
* *September 19th: Client refused to take medication. Walked away during meeting.*
* *October 1st: Client expressing disorganized thoughts.*
* *October 11th: Client unstable, verbally aggressive.*
* *October 15th: Attempted meeting, client not at ALF.*

At this point, Sanbourne was forcibly hospitalized again. This time, she stayed two weeks.

* *November 12th: ALF staff reports client is continuing to steal possessions of other home members.*
* *December 10th: Client is wearing new clothing coming from unknown source. Shoplifting by client is suspected.*
* *January 21st, 2003: Visited ALF, client not there.*
* *February 4th: Spoke to client through door to bedroom. Client did not wish to meet with monitor.*
* *February 18th: Visited ALF, client not there.*
* *March 4th: Client refused to open her door.*

Again, Sanbourne had to be admitted to a psychiatric ward. This was the fourth time she had had to be hospitalized since her doctors at Atlantic Shores Healthcare had deemed her well enough to be released.

And what of those glowing promises written by her discharge team—

the notes in her file that stated Deidra Sanbourne would be trained to ride a bus, budget her own money, cook for herself, even enroll in college and ultimately find a job?

"No one did anything there to help her," Wagner recalled bitterly. "When I stopped by, she was out wandering the streets."

Sanbourne's life became predictable. About every twelve weeks, she would become so ill that she would have to be hospitalized. Between those admissions, she fought with other residents, walked aimlessly though the neighborhood, sat next to the canal smoking cigarettes, and told strangers that she met on the street that she was the Virgin Mary and didn't know how to find her way back to New York.

"That was my sister's new wonderful life outside the state hospital," Wagner later complained. "She had been dumped into this boarding-house and forgotten, and there was nothing we could do about it."

In March 2003, Sanbourne was, once again, admitted into a psychiatric ward. But this time, when she was ready to be discharged, the manager at Delta House refused to accept her back. He told the FACT monitor that she was too sick and disruptive to continue living there. The FACT team worker drove Sanbourne to Garden Plaza, a much smaller ALF in Miami Beach. The day after she arrived, Sanbourne disappeared. No one knew where she had gone, and she stayed missing for two days. Finally, paramedics brought her back after a good Samaritan called and said that he'd seen a "crazy woman" slip and fall while walking on a sidewalk. Sanbourne had a gash on her head, and her right arm and right knee were cut and bruised. She was in such bad physical shape that the manager at Garden Plaza refused to let her live there. The FACT team monitor drove her to Palm Breeze, another boarding home, but its manager also wouldn't take her. He urged the FACT team monitor to admit her into the Westchester General Hospital, where she was put into a psychiatric unit.

Hospital records described her as being "withdrawn, paranoid, and delusional." A nurse's log noted that on April 19, Sanbourne woke up howling and was so disoriented she had to be given a shot of Haldol to bring her under control. She became incontinent, refused to eat, and spent much of her time trying to pick up "invisible objects."

No one told Wagner or her mother where Sanbourne had been taken. Neither of them could find her. When they called Delta House, the manager said he didn't know where she'd been relocated. For more than a *month*, Sanbourne was in the hospital without anyone coming to see her, including her FACT team monitor. She had been left on her own.

On May 29, a nurse checked Sanbourne's vital signs and found her pulse racing. A quick examination revealed that she had an obstructed bowel. She was taken into an operating room, but the surgeon couldn't repair the problem. Deidra Sanbourne fell into a coma. At that point, the hospital began searching for her next of kin.

"One day the phone rings and I'm told my sister is on life support," Susan Wagner said. She and her husband raced to the hospital. Sanbourne died an hour later. Her sister was livid. "I wanted to sue someone. She never should have been put out into the street like she was. She never should have been allowed to wander the streets. She never should have been dropped off and abandoned at that hospital."

Wagner called Judy Robinson at the Miami NAMI office for advice. Robinson gave her the telephone number for the Advocacy Center for Persons with Disabilities. Ironically, that was the watchdog group that had first investigated the inhumane conditions at South Florida State Hospital in 1988. Gayle Bluebird, an investigator at the center, promised to look into Sanbourne's death. As soon as Bluebird hung up from talking to Wagner, she telephoned Alice Nelson, the civil rights lawyer who had persuaded Deidra Sanbourne to put her name on *Sanbourne v. Chiles*.

Two weeks later, Gayle Bluebird called with the results of her probe. She told Wagner that her sister had obviously received "less than ideal health care." But she said there was no evidence of any criminal or civil wrongdoing by Atlantic Shores Healthcare, the FACT team, or Delta House. Although she was still fuming, Wagner gave up her idea to sue.

At a memorial service, Alice Nelson described Sanbourne as "yet another tragic victim of a coldhearted policy of dumping folks in the name of community placement without an adequate system of supports and services."

The Miami Herald noted Sanbourne's death in a brief item. It called *Sanbourne v. Chiles* a "groundbreaking" class-action suit and credited it with sparking a "movement across all of Florida" that "improved the lives of thousands of mentally ill Floridians" by helping them receive "equal—and more humane—care outside large, costly and often dangerous institutions."

Susan Wagner cried when she read that clipping. "How can anyone describe what happened to my sister as more 'humane care' than what she was getting?" she asked rhetorically.

A few days later, Wagner got even more insulting news. She was told that the management of Atlantic Shores Healthcare had installed a tribute to her sister in the lobby of the company's administration building. Under a photograph of Sanbourne, an engraved plaque read:

> She died a quiet death but she will not be forgotten. She probably forgot the significance of her one simple act and never realized the benefits of how the settlement of the lawsuit changed conditions in the hospital and led to people being discharged into the community. . . .

Wagner was indignant. "They threw her out and then they put her picture in the lobby." She shook her head in disgust. Later, she said, "My sister was famous in the mental health community because of that lawsuit and what good did it do her?"

I asked Wagner if her sister had ever visited any of the drop-in centers that had been opened with the $3 million award paid to settle *San-bourne v. Chiles*—the so-called Sanbourne funds.

She hadn't. None of the centers was located near Delta House, so Sanbourne couldn't visit them. "Since her death, I've learned a lot of people, who she knew in the state hospital, go to the centers. I don't know why she wasn't put in a home near one of them, but she wasn't. At Delta House no one knew who she was or anything about the lawsuit," Wagner said. Then she added, "You've got to wonder: If this is how the system treats someone who is famous, what happens to the ones who aren't?"

I had set out to find Deidra Sanbourne to learn if mentally ill patients were any better off now in Florida than they were in those horrid days when they had been locked in inhumane state hospitals. I had wanted to discover if the civil rights protections that had been passed were truly keeping patients from being abused. In investigating Sanbourne's life and death, I had uncovered an ugly truth. Sanbourne had been warehoused for nearly two decades in a state mental hospital, only to be discharged and warehoused again—this time in an ALF boarding home. Her life had not gotten better after she was discharged. She had become more confused and had regressed mentally. How many others were there living in Miami in rooming houses? They'd not been saved, they'd simply been better hidden. They had become even more invisible.

PART THREE

" A DAMN CRUEL DISEASE "

It must be remembered that for the person with severe mental illness who has no treatment, the most dreaded of confinements can be the imprisonment inflicted by his own mind, which shuts reality out and subjects him to the torment of voices and images beyond our powers to describe.

—*Anthony M. Kennedy,*
U.S. Supreme Court Justice

T he Fairfax County prosecutor's decision to give Mike a continuance meant we had three months to convince the homeowners that my son should be allowed to plead guilty to two misdemeanors rather than a felony that would bar him from entering his chosen occupation and brand him forever as a criminal. Actually, it was Mike's attorney, Andrew Kersey, who would try to do the persuading. Mike's mother, his stepmom, and I were busy meeting with Mike's therapist, Hossein Bakhtar, who was counseling him at Penny Hinkle's day treatment program. Bakhtar was a soft-spoken man in his early thirties. He asked us to call him Miki. During our first family session, Mike sat in a stupor while we talked about him. Miki interrupted us and insisted that Mike join in. "This is your life," he said. "Your parents can't make decisions for you."

Although Mike now admitted that he was mentally ill, he didn't enjoy reporting to the treatment center every day. He didn't want to learn about his illness. He didn't want to hear about other patients' problems. He went because he had to. Our attorney had warned him not to miss a single session. One night, he turned to me and said, "I want my old life back. I wish we could just forget this happened."

I did, too.

Later, I spotted him staring at an old photograph held by a magnet on our refrigerator. He'd been a thirteen-year-old when it was snapped. "I loved being a kid," he said. "Everything was so simple."

What Mike disliked the most was being constantly asked how he felt. Are you okay? He realized that everything he said, each time he laughed, every thought he expressed, was being analyzed. Could you blame us?

Kersey faxed me a letter that he had composed to the owners of the house that Mike had broken into. In it, he explained that if Mike pleaded guilty to a felony, the judge would sentence him to one year of probation. But if the victims would allow Mike to plead guilty to two misdemeanors, he would agree to a much tougher set of restrictions. Mike would serve a year of probation for each misdemeanor count, which meant he would be under the court's thumb for two years rather than only one. He'd remain in Hinkle's day treatment program as long as its counselors deemed necessary, and after he was released, he'd continue to see a psychiatrist. If necessary, he'd submit to blood tests to prove he was taking his antipsychotic medicine. Kersey also promised to help the couple obtain a restraining order against Mike that would forbid him from coming near their home. Having offered the victims these extra layers of protections, Kersey asked them to show Mike compassion. He reminded them that Mike had a clean record, was truly remorseful, and was embarrassed. He also reiterated that Mike had chosen their house completely at random. He still didn't know them and wouldn't recognize them if they bumped into each other.

"This gives this family much more protection than they'll get if he pleads guilty to a felony," Kersey said confidently. "I'm sure they'll go for it."

But a few weeks later, an annoyed Kersey telephoned and read me the couple's harshly worded letter reply. They had no pity for Mike. None. Instead, they explained that they were disappointed he was not being put in prison, which is where, they added, he belonged. They flatly rejected all of Kersey's proposals. When we next met in court, they would insist that Mike plead guilty to a felony. There would be no more negotiations, no more let-

ters. If anyone deserved sympathy, they added, it was them. Their house was being put up for sale and they were going to move out of the area because of the break-in.

I was furious. How would ruining Mike's future bring back their sense of security?

"I'll try talking to the prosecutor again," Kersey volunteered. But he ended our telephone call with a dire prediction: It looked as if Mike was going to have to plead guilty to a felony. "You need to prepare him for that. I don't think this couple is going to change their minds."

By this point, two months had passed since our last court session. I broke the news to Mike. "I don't want to be a felon," he said. I told him that we didn't have a choice. And then I explained, once again, how felons were barred from obtaining professional licenses. He'd have to rethink his career.

"What will I do?"

I didn't know.

"I need to find a job," he suddenly announced. His hospitalization had cost more than $35,000. His medicine ran $400 a month, and the treatment program was a couple hundred more each week. Luckily, his health insurance paid the bulk of these expenses, but he needed money to pay the difference. And then there were Kersey's legal fees. But the main reason Mike wanted to work was that he desperately needed to feel as if he was getting his life back on track.

During another family meeting with Miki, we all agreed that it would be easier for Mike to find a job now—before he was forced to plead guilty to a felony. But Miki warned him not to try anything too stressful. Recovery takes time. For many, up to two years. For others, their entire lives.

Mike began applying wherever he saw a "Help Wanted" sign and was hired as a waiter at a neighborhood restaurant. Patti and I both thought it was a mistake, because it required him to work late each night, after he had already spent a full day attending his treatment program. We urged Mike to look for part-time work, but he insisted he could handle it. He wanted to feel

*normal again. After several frustrating weeks, he quit. He was having trou-
ble keeping track of orders and was falling asleep at the treatment program.
It had been too much, too soon. His failure depressed him even more.*

*Patti and I were uncertain how to react. How much should we expect
from Mike now that we knew he was mentally ill? How hard should we
push him? Or should we be pushing him at all? Where was the line between
encouraging him and crippling him? We were told that Mike probably would
qualify for federal assistance if he applied. The government would pick up
the tab for his medicine, plus send him a monthly Social Security Disability
Income check, help with housing, even food stamps. The trade-off would be
that he couldn't work or he'd lose those benefits. Neither of us wanted that.*

*The day for his plea arrived and we drove to the courthouse. Mike was
wearing his new suit again, and we stood in the exact same spot as before,
waiting for Kersey. Just before court was about to begin, he came hurrying
up to us.*

*"I've just spoken to the prosecutor," he announced breathlessly, "and we
may have another shot at a plea bargain." Kersey said the victims had
called the prosecutor's office the night before and asked for a continuance.
Apparently, the husband had to leave town this morning on a business trip.
The wife didn't want to come to court alone. But the prosecutor had refused
to reschedule.*

*"If the wife isn't here, there's a chance the prosecutor will let your son
plead to the two misdemeanors," Kersey said. He had already shown the
prosecutor the list of additional requirements that Mike was willing to accept. "Our offer really makes sense, and this case should have been plea-
bargained months ago," he added. "I think even the prosecutor sees how
out-of-hand this has gotten."*

*It was time for us to enter the courtroom. We sat down, and every time I
heard the doors open behind me, I turned to see if it was the wife. I found
myself whispering a prayer.*

The judge entered. The wife still hadn't. The clerk began to call the docket. When he got to Mike's case, Kersey stood and Mike joined him at the podium. At that very second, I heard the door swing open and I felt betrayed. I assumed the wife had been hiding, mustering her courage, waiting to make a dramatic entrance. But when I glanced around, I didn't recognize the person who had entered the room.

She wasn't coming!

Still, none of us knew what the prosecutor would do. "Your Honor," he said matter-of-factly, "we have reached an agreement in this matter."

That was Kersey's cue. He outlined all the hoops that Mike was willing to jump through. In fewer than three minutes, it was over. Mike had pleaded guilty to two misdemeanors and had been placed on two years of probation. Even though I still deeply resented that the Fairfax prosecutor had charged Mike with two felony crimes, knowing that he was clearly mentally ill, I found myself thanking him outside the courtroom. Mike would not be marked forever as a felon. He would have a chance to pursue his dream.

I felt a huge sense of relief. It was over. Or at least the criminal case was.

As we left the courtroom, I thought about the victims, especially the wife. Before this moment, I had honestly come to despise her. As a reporter, I had been trained to put myself into someone else's shoes. And if my son had not been the one who had broken into their house, I'm certain I could have easily slipped into that role. But I hadn't been able to do that.

Now that Mike's case was over, I tried. I wondered how I would have felt if I had come home and discovered a madman had thrown a lawn chair through my plate-glass patio door. How would I have reacted if I'd suspected that he had urinated on my carpet and had taken a bubble bath in my teenage daughter's tub? If it had been my life that had been intruded on, if I had been so distraught that I had felt compelled to put my house on the market, would I have demanded a pound of flesh, as they had done? Or would I have understood that mental illness was a chemical brain malfunction? Would I have shown mercy? Because it was Mike who was psychotic, the answer had seemed obvious. But sadly, when I stripped away his face *and replaced it with the hollow look of a deranged stranger, I was forced to admit that I might have reacted much as they had. I felt conflicted. The wife who had wanted Mike in prison did not have the knowledge that I now had about mental illness. But I would not have had that information either, had it not been for Mike's unexpected plight. It was wrong for me to detest her. Yes, I still thought she had overreacted. Yes, I still thought she had become hysterical. But I began to see her differently. I began to see her as the reader of this book whom I most wanted to reach. She was the audience that I most needed to persuade. The anger that had made me come to hate her now made me want to invite her inside my world—to share with her the information that I had learned. I was forced to admit that she truly was a victim. And it was my son who had victimized her. I only prayed that she would eventually come to see that Mike had been a victim, too.*

M   *ike's psychiatrist switched him to Abilify, the drug that I'd learned about during Rachel Diaz's NAMI meeting in Miami. Almost overnight, he began acting more like his old self. He wasn't always starving or as lethargic as he'd been on Zyprexa. Miki decided that Mike had attended enough daily sessions at the treatment center. He passed Mike over to a new therapist, Robert Straub, who began meeting with him once a week.*

Now that Mike had more energy and didn't have to report to the center each morning, he started filling out job applications again. Straub suggested he try something different from being a waiter, a job with regular hours, so Mike hit the streets, and he immediately ran into a new obstacle. Nearly every application asked if he'd been convicted of a crime. Mike didn't lie. He admitted he had pleaded guilty to two misdemeanors. When he was asked during interviews about them, he said he was being treated for bipolar disorder. Mike didn't believe his illness would be a problem. After all, his doctors and therapists had been telling him for months that there was no reason for him to be embarrassed. His mental illness was no different from the flu.

It was a brain disorder. But as soon as he uttered the word "bipolar," every interview abruptly ended.

At one point, Mike applied for a job bagging groceries. The store manager, who wasn't used to getting applicants with college degrees, was enthusiastic until Mike mentioned his illness. He didn't get the job, and he came home understandably frustrated.

"I can't even get hired to put cans and jars in a shopping bag," he complained.

I called a friend who worked as the human resources director at a large company, and asked for advice. Mike was being too candid, she warned. If an employer hired him, knowing that he had once had a mental breakdown, the company would be liable if Mike hurt someone during a psychotic fit. It was better for Mike and for potential employers if he didn't tell anyone about his past. If asked, he should admit he'd pleaded guilty to two misdemeanors, but should only say that the charges had nothing to do with illegal drugs, theft, or violence. "No one is going to hire someone who is bipolar," she warned.

For three weeks, Mike kept trying, growing more exasperated with each rejection. And then, finally, he landed a job. Within days, he'd regained his confidence. He loved going to work each day. He was happy for the first time in months, and so was I. Even though he was working full-time, he kept his weekly appointments with Straub and continued taking his antipsychotic medicine. I didn't bring up his mental illness as often as I had. But whenever I did, he told me not to worry.

"That's the past," he said. "I live in the now."

He'd been at work for about a month when he got a call from the company's personnel office. It'd taken a while for the firm to complete a background check, and the investigation had revealed that Mike had two misdemeanor convictions. His boss had pulled Mike's original application, and it showed that Mike had disclosed the charges. He hadn't lied. But there was a new problem. The company had a strict policy against employees being on proba-

tion, and Mike had two years of it to serve. He was told to resign. He was heartbroken. It seemed that each time he took a step forward, he got knocked two steps back. Mike was keeping all his promises to the court. He was still in treatment, still taking his medicine. But no matter what he did or how hard he tried, he could not return to how his life had been. Mike had avoided being labeled a felon, but he was discovering that being mentally ill carried a life sentence of its own—one that was not easily forgiven and apparently was never forgotten.

B efore I returned to Miami, there was someone I wanted to interview. *The Washington Post* had described E. Fuller Torrey as "perhaps the most famous psychiatrist in America." He'd written more than a dozen authoritative books, but it was testimony that he gave in March 1997 before a congressional subcommittee investigating homelessness that really piqued my curiosity.

"Between twenty-five [and] forty-five percent of homeless individuals have a severe psychiatric disorder," he told the panel. "The quality of life for them is a national disgrace. Twenty-eight percent get some food from garbage cans . . . a third of homeless mentally ill women have been raped." And then, in an unfaltering voice, he pointed a finger of blame: "This problem has been exacerbated by well-meaning but misinformed lawyers who changed state laws to make involuntary treatment virtually impossible in most states. These lawyers, under the American Civil Liberties Union and Bazelon Center for Mental Health Law, argue that mentally ill individuals should not take medication unless they wish to do so. But since half of these mentally ill individuals do not think there is anything wrong, they will not take medication."

Continuing, he predicted America would always have homeless, crazy people babbling on sidewalks until states passed laws that allowed doctors to forcibly treat them.

As expected, his testimony enraged the Bazelon Center and former state hospital patients who had been forcibly treated. Demonstrators armed with oversized mock hypodermic needles protested outside his office. Off-duty policemen were hired to protect him when he spoke at conferences. But Dr. Torrey refused to back down. Instead, he founded a nonprofit advocacy group called the Treatment Advocacy Center to challenge "restrictive" mental health laws and to battle the Bazelon Center. His adversaries were bigger, better financed, and more established. But Dr. Torrey's fledgling TAC organization soon began winning a slew of David-versus-Goliath victories.

His modest office was on the edge of the giant Washington, D.C., beltway, the highway that rings the city. He looked the part of a psychiatrist, with a salt-and-pepper beard and eyeglasses.

"Your critics have compared you to Adolf Hitler," I said.

"The most important thing for me is to make changes and improve whatever I'm trying to make changes on," the sixty-three-year-old doctor replied. "So if I'm called Hitler in the process, that's almost incidental."

Dr. Torrey had spent much of his life as a renegade, despite a privileged upbringing. Born into a wealthy family in upstate New York, he first encountered mental illness when his widowed mother called in a panic while he was studying religion at Princeton University. His younger sister Rhoda was standing in the front yard yelling, "The British are coming!" Torrey and his mother rushed her to a hospital, where she was diagnosed with schizophrenia.

"The doctor told us it was the result of my father dying when she was young. I remember scratching my head and thinking, 'This really doesn't make any sense at all. If schizophrenia is caused by trauma, then why don't I have it?'" Torrey had been seven years old when their father died.

When he returned to school, Torrey got a part-time job delivering frozen foods, and two mental hospitals happened to be on his route. Together, they held 25,000 patients. He couldn't believe all of them had become mentally ill because of a parent's death or some other trauma. "It looked more like an epidemic, some sort of sickness, than a trauma-induced illness."

After he graduated magna cum laude, he was offered a slot at a prestigious New York City medical school. But he enrolled in a Canadian university—in part because he'd become uncomfortable with the noblesse oblige that he saw in his Ivy League colleagues. It was the start of a series of against-the-grain moves. He went on to two years in the Peace Corps in Ethiopia and then worked in a South Bronx clinic.

While doing his psychiatric residency at Stanford University, Dr. Torrey also earned a degree in anthropology and published his first book, *Witchdoctors and Psychiatrists*, a droll comparison of the treatment techniques used by primitive healers in Ethiopia and Malaysia and his learned colleagues. He concluded that both had about the same success rate when it came to helping the mentally ill. He was immediately criticized for belittling his profession, but during our interview Dr. Torrey insisted that he had been making a worthwhile point.

"I believe patients can be divided into two categories. The first includes individuals with schizophrenia, bipolar disorder, and severe depression. But it seemed obvious to me, even back when I was first starting out, that these patients had brain diseases. They really needed to be treated by a neurologist, not a psychiatrist. The other patients were people who were having trouble living in our society, and they really didn't need psychiatrists either. They could be treated by therapists or people trained to help them learn everyday coping skills." This was why witch doctors and psychiatrists both achieved similar results. Neither really had a clue how to treat a brain disorder, but both could help troubled people live happier lives.

Dr. Torrey's belief that mental illnesses were diseases put him at odds with most of his colleagues at the National Institute of Mental Health, where he was hired in 1970. The psychiatric profession was still stubbornly clinging to Freud's theory that mental disorders were environmental, most likely caused by overbearing mothers or severe trauma. From the start, Dr. Torrey didn't fit in at the government institute. He accused it of spending too much money on what he called "the worried well—patients divorced by their third husband or fourth wife who were simply unhappy." Those tax dollars would have been better spent investigating schizophrenia, he charged. When Dr. Torrey suggested in 1975 that any psychiatrist who had received government educational loans should be required to spend two years working in subsidized clinics rather than establishing private practices in the likes of Beverly Hills, the heads of fifteen university psychiatry departments demanded that he be fired. Instead, he was sent to the most remote government outpost possible: an Indian Health Service clinic on a tiny island off the coast of Alaska. Dr. Torrey enjoyed it, and when his tour ended, he asked to be stationed at St. Elizabeths Hospital in Washington, D.C., a post that was considered to be another dead-end job. At the aged federal facility, Dr. Torrey took on the most hopeless cases: chronic schizophrenics.

"I read everything I could about the disease, and in two or three weeks, I knew everyone who was an expert in the field—that's how few people were focusing on schizophrenia in those days."

Seven years later, Dr. Torrey published *Surviving Schizophrenia*. It quickly became the bible for patients and their families. During an appearance on Phil Donahue's television talk show, Dr. Torrey urged people to contact the National Alliance for the Mentally Ill (NAMI), which had fewer than 50,000 members at the time.

"Nobody had ever said the word 'schizophrenia' on popular television, and people came out of the woodwork seeking help," Laurie Flynn, NAMI's executive director, later told *The Washington Post*. "For many years, mothers were told they were the cause of the problem, and here comes Fuller Torrey saying, 'Wait a minute, this isn't the family's fault. These are brain diseases.' Here was a psychiatrist saying, 'I know what you're going through, because my sister has the problem.' It's hard to overemphasize what a hero he was back in the early days."

Dr. Torrey hit the road to help organize new NAMI chapters. He donated all of his best-selling book's royalties to the group, and before long NAMI became a national political force. Meanwhile, he retired from the government.

But fate was not done with him.

After *Surviving Schizophrenia* was published, a college student named Jonathan Stanley began showing signs of bipolar disorder. His parents, Ted and Vada Stanley, were wealthy New Englanders, and their paths would soon cross with Dr. Torrey's.

Ted Stanley was rich from selling decorative plates, commemorative postage stamps, and other collectibles through the mail. Their son was studying for a career in finance, but during a trip to Manhattan to visit a friend, Jon became convinced government agents were after him. He began running and he kept running for three days. He didn't eat, didn't sleep, and didn't stop moving. He spent all of his cash on cab and subway rides, leaping off one train to board another. Finally, he ducked into a deli, certain that he had been surrounded. When the police arrived, he was standing naked on a milk crate.

The cops dropped him off at a hospital, and by the time Ted Stanley got there, his son was about to be discharged. Although delusional, he wasn't considered in "imminent danger." The senior Stanley demanded to be left alone with his son, and a few minutes later emerged with Jonathan's signature on a voluntary hospital admission form. No one questioned if he'd actually signed it. As soon as they could, the Stanleys moved him into a private facility.

Jonathan Stanley would later describe this period of his life to me during an interview. "Have you ever cleaned your house with the television on?" he asked rhetorically. "You walk through the room where the TV is, and every once in a while, you get a glimpse of it. Then you walk down a hall and don't see anything on the TV for a while, and then you come back. That's how I was when I was in the hospital. I only caught glimpses of what was really happening—what was showing on the TV. Everything else was being played out in my imagination."

Stanley was given lithium and Tegretol (carbamazepine), an anti-convulsant used to prevent seizures and to treat bipolar disorder. After five weeks, he seemed stable enough to be discharged. But the doctors decided to test him first. They suggested he walk from the hospital to a nearby barbershop to get a haircut. He strutted confidently through the facility's front door, convinced he was fully recovered. But by the time his shoes touched the street, he was trembling and believed government agents were again watching him. He dashed back to the hospital.

"Any doctor in the world would have discharged me," he recalled, "because—on the surface—it appeared I was doing fine. Even I believed I was. But I wasn't. It took me another month of treatment to be able to go outside and not see the agents."

When Stanley's mental stability returned, he moved home, and later went on to graduate from college and law school. To date, he has taken his medicine and never had another incident.

During their family crisis, Ted and Vada Stanley read *Surviving Schizophrenia* and called Dr. Torrey for advice. After their first conversation, Ted Stanley offered to donate $50,000 for mental health research. Dr. Torrey told him to make the check out to NAMI. Sometime later, the Stanleys called Dr. Torrey again. They knew he didn't believe the federal government was doing enough research into the causes of schizophrenia. So they offered to donate a million dollars a year for a minimum of ten years to study it. There was only one catch. They didn't want to give their money to NAMI. They wanted to create their own research foundation, and they wanted Dr. Torrey to come out of retirement to run it. He agreed, and since then Ted and Vada Stanley have pumped more than $200 million into the Stanley Medical Research Institute for studies of mental illness.

In 1997, Dr. Torrey published *Out of the Shadows*, a powerful exposé that documented how deinstitutionalization and failed government policies had created a "mental health crisis" in America. Vada Stanley read it and asked him if there was something more that she and her husband could do. It was at this point that he suggested creating the Treatment Advocacy Center to challenge involuntary commitment and treatment laws. The Stanleys donated another half million, and Dr. Torrey launched TAC. He hired Mary T. Zdanowicz, an attorney, as its executive director, and asked Jonathan Stanley to join its board. Dr. Torrey had met Zdanowicz while she was trying to stop New Jersey from shutting down a state mental hospital where her schizophrenic sister was living.

Dr. Torrey's national reputation and the Stanleys' financial backing got TAC off to a running start. Their cause was helped on January 3, 1999, when a crazed man shoved Kendra Webdale in front of a speeding subway car in Manhattan. The attractive and vivacious Webdale had been waiting on a train platform when Andrew Goldstein, a chronic schizophrenic, felt "an uncontrollable urge to shove a blonde woman."

Webdale's murder alarmed the city, especially after *The New York Times Magazine* published an eye-popping account about her killer. The newspaper had gotten Goldstein's confidential 3,500-page medical record from a disgruntled social worker. The documents revealed that Goldstein had attacked eight people before shoving Webdale, and he'd been hospitalized fifteen different times in the previous two years. Only a few weeks earlier, he had punched a woman, and a few days before Webdale's murder, Goldstein had walked into a Queens hospital complaining about voices in his head. Sadly, he had been turned away untreated.

Mary Zdanowicz read the magazine account and decided to contact Webdale's parents. In a letter to Ralph and Patricia Webdale, she explained how TAC was trying to change New York's mental health laws. Zdanowicz wasn't certain how the couple would react, but she received a passionate response from them. Patricia Webdale said that she and her husband did not want Goldstein punished, because they understood that he was mentally ill. They wanted him treated. "What's ironic is that Kendra was the kind of person who would have tried to help the kind of person who pushed her," Patricia wrote.

As soon as the Webdales joined TAC's campaign, its lobbying efforts took off. With help from state legislators, a new statute called Kendra's Law was drafted.

The ACLU and the Bazelon Center fought to stop it from being approved. They claimed it would lead to the police sweeping through Manhattan, herding up thousands of homeless mentally ill people, who would then be force-fed mind-altering drugs.

Nonsense, TAC replied. It claimed Kendra's Law contained safeguards that protected the mentally ill from being abused, and also the public. A mentally disturbed patient had to meet six specific criteria before the state could step in and order him to take medicine. There had to be proof that the patient had a history of not taking medication, plus he had to either be violent or have a history of being repeatedly hospitalized. Even then, an unbiased psychiatrist had to interview the patient and agree that he needed to be forcibly treated.

In the middle of this bitter dispute, another tragedy happened. Edgar Rivera was waiting at a subway platform when a homeless, psychotic man pushed him into the path of an approaching train. Rivera survived but lost both legs. Zdanowicz contacted him, too, and he also joined TAC's campaign. Days later, a disturbed Long Island man was shot by police after he began swinging a sword inside a commuter train in Penn

Station. Zdanowicz contacted the man's family and they agreed to help TAC.

Kendra's Law was signed August 9, 1999. TAC had won its first major victory, and it had also learned an invaluable lesson. "Nobody cares about people with brain disorders," Don Lyle Jaffe, a TAC board member, bluntly explained in a speech. "Laws change for a single reason—in reaction to highly publicized incidents of violence. . . . I am not saying it is right, I am saying this is the reality." In order to continue changing the law, TAC had to take the "debate out of the mental health arena and put it in the criminal justice/public safety arena," he said.

TAC began posting "Preventable Tragedies" on its Internet Web page. These were cases similar to Kendra Webdale's that involved a crazed person who killed himself, a police officer, a family member, or a bystander. The list soon contained hundreds of incidents. Dr. Torrey told reporters that nearly a thousand homicides each year were being committed because of mentally ill people who were going untreated. That was *nineteen* preventable deaths per week!

"The Treatment Advocacy Center's strategy is to scare the bejesus out of the public to get these outpatient commitment statutes enacted," the Bazelon Center's legal director, Ira A. Burnim, complained. He accused TAC of further stigmatizing the mentally ill.

But TAC continued to push. And win.

After New York, it turned its sights on California, and once again put a human face on its efforts. This time it was Laura Wilcox, a teenager murdered by a disturbed man who'd stopped taking his medicines. Despite fierce opposition, Laura's Law passed in September 2002. TAC next turned its attention on Florida.

During our interview, I asked Dr. Torrey if Kendra's Law would have enabled me to force Mike to take antipsychotic medication when I took him into a hospital emergency room. No, he answered, the statute was aimed at the chronically mentally ill who had a history of violence or multiple hospitalizations. But it was a first step. The passage of Kendra's Law showed that New Yorkers' attitudes about the mentally ill had changed dramatically from 1987, when Mayor Ed Koch had been successfully challenged by the ACLU after he had forced a psychotic Joyce Brown into a hospital during a freezing night. New Yorkers had had enough, and so had the rest of the nation, Dr. Torrey claimed. The pendulum was beginning to swing in the other direction, because Americans had grown weary and also afraid of homeless, crazed men and women living untreated on sidewalks.

Chapter 2 0

T   he first person I wanted to see when I returned to Miami
         was Judy Robinson. I was curious about how she and the
         regulars who attended her monthly NAMI support
         group meetings were doing. But I also had a personal
reason. I wanted to know how she managed to deal with her son's mental illness without its crippling her life.

"How would you like to meet my son Jeff?" she asked when I called.
They were going to dinner to celebrate her seventy-fifth birthday, and
she suggested that I join them at her favorite Miami bistro.

All I knew about Jeff was that he had been arrested more than forty
times and had been struggling with mental illness since his early teens.
When I met them, Jeff stuck out his hand confidently and introduced
himself. He was fifty-three, had thick black hair and a handsome face,
and was fashionably dressed. There was no outward sign that he was ill.
We sat at a corner table, and as we made small talk, I looked for a clue.
There was none.

Jeff recalled how he had acted as his own attorney once while he was
in jail. Although he hadn't had any legal training and didn't have a college degree, he'd filed a court brief that had been so well argued that a
county judge had complimented him in court on his acumen. As we

talked, Jeff recited specific legal citations from his brief. When he excused himself to use the men's room, I turned to his mother and said, "Jeff is really impressive! Quite frankly, I expected him to be in much worse shape."

"He took an extra dose of his medicine before coming tonight," she replied. "He's been nervous about meeting you. This sort of thing is tough for him."

I asked her when she had first discovered that Jeff was mentally ill. "In 1962," she said, "during a family trip to Wheeling, West Virginia. Jeff was only twelve years old."

"Twelve?"

"Yes."

Robinson had lived in Wheeling when she was first married. In 1957, she had divorced her husband, a local attorney, and had moved with her two children, Jeff and Patrice, to Florida. It hadn't been easy. She was a professional singer who had once worked on Broadway, but theatrical work in Miami had been difficult to find. She took other jobs. Five years after the divorce, she was invited to return to Wheeling to perform in a city concert. She thought the trip would be a good way for her to earn a few extra dollars, visit friends, and allow her children to visit with their father. Everything had gone smoothly until Jeff was forced to choose between going to a movie with his dad and attending his mother's performance. Robinson had urged her son to stick with his father. But she would later become convinced that the stress of that moment had somehow tripped a hidden switch inside his brain. When she and her children returned home, Jeff spent the next ten days in bed. After that, he never was quite the same. His grades fell and he began getting into trouble, usually for making rude public outbursts or arguing with his teachers.

Jeff was diagnosed as having manic depression, the term then used to describe bipolar disorder. Later, his diagnosis would be changed to schizoaffective disorder. Her son's first psychiatrist blamed Robinson for the illness. He said Jeff was sick because he lacked a strong father figure, and he accused her of being overbearing. She was hurt, but called that reasoning "bunk."

Her son's condition gradually worsened, and she soon found herself bailing him out of jail and then fighting with hospital officials to get him into treatment programs. "If I hadn't stepped in, my son would not be here today," she said. "He'd be dead. I'm not patting myself on the back. I'm telling you this because that's how ghastly this system was and still is."

In 1980, Jeff's symptoms improved. He rented his own apartment and began dating. A California company offered Judy a marketing job, so she moved to San Jose. Her brother Ron lived there, and the two of them had been close as children. On the Fourth of July weekend in 1981, Ron left with a friend on a motorcycle trip up the West Coast. As they were cresting a hill on Interstate 5 just outside Eugene, Oregon, a station wagon came speeding toward them. It was traveling the wrong way, against traffic. Neither biker had a chance. The car killed them instantly. Its driver was a woman who had been "deinstitutionalized" ten days earlier from the Oregon State Hospital. She had chronic schizophrenia. An hour earlier, she had telephoned the police and claimed that someone was trying to murder her. After the collision, a judge declared her insane and sent her back to the same hospital that had released her.

"Do you see the irony?" Robinson asked me. Her eyes welled with tears. "My son is mentally ill and then my brother is killed by someone who is mentally ill. I couldn't seem to escape it."

Robinson felt adrift in California, and when Jeff began getting into trouble again, she quit her job and returned to Miami. In 1991, Jeff was accused of an attempted kidnapping, the most serious charge ever filed against him. A woman staying in a Miami Beach hotel told police that a man had tried to abduct her. Jeff lived a few blocks away but swore he had not been anywhere near the hotel. It was a case of mistaken identity.

Robinson hired an attorney and the charge against Jeff was eventually dismissed for lack of evidence. After that incident, he moved in with her. Since then, he had not been arrested or hospitalized.

"What changed?" I asked.

Robinson credited his therapists for helping him get the symptoms of his illness under control. He had two—a married couple who operated a unique Miami practice. Rather than asking Jeff to report to their office for appointments, they met him at a local coffee shop. They invited him to their house for dinner. They even went with him to see a movie. "They became part of his life," his mother said. "They showed him that they actually cared about him. They just didn't write him a prescription." In addition to therapy, they spent months fine-tuning his antipsychotic prescription. "It was individualized care, real one-on-one stuff, and it made the difference."

At this point in our conversation, Jeff returned to the table. His mother didn't hide the fact that we had been discussing him.

"When I was twelve years old, we went to West Virginia," Jeff volunteered, unaware that Robinson had already told me about that trip. "And I got to spend time with my dad, and he told me when I left he was sending investigators to keep an eye on me back in Florida. My dad said, 'You will never know where they are and they may not excavate you from difficult situations, but they will always be around, watching you and documenting things.' Now, I don't know if my father really did this or not—my mother and my therapists tell me it isn't true—but I believe my dad did do this, and I am being watched and tested, even right now."

Robinson sighed and said, "Jeff, we've been over this. There is no one watching you."

The dinner check came, and we drove to Robinson's house for ice cream and coffee. While she was in the kitchen, Jeff and I went for a walk so he could talk to me privately. As soon as we stepped outside, he said, "I've been beaten in the Miami jail. I've been hog-tied on the ninth floor. Other inmates have struck me in the face so many times I can't recall them all, and because of those hits and all of the different medicine I've taken, I have almost no short-term memory. But I remember being in jail once, and I was given a milk carton, and I could remember every nutrient listed on that carton, and I think that was one of the tests the people watching me give me from time to time."

Continuing, he said, "I believe the government can use gas to induce many, many different states of mind, and I think that while I was in jail, I was given a gas by osmosis and that is how I could memorize the nutrients on that milk carton. It was all a secret government experiment."

Jeff explained other tests that he believed federal agents had given him. Then he added, "I remember being so sick once when I was in jail, I drank water from the toilet in my cell, like a dog, because I believed I was dying of dehydration. My mom saw me when I was in that condition. I hate that. But I feel all of these things have happened to me for a reason. They indicate I'm being studied, and I think some day there will be some vindication of my name and these events will give me credibility and enhance my image rather than diminish it, as they do now, because I will be able to show how I have transcended these adversities. I honestly believe I am being groomed to do something important in my life. I don't know exactly what it is, but because of the intense pain I've suffered, I believe it's going to be something really big and important. Maybe I'm being groomed to become president of the United States. I think so. Yes, that's a real possibility. When people see what I've been through and how I've handled myself accordingly. Yes, I really do believe someday I will become president."

By the time we returned to the house, I noticed that Jeff's demeanor had changed. He had become jittery. He couldn't sit still in a chair. His hands had begun to shake, and he was having trouble speaking without a stutter. I checked my watch. Four hours had passed from when I'd first met Jeff at the restaurant. In that short time period, he had gone from being poised to being shaky.

A few minutes later, his mother and I were alone in her kitchen. "How do you do this?" I asked. "How do you handle seeing your son like this?"

"Who said I have a choice?" she replied.

For the second time during the evening, I saw tears form in her eyes. But she held them back.

"This never gets any easier," she said. "I've been doing this for forty-one years, and you'd think I'd reach a point where it doesn't hurt anymore. But it still does. Seeing your son suffer always is painful."

Because Jeff had stayed out of jail, hadn't been hospitalized in several years, and could handle himself for short periods in public, people assumed that he had been "cured," she explained. What they didn't see were his private moments when he was so fidgety that his entire body twitched. What they didn't hear was him talking about how CIA agents were lurking outside the window. Nor did they know that he didn't have many close friends and that he longed to meet a woman, fall in love, and begin a family. It was Robinson who saw those sights, listened to his fears, heard his dreams.

Since she had just celebrated her birthday, time was on her mind. "I've set up a support system for Jeff for when I'm gone," she said. Jeff's sister was next in line to watch over him. If something happened to Patrice, then Patrice's children were supposed to take responsibility for their uncle Jeff.

"At this stage of my life, I do what I can, and I really work very hard to do what I can both for Jeff and for everybody in my NAMI support group. I work hard as an advocate on the local and on the state level. But no matter how hard I work, there are no guarantees when it comes to Jeff's future. I've had to learn and to accept that. And you will have to learn and accept that about your son, too."

She paused to let that sink in. "This is an illness that you can't predict and you just *can't* fix," she continued. "All you can do is fight it, every day. You can't lose your patience with it, and most of all, you must *never* give up. You can sit around and complain, or you can empower yourself and tell yourself, 'Okay, life isn't fair—so what! What can I do to make this situation better?' That's the path I've chosen, and I will continue taking it until the day I die. What happens after that?" Robinson shrugged and gave me a sad smile.

Again, I spotted the tears. She turned away. It had been an emotional night. Then I heard her say in a hushed voice, "Mental illness is a damn cruel disease."

A s he did on most mornings, Dr. Poitier began his rounds searching for room in C wing to accommodate inmates who'd been booked into jail overnight. He needed space for six. The air conditioning wasn't working, so the entire ninth floor was hot and smelled like a teenager's unwashed gym socks. A schizophrenic prisoner in cell five was chanting: *Jehovah—Jehovah—Jehovah*. His drone caught the attention of another inmate and he began slapping the stainless-steel toilet in his cell. *Jehovah*. Bang! *Jehovah*. Bang! *Jehovah*. Bang! The sounds mixed with the normal dissonance: the banging of cell doors, the officers' shouts, the morning chorus of inmates coughing, spitting, pissing, moaning.

Dr. Poitier moved through C wing seemingly unaffected. When he reached cell three, he recognized someone from his past.

"How's your arm?" he asked.

A thin man lifted his left wrist, revealing a three-inch-long scar. The wound had been made twenty years ago when he was in the state forensic hospital where Dr. Poitier had worked. Convinced an evil spirit was living inside him, the prisoner had chewed through the flesh on his arm to create an exit for the ghost to flee.

"Do you remember me?" Dr. Poitier asked.

He didn't.

Dr. Poitier continued his rounds.

A man's naked butt was pressed against the glass wall in cell four, and when Dr. Poitier and the two women with him—a social worker and nurse—reached it, the inmate began wiggling his buttocks. Officer Michael Urbistondo hit the glass with his hand.

"Stop that!" he ordered. "Get dressed. Now!"

The inmate turned, revealing an erection, and picked up his paper gown.

Moments later, Dr. Poitier reached the cell where the prisoner was chanting. He asked him to stop so they could talk, but the inmate began yelling louder and faster. His new cadence caught his accompanist by surprise. *Jehovah. Jehovah.* Bang! *Jehovah.* Bang! *Je*—Bang!—*hovah.*

In the next cell, Dr. Poitier encountered an inmate with only one leg. The man said he'd been tortured in jail in Liberia, Africa, and he was afraid someone in the Miami jail was going to cut off his other leg.

"We don't do that in our jails," Dr. Poitier said.

A sign posted outside the next cell warned: SPITTER AND CHRONIC MASTURBATOR. The inmate inside was sleeping.

The prisoner in cell twelve had fresh bruises on his face.

"Those happen before or after you were arrested?" Dr. Poitier asked.

"Before." He'd been beaten on South Beach by four men who had caught him masturbating not far from where their girlfriends were sunbathing topless.

By the time Dr. Poitier reached cell nineteen, he had found space for four of the six new arrivals. He exited C wing to look for room in A and B cell blocks. A few moments after he was gone, a prisoner in cell ten yelled out to Officer Clarence Clem.

"Where's lunch?"

Clem, who was seated a few feet away, glanced at his watch. "You've got at least another hour," he replied.

The inmate began complaining.

"Hey, man," said Clem. "This ain't Burger King. You don't get it your way."

Another inmate yelled. "Officer, I need a favor!"

Clem replied, "I don't do favors. I do my job. Now, if you want something that's part of my job, then we'll see, but don't be asking me for no favors."

"I need toilet paper."

Clem sent a trusty to fetch some.

A few moments later, Clem spotted a prisoner "jerking" in his cell. It was the chronic masturbator. Clem positioned himself between the inmate and the nurse whom he was watching. "You know better than that!" Clem said. The inmate removed his hand from under his paper gown and retreated to his bunk.

Jehovah. Jehovah. Jehovah. The prisoner in cell five had been chanting nonstop for *thirty* minutes now. Thankfully, his accompanist had gotten tired of beating the toilet and stopped.

It was just another ordinary day in C wing.

The phone at the officers' workstation rang, and the officer closest to it answered and then yelled to Clem, "Someone downstairs to see ya. Wants you to come down to the lobby."

"And who'd that be?" Clem asked.

As soon as the officer said the visitor's name, the others groaned. It was a drug addict who'd been in and out of jail for years. The last time Clem had seen him, the derelict had needed bus fare and Clem had given him a few dollars.

"Better take some quarters with you, Clem," Urbistondo taunted.

Minutes later, Clem returned, triumphantly waving a five-dollar bill. The drug addict had come to repay him.

"Three months ago, he gave himself to Jesus," Clem proclaimed. "He claims he's off drugs now. I told 'im I didn't want his money, but he told me to put it in my church's offering plate on Sunday." Clem tucked the bill into his shirt pocket.

By 9:30 A.M., Dr. Poitier had found room for the new prisoners. After leaving instructions about where to move them, he reported across the street for a court hearing. Officer Clem and the others began shuffling inmates on and off C wing. After that, they started releasing prisoners one at a time from their cells so they could use the C wing shower stall. The inmate in cell five was still chanting *Jehovah*. He had been repeating it for a solid hour.

When it was his turn to be escorted to the shower stall, the prisoner in cell three refused to come to the front of his cell to be handcuffed.

"I ain't going," he declared, even though his body stank.

"We don't care what *you* want," Clem replied.

The inmate backed up and raised his fists. "Come in here, and I'll kill you!"

Sergeant Michael Alonso, who was in charge of the ninth floor during the day shift, was summoned, and he tried to persuade the inmate to come up to the cell door. But he refused, so Alonso ordered his officers to begin clearing everyone but the prisoners out of C wing. He had decided to "gas" the inmate.

I walked with him to get a canister of oleoresin capsicum (pepper) spray. Along the way, he explained that jail administrators had only recently decided to allow officers to spray gas on the ninth floor. He was hoping the inmate would change his mind when he saw the can, which was called a one-pounder. It resembled a small fire extinguisher. But if he didn't, Alonso felt justified. The inmate was disobeying a direct order and was threatening his officers.

"I'm through playing with you," Alonso declared when he returned to the cell front. "Cuff up, otherwise you're getting sprayed."

"Fuck you!"

Alonso pulled a steel pin from the canister's spout and aimed its nozzle through the cell door's food slot. He squeezed the trigger and a burst of gas blew out, instantly filling the cell with a fog of irritating spray. It was so potent that Alonso coughed even though the device had been aimed away from him. The inmate collapsed and began crying and wiping his eyes. Alonso waited a few seconds for the fog to clear and then unlocked the cell. The prisoner didn't resist. He let the officers take him to the shower. As he stood under the showerhead, washing his face, he moaned, "Why'd you do that?"

"'Cause you wouldn't listen and take your shower when you was told to," Clem answered.

Some of the spray's residue drifted across C wing, causing the other prisoners to cough. For the first time that morning, the inmate in cell five finally stopped chanting. He, too, was hacking from the spray.

Alonso had not insisted that I leave during the incident. That was unusual.

D uring my trips to the jail, I was ordered four separate times to leave C wing. Each time, I was told it was for my own safety. But I never believed that. An incident one afternoon was typical. Dr. Poitier was at the courthouse, but I had stayed behind. I was standing at the mouth of C wing, listening to an exchange between an officer and an inmate who was handcuffed to a steel table there. The inmate had been complaining about how he had not been fed, and he was being obnoxious about it. I had started my handheld tape recorder, which I was holding out of sight in my palm, because I wanted to record the inmate's abusive tone and the other noises in C wing. Here is what I taped:

Officer: Okay, that's it. You've been jumping around here, shooting your mouth off, so now I'm going to let you do some *real* jumping.

Inmate: Well, thank you! Thank you! I'm finally getting fed!

Officer: Oh, no, no, no. You're not getting fed and you don't need to be thanking me because you ain't gonna like what I've got in mind.

Inmate: Don't hurt me. I'll be quiet. I'm sorry.

Officer: Oh, it's just gonna hurt a little.

Inmate: I'm sorry, okay? You're joking, right? You're not going to hurt me?

Officer: Oh, the time for joking is long past, and yes, it is gonna hurt you, but just a little.

The officer called two of his colleagues to the table. He was starting to unfasten the prisoner's handcuffs when one of the officers nodded toward me. I was ordered to leave because, as one officer put it, "We need to take care of some business."

I'd promised jail administrators that I would obey orders from correctional officers. It was one of the conditions of getting access to the ninth floor. Still, I felt uneasy about walking away. I stepped into the lobby and stood next to the glass-enclosed control booth there. It contained monitors connected to video cameras that were mounted at strategic spots in the ninth floor's three wings. There were two cameras hanging from the ceiling of C wing, and I quickly found their screens. As I watched, the officers took the inmate from the table into a cell. Because the cameras showed only what was happening in the center of the cell block, there was no way for me to witness what happened next. But I had a pretty good idea when I heard a man scream. After the shift change, I walked to the cell and asked the inmate what the officers had done to him. But he refused to discuss it, and I couldn't blame him.

Ironically, the officers who'd taken part in the incident were nonchalant when I approached them the next day. All three spoke to me separately in return for my promise that I would not disclose their names—in this book, to their supervisors, or to anyone else. The fact they were so candid confirmed to me what I had come to suspect. Sadly, this sort of "discipline" was not a freak happening.

I was told the inmate had been punched several times in his kidney area and his arm had been twisted behind his back while, as one officer said, "he was given a talk-to about his lack of respect and manners."

Obviously, it was against federal and state laws to strike a prisoner while he was handcuffed and was not putting anyone's life in a threatening position. But all three officers said they felt justified in punching him and twisting his arm.

"You need to instill fear in these inmates or they won't listen to you," one explained. "Especially crazy inmates, 'cause if you don't scare them, then they will hurt you." He claimed jail officials had created a "no-win" situation on the ninth floor. At the time of the incident, the jail did not allow the use of four-point restraints, which was a punishment that often was used in jails and prisons. It involved tying an inmate's wrists and feet to different corners of a rectangular bed so he couldn't move. The jail owned a steel "restraint chair" that could have been used for the same purpose. But the officers had been barred by administrators from using it.

"We don't have any way to control these inmates except with behavior modification, which is a nice way to say: putting our hands on them if they get out of line. I mean, how else can we keep them under control? You tell me?"

There was little the officers could take away from the inmates on C wing as punishment, because they had nothing in their cells.

"Having OC spray helps," one of the officers told me. But only a few supervisors, such as Sergeant Alonso, were authorized to use the gas. "We're supposed to control these inmates, but the people at the top don't give us the equipment we need to do it safely. The bottom line is: If I have to break someone's arm to feel safe around here, I'm going to do it."

When I asked if the officer was worried about being prosecuted or fired, I was told, "Look, it's our word against an inmate's word—against a crazy inmate's word. Now, who do you think they are going to believe?"

One of the others said, "You've got to be smart about it. There are some officers who will rat you out and there are some who will back you up. I know guys who would back me up even if I went into a cell and cut a guy's head off. But those guys are my good friends. Most people around here aren't going to do that. It's like swimming. If you stay close to the shoreline, you'll probably be okay, but if you get carried away and swim out into the ocean, you're going to be out there all alone."

The officer added, "No one likes it when this sort of thing happens, but sometimes it happens a lot. It depends on who you work with and how good they are at their jobs. What people who've never worked in a jail or with crazy people don't understand is, this world in here, it is a twenty-four-hour war. You always have to have your armor on."

I'd spent enough time on C wing to understand how the inmates' actions could cause tempers to flare. I thought about how a prisoner had thrown urine and feces on Nurse Evelyn Johnson and recalled the morning when the inmate in cell five had chanted *Jehovah* for more than an hour. Prisoners could be seen masturbating, and psychotic inmates were unpredictable and could be violent. There was no question that the men and women who worked on the ninth floor had an extremely difficult job.

But I also pointed out to the three officers that the prisoner whom I'd seen them take into a cell had not posed any immediate threat. He had been complaining about not getting fed.

"Listen," one of them snapped, "prisoners do get their asses whipped sometimes for smarting off and it's just part of what happens. It doesn't just happen on the ninth floor. It happens everywhere in this jail, and I'll bet in any jail. You keep control in a facility like this through *fear* and *intimidation*. People don't come here to make friends."

Another told me about a previous incident. "We had a really crazy guy in here once, and we couldn't get him to stop jerking himself and it was really pissing off the female correctional staff, so one afternoon three of us went in his cell and we beat the living shit out of this guy. I think his arm got broke. I mean, we did a number on this guy. That night I felt really bad, because this guy was clearly crazy and we really had worked him over. A few months later, I was in a store in the mall with my kids and this same guy sees me and comes over and I'm thinking, 'Oh shit, this is going to get bad.' But he said he wanted to apologize to me for the way he acted in jail. Can you imagine? He was apologizing to me! He said he understood why we had kicked his ass, and I didn't feel so bad after that. Like I said, even a guy who is out of his skull doesn't want to get his ass kicked, so he'll listen to you."

A few days after I interviewed the three officers, I spoke to another one who had a reputation as someone who wouldn't tolerate abuse of the prisoners. She told me that she wasn't trusted by many of her co-workers because of her attitude. "It's tough. Sometimes they want you to look the other way. I ain't going to do that and put my job and my own future on the line just because someone wants to put their hands on an inmate who's being a pain."

She especially hated working on the ninth floor.

"Is it because it is more violent than others?" I asked.

"No," she replied. "On the other floors, you know who you are dealing with—they're criminals. You know what to expect. But here you never do. There's something else creepy about this floor. I know I'm not ever going to rob a bank or kill someone. But on the ninth floor, you're dealing with people who have lost their minds. They didn't choose to become crazy, and it don't take long working here for you to realize this could happen to anyone. It could happen to you and it could happen to me. We could become one of *them*. That's what's really frightening about working here and seeing this."

It was why, she said, everyone dreaded the ninth floor.

Chapter 22

F reddie Gilbert was being treated at the Jackson Memorial Hospital Mental Health Center, less than four blocks away from the jail. The homeless chronic schizophrenic had been involuntarily committed there nine weeks ago, mostly because of Dr. Poitier's testimony. A nurse let me into the locked ward and reappeared moments later with Gilbert.

I didn't recognize him. His wild afro hair had been closely trimmed, his whiskers shaven. He was freshly showered and wearing brown slippers, a pair of baggy black sweatpants, and a navy-blue T-shirt.

Before I could say anything, he asked, "You got any cigarettes?" I was surprised because his voice was high-pitched and seemed out of place coming from such a big frame.

I told him that I didn't smoke and then asked, "Do you remember seeing me in the jail?"

He looked hard and said, "I didn't know you was real."

I asked what he meant.

Once again, he asked me for cigarettes. Then he said, "I see people who aren't there. I wasn't sure you weren't one of them."

"I used to wonder what you were thinking when you were standing in your cell and didn't talk to anyone," I said. "Do you remember what you were thinking?"

He asked me for a third time if I had any cigarettes, and after I said I didn't, he rubbed his chin with his right hand and tapped his foot nervously against the floor. He glanced downward and then looked up and said, "He was talking to me a lot in jail."

"Who's he?" I asked.

Gilbert looked to his left and then swung his head slowly to his right to make sure we were alone. Then he raised his forefinger in front of his lips and went "Sssh."

I didn't understand, so I decided to switch subjects and ask him about his background. "Where are you from?"

"California."

Gilbert said he had two brothers and a sister who lived there. Or he thought they did. He hadn't talked to any of them in more than a decade.

"Do you know what year it is?" I asked. I had heard Dr. Poitier pose this question during his morning rounds to assess if inmates were thinking clearly.

Gilbert gave me a date. But he was off by three years.

I asked him when he first began hearing voices. He told me they'd started when he was a teenager and had started smoking marijuana and using illegal drugs. "The drugs made me sick."

"You think the drugs made you mentally ill?" I asked. It was a common misconception that illegal drug use can cause schizophrenia. While people who hallucinate or become delusional after taking illegal substances often act like someone with a thought disorder, the federal government has concluded that drug abuse does not "turn" anyone into a schizophrenic.

"I don't like drugs," he said.

I asked him if he understood that he had schizophrenia. He said yes.

But when I asked him if he knew what it was, he said no. "The drugs did it. Drugs are for weak people."

He said the police had taken him to a state mental hospital in California when he was younger. After he was discharged, his mother refused to let him move in with her, because she was afraid of him.

"How did you get from California to Florida?"

"A man put me on a bus."

"What man?"

Based on bits of his mumbling, I pieced together his story. Apparently, he had become a squatter in the alley behind a restaurant and the owner had decided to send him away.

"His wife made me sandwiches and gave me two Cokes for the ride."

Gilbert hadn't realized the bus ride was going to take so long.

I asked him if he liked being in the treatment center and if he knew why he was confined here.

"It's okay, but I'd rather be out. I don't like medicine."

"Why? Doesn't it help you think clearer?"

"Drugs aren't good."

He glanced again to his left, then to his right, and whispered, "I don't hear him when I take pills."

"Who?"

"Him."

"Who's him?"

Gilbert lifted his finger to his lips. "Sssh," he whispered, and then he said, "God."

"God speaks to you?"

Gilbert nodded. "But not all the time. Only when He wants to."

I asked him what God said to him.

"He tells me to watch out for devils."

"You see devils?"

"People look like they're real, but only I can see them."

I asked him if he intended to keep taking antipsychotic medication for his schizophrenia after his six months of forced treatment ended.

"Yes. I will," he instantly answered. But his response seemed rote.

"Will you go back to living on the streets?"

Again, a conditioned response: "No, I need to live indoors."

The nurse interrupted us because it was time for lunch. Gilbert stood. I stuck out my hand. He had a strong grip. He asked if I had any cigarettes and when I said, "No," he replied, "Oh, okay then, bye."

Having checked on Freddie Gilbert, I decided to call Ted Jackson in South Beach. One reason I was shadowing him was that a social worker in the jail had referred to Jackson as an "on the brink" case. That was how she described mentally ill inmates who weren't as obviously sick as Gilbert or Alice Ann Collyer, the homeless schizophrenic riding the Chattahoochee bus. "Someone who is hallucinating and yelling on a street corner is going to get everyone's attention," the social worker explained. "But there are mentally ill people amongst us who are always on the brink because of their illnesses. They can cope for a while, but eventually it always brings their world crashing in."

Jackson fit that description. He willingly took his antipsychotic medication, rented an apartment, owned a cell phone, shopped for groceries, cooked, cleaned, did laundry, and on most days avoided trouble. He survived meagerly, living off his $1,000 monthly family stipend.

But Jackson had bipolar disorder, and despite his medication and his monthly visit with a VA psychiatrist, his sickness constantly complicated his life. In jail, he'd told me about the male prostitute who robbed him after he'd naïvely taken the teenager fishing and given him a place to sleep. Then there was Charlie, the "friend" who had charged $500 worth of stereo equipment to Jackson's credit card and never repaid him. Because of his belief that God had personally chosen him to prepare for the Second Coming of Jesus Christ in 2007, Jackson had been arrested twice by the Miami Beach police for writing graffiti and had been brought to jail battered both times. So I was not surprised when I telephoned Jackson and he disclosed that he was facing a "tricky issue" that he needed to discuss.

By this point, he had stopped cowering in his apartment, and he offered to meet me at a fast-food joint in South Beach. As soon as I got there, he came rushing up and exclaimed, "I need advice!"

Jackson was tanned and fit, and had added blond highlights in his short brown hair. He said the Miami Beach police had been leaving him alone, and then he announced that he'd come up with a surefire way to get out of debt.

Plucking a napkin from a table dispenser, he began jotting down figures. He still owed $500 to a credit card company for charges that Charlie had made. Kinko's was bugging him about the $4,000 in unpaid fees for copies that he'd made of his Puppet Master flyer. And there was $649 in court fees that had been assessed against him after his first arrest.

"That's a lot of moola," he explained, "but God has been taking care of it for me."

"What do you mean?"

A week before the court fees were due, he'd received a credit card application in the mail that said he'd been preapproved for a $1,000 credit limit. He'd used his new card to pay the $649 court fine. He still owed the money, but now the credit card company was trying to collect the debt, not the court. "I'm sure God had something to do with that application showing up then."

He slid the napkin across the table to me.

Credit Cards: $649 + $500 = $1,149
Kinko's: $4,000 + $1,149 = $5,149

While I was looking at his figures, he launched into a long-winded story. He was no longer going fishing during the day, because a Miami Beach land developer had erected a chain-link fence at the spot where he always fished, blocking his access to the bay. Now he was concentrating on his dancing. Most days, he would sleep until one P.M. Then he'd head to South Beach to sun himself. He'd usually fall asleep, because his medications were still making him feel drowsy. Around five o'clock, he'd return to his apartment, fix dinner, shower, and get ready to go out. There were three nightclubs that let him come inside to dance even though he never bought anything to eat or drink. The managers, however, limited him to one admission per week. That meant he had to rotate where he went and also space out his nights.

What any of this had to do with his debts wasn't clear, but after several more minutes of chattering, it all came together.

"I was coming off the dance floor the other night when this Mexican comes up to me with this young girl and he compliments me about my dancing, and I said, 'Thank you, sir.' Then he invited me to join them at their table and he said he had a business proposition for me."

"How did he know you?" I asked, interrupting.

"This bartender at this nightclub had pointed me out. Everyone knows me because my dancing is unique. Anyway, this guy tells me this girl with him is from Peru, only she is living in the U.S., only she is about to be kicked out. He said the two of them were willing to pay me five thousand dollars if I'd marry her so she could stay in Miami and become a U.S. citizen. Now, I figure that five thousand would let me pay off most of my debt. Do you think I should do it? Maybe God wants me to."

Before I could answer, he added, "The girl is pretty cute, but she don't speak no English. This Mexican bought me a Coke, and the girl and I kind of, like, just listened to the music together, and she seemed really nice."

Jackson pulled a sheet of paper from his pants pocket. I thought it might be another copy of his Puppet Master flyer because he'd been carrying one with him when we'd first met in jail. But he told me that this sheet was his "résumé."

"There are a lot of foreigners who come here," he explained, "and sometimes women see me dancing and ask if I want to go on a date with them. What they really mean is: will I have sex with them. I tell them I'm not interested in casual sex. I tell them I don't want anything to do with you if you don't believe in Jesus as your personal savior."

Jackson said he got tired of being approached, so he prepared a résumé that explained what he was seeking in a woman. His full name and telephone number were typed at the top of the sheet. The first paragraph described his personal history, including where he had attended high school, what sports he'd played, and his military career. In the second paragraph, he listed his attributes. Just as he had on his Puppet Master flyer, Jackson had misspelled several words, but most were easy to decipher.

I'm sweet, generous, kind of witty, helpful to others, interesting with lots of stories, very intelligant, true blue down deep on earth person, stays 3–5 steps ahead of games, recieves self graduificition, TO MUCH MORE TO LIST. . . .

The third paragraph was printed in all capital letters for emphasis, and it listed what sort of person he was *not* interested in associating with:

INSTAGTORS. DECITFULL, MUANIPUATIVE, DISRUP-TIGVE, DESPERATE, DISTRACTIVE, ALTERIAL MOTIVES, TOW FACED, EGOTHISTIC, WARPED, NIAVE, CONTRA-

DICTORY, HYPOCHONDRIAC, IMBECILES, SHREWD, SHOVANISTIC, LUNATIC, COMPULSIVE LIARS AND SCHIZOFRIENDICS.

Jackson had shown his résumé to the girl from Peru, but she couldn't read English. He'd then asked her male escort if the woman was planning on having sex if they were married. The man had said it would be up to them and had explained that they would stay together only until she got whatever papers she needed to qualify for her U.S. citizenship. After that, they would get a divorce.

"You realize what he is proposing is illegal, don't you?" I asked.

"I figured it probably was," he replied. "But how would the cops know?"

"I'm not sure, but the woman would probably be able to sue you when you got divorced and demand half of your assets, maybe even some of your trust fund," I said.

That scared him. We talked for a few more minutes, and then Jackson offered to show me his apartment, which was three blocks away. It was in an old two-story motel that had been converted into efficiencies. There was a bicycle chained to a tree outside the door of Jackson's ground-floor unit. The bike had been painted fluorescent orange and had a banana-shaped seat and sissy handlebars with blue streamers dangling from their ends.

"This here is a one-of-a-kind bike in South Beach." He beamed.

His apartment was clean and orderly. He had erected a trifolding Oriental screen to divide the room into two living areas. In the first half was a love seat, a coffee table, a desk, and a television. The second contained a table large enough for two and a double bed. A kitchen and a bathroom were at the end of the unit. Jackson had hung photographs on the walls that showed him with his parents and in his Army uniform. He pulled a scrapbook from under the bed.

He'd been born in a rural town southwest of Akron, Ohio. In high school, he'd played football, baseball, and track and had won a statewide Golden Gloves boxing championship. The University of Toledo had recruited him to play football, but he'd dropped out his freshman year to enlist. At first, he'd excelled, advancing quickly while earning "expert badges" in parachuting, the M16 rifle, hand grenades, and jungle survival. He'd eventually become a paratrooper in the 82nd Airborne Division. As he talked, Jackson showed me various military certificates that he'd been awarded, carefully holding each longer than was necessary.

His mental problems had surfaced in March 1983, after a new sergeant had taken charge of his squad, he recalled. They hadn't gotten along, and Jackson had become convinced the sergeant was picking on him. He showed me a copy of a complaint that he'd filed against him.

This sergeant has tried everything in his power to break me and make me look bad. He called me names. He even talked dirty about my mother. He put so much pressure on me that it drove my mind to where it might break.

Jackson was ordered to undergo a psychiatric evaluation. While no one knows for certain what causes mental illness, the federal government has found that stress frequently appears to trigger it. Schizophrenia and bipolar disorder also typically surface when a person is in his early twenties. Jackson was twenty-two, and he showed signs of "paranoia and rage" brought on by "stress and pressure," according to his psychiatric report. Despite this, the Army didn't intercede. Jackson was left under the sergeant's command and his condition continued to worsen. On October 25, 1983, Jackson's unit took part in the surprise invasion of Grenada, and during the fighting on that Caribbean island, the sergeant was killed. Jackson became convinced that God had orchestrated it. "He wanted to punish that sergeant for how he was treating me." After the invasion, Jackson was sent by the Army for another evaluation, and this time he was diagnosed as having bipolar disorder and was discharged. But instead of going home, Jackson slept in his car for nearly a year outside the military base because he didn't want his parents to know. By the time he got back to Ohio, he was so delusional the police arrested him. He was taken to a psychiatric ward. It was the first of three long hospitalizations.

For a while, Jackson lived with his parents, but he met a divorcée with three children and stayed with her for the next thirteen years. When her kids became teenagers, they refused to listen to him, and he decided to move to South Beach by himself.

Looking through his scrapbook and military records, I was again struck by the randomness of mental illness. Jackson had been an average midwestern farm kid.

He checked his wristwatch, told me it was time for him to go dancing, and asked if I wanted to tag along.

"This guy threw a twenty-dollar bill out on the dance floor at me one night because I was working so hard. Other people began laughing and tossing out money, and I got eighty bucks that night."

He changed his shirt and we walked toward the beach. He was heading to the Clevelander, a well-known South Beach bar, restaurant, and hotel complex at the corner of Tenth Street and Ocean Drive. Jackson cautioned me to walk slower as we approached the entrance to its outside café. He was pacing us so we'd arrive while the hostess was busy talking to guests who were putting their names on a reservation list. She was occupied when we scooted up a sidewalk ramp near her. To our right was a swimming pool, and next to it was the outdoor dance floor, where a DJ had just started playing music. I followed Jackson into the center of the restaurant and took a seat next to him on a knee-high wall of cinder blocks that encircled a palm tree and tropical plants.

"This is risky," he whispered. He had come here last night, and the

Clevelander's manager had seen him. "I didn't plan on being back tonight, but I met these two guys and I'm supposed to meet up with them."

"Who are they?" I asked.

They were tourists from Belgium. They had invited him last night to join them at their table after he'd finished dancing and had asked him about tourist sights. "I told them to go see the Florida Keys, but they really didn't care about that. They wanted to know where they could buy marijuana and find some hookers, and I told 'em I didn't mess with any of that. Then I told 'em I would show 'em some fun clubs in Fort Lauderdale if they wanted to drive me up there, because all I got is my bike. That's when they told me to meet them here tonight so we could all go up there together."

I asked if Jackson knew the men's names. He didn't. I asked if he knew what hotel they were staying in. He didn't. "But they seemed like okay guys and they told me to meet them here promptly at ten-thirty tonight." He had taken them seriously.

Jackson began tapping his cherry-red Nike sneakers on the concrete to the beat of the music. All around us, diners were eating cheeseburgers and chicken fingers, drinking beer and cocktails. Jackson checked his watch again. It was 10:15 P.M. He tried to relax. But thirty minutes later, the two Belgians still hadn't arrived. He continued twitching on the planter seat until 11 P.M., when he decided they weren't coming.

"I would have liked going to Fort Lauderdale," he said wistfully, "but I guess they found themselves some drugs or hookers." Springing to his feet, Jackson declared, "I'm going to dance now, so I'll be saying good-bye, because I dance for two hours and then I go home to bed, so you might not want to stick around that long." He started toward the floor but stopped and returned to speak to me. "I don't think I'll marry that girl from Peru. I'll find some other way to pay them bills. Call me the next time you are in Miami and we can do something."

I watched him stake out a corner near the DJ and begin a vigorous set of jumping jacks. After about ten minutes, he dropped to the floor and did push-ups. The other couples stepped away from him. Returning to his feet, Jackson began a series of martial-arts thrusts. I noticed most of the restaurant's patrons were now watching his gyrations. Several were laughing, but if Jackson realized it, he didn't care.

I wanted to interview a mentally ill woman—someone Mike's age. I began plowing through arrest records at the courthouse, and I asked Dr. Renoso at the women's detention center, and Judy Robinson and Rachel Diaz at the Miami NAMI office, for help. After several weeks of searching, I knocked on the door of an apartment in a seedy Miami Beach neighborhood. A woman in her early twenties answered. April Hernandez wore her dyed black hair cut short and favored goth makeup. She introduced me to her boyfriend, Jason Gilly, who was in his thirties, a bodybuilder and a former guitar player in a rock band. He had just quit his job, so they were living off the $600 a month in Social Security Disability Income payments that she received because of her mental illness. Her rent also was subsidized. Their efficiency contained a double bed, an old dinette set, a dresser donated by Hernandez's mom, and a kitchen table. A compulsive smoker, Hernandez lit one Marlboro as soon as her last was snuffed out. She and I sat on worn dinette chairs. Gilly lay on the bed, strumming his unplugged electric guitar. During the next six hours, Hernandez described her painful descent into madness in unflinching detail. It was an especially difficult story for me to hear, because she had been diagnosed as having the exact same illness as Mike.

Hernandez's life first began to unravel when she was only fifteen and her younger brother Raphael became sick. They were staying at their father's house because their parents, Ramon and Jackie, were divorced and shared custody. Hernandez took charge—because her father wasn't used to nursing sick children. She decided Raphael had the flu, and said there wasn't anything they could do about it. But on Sunday morning, he blacked out, and within a few hours he was dead from untreated bacterial meningitis. Hernandez blamed herself, and her mother also berated her.

Before Raphael's death, Hernandez and Jackie had been close. But after the funeral, they became estranged and Hernandez began running around with a rough crowd in high school. She began experimenting with drugs and tried X (shorthand for the drug ecstasy) during a week-end rave. Her first trip was a nightmare—she flopped around in the mud, screaming that insects were biting her—but that didn't stop her from bringing home a plastic bag filled with ecstasy tablets. She spent the next four days tripping in her bedroom while Jackie was at work. On day five, Hernandez rode her bicycle to a nearby field and slit both her wrists.

"I cut lengthwise," she recalled, turning her wrists so I could see the scars. "I knew that was how you did it if you were serious."

When blood began spurting out, she panicked and ran up an embankment onto a highway. A driver called an ambulance. At first, doctors blamed her attempted suicide on the ecstasy, but when she was still paranoid several days later in a hospital, they began to reconsider. Hernandez claimed the nurses were trying to poison her and steal her thoughts. Lithium helped her calm down, and after two more weeks, she was discharged.

But she didn't stay sane for long.

She stopped taking lithium as soon as she felt better and quickly became psychotic again. During a manic outburst, she broke into her boyfriend's house, took one of each of his shoes, and burned them. Jackie didn't understand why her daughter was acting so rebellious. She accused her of using drugs. And she was right. Hernandez had begun snorting cocaine. Jackie kicked her daughter out of the house. It was the first in a series of moves that she would make between her parents' homes.

One afternoon, Hernandez was taking a nap at her father's house when she heard a woman scream *Boo!* She opened her eyes, but there wasn't anyone around. Another voice yelled at her. And then another. All of them told the then seventeen-year-old that she was worthless. They urged her to kill herself. Her father found her crouching in the corner of her bedroom, shaking and terrified. He drove her to an emergency room, where she was given antipsychotic medication. The drugs silenced the voices, but after she was discharged, she stopped taking them, as they made her hungry and caused her to gain weight.

A cycle developed. Hernandez would begin hearing voices, become delusional, be hospitalized, be given antipsychotic medication, get better, be discharged, stop taking her pills, and become manic again.

When Hernandez turned eighteen, Jackie and Ramon were told they could no longer force her into a hospital against her will whenever she became psychotic. They began filing Baker Act petitions to commit Hernandez, but their daughter quickly figured out how to thwart them. Each time her parents had her picked up, she called the public defender's office and it got her released.

Hernandez's symptoms, meanwhile, grew worse with each episode. When she scratched the words "slut" and "whore" into the paint of her mother's new car and also threatened to kill her, Jackie got a restraining order. It prohibited her daughter from coming within fifty feet of her or her house. Ramon also had reached his limit. He told her that she could no longer live with him.

Hernandez started sleeping in a chaise longue at night at a neighborhood swimming pool. Her mood swings were now coming in what psychiatrists call "rapid cycles." She would feel invincible one moment, suicidal the next. Marijuana helped calm her nerves. She was still using cocaine, too, whenever she could afford it. A friend told her about a woman in South Beach who sold drugs cheap to young girls. Hernandez contacted her, and the woman invited her to live with her. She also gave her crack cocaine.

"I couldn't get enough of it," Hernandez remembered. "I used it three or four days straight, and then the woman began pimping me out. She had men come into the house to have sex with me in return for money. She was a crack whore and she was using me to pay for her habit."

"How old were you?" I asked.

"Nineteen."

After several days of smoking crack and having sex with strangers, Hernandez panicked. "I was desperate. I just wanted to go somewhere safe, away from guys having sex with me. I wanted to turn the clock back." She called her father, and he got her into a private hospital, where doctors weaned her off crack cocaine. She promised her dad that this time she would stay on her antipsychotic medicine and away from illegal drugs. He rented her an apartment and she was hired as a waitress. For two months, Hernandez stayed sane and sober, but a coworker offered her crack one night, and within a week she had lost her job and spent every cent that she had saved on drugs. Ramon refused to rescue her.

Hernandez vanished. Neither Ramon nor Jackie had any idea where she had gone. Two months later, a court clerk in Charleston, South Carolina, telephoned Ramon and told him that his daughter was in jail. She'd been picked up on a prostitution charge and was delusional. Ramon paid to fly her home.

"On the plane ride, I thought I was an angel soaring through the clouds," Hernandez remembered. "I was so out of it, I didn't even realize there was an airplane around me."

Ramon and Jackie got her into a day treatment program for drug abusers. But she dropped out and was arrested within days for petty theft. The police took her to jail, where she was put into Judge Leifman's misdemeanor diversion program. She spent a week at a crisis treatment center, and the theft charge was dismissed. A few days after she was freed, she got high on crack and showed up at Jackie's house. Her mother called the police, and by the time they arrived, Hernandez had stripped down to her underwear and was running through an outside sprinkler because it was hot. She turned the water on the cops. They found the keys to a stolen car in her pants pocket, so they took her back to jail.

A judge gave her a six-month sentence but agreed to suspend it if she enrolled in a mental health treatment program. Hernandez signed up, but stuck at it for only a week. Then she began using drugs again. She was arrested for violating her probation, but the judge offered her a second chance. This time, she stayed in the treatment program for four months. Her parents were hopeful, but Hernandez got high on cocaine one night with a boyfriend and, once again, ended up in front of the judge. This time, he invoked his original sentence, and Hernandez was sent to the women's detention center for six months.

In jail, Hernandez became paranoid and hallucinated. She began taunting black inmates with vulgar racial slurs. "Everyone was afraid I was going to get killed. The other Hispanic prisoners told the guards to transfer me to the psych floor before I started a race war."

Dr. Renoso put Hernandez on antipsychotic medication. The drugs helped stabilize her, but Hernandez continued to regularly smoke marijuana and use harder drugs that were smuggled into the jail. She felt twice trapped. Whenever she would get her mental illness under control, her addiction would kick in.

Hernandez returned to South Beach after she was released and began panhandling on Lincoln Road, a boulevard that had been turned into a popular pedestrian mall. At night, she "crashed" with other potheads and addicts. "I'd do a guy if he'd let me take a shower in his apartment or sleep on the floor."

Now that she was no longer in jail taking antipsychotic medication, her mental illness came roaring to the surface. She thought she was a vampire, capable of dividing herself into two different people. On the street, everyone called her "Schizo." The voices in her head were relentless. She watched angels descend from the sky. One day, she crawled on the sidewalk on her belly because she thought she was a snake. Her behavior became so outrageous that men stopped paying her for sex.

"When you smell like shit and talk crazy, no one wants you around, not even for a blow job." Even other crackheads shunned her. Hernandez began sleeping in front of a store on the sidewalk. One night, four teenagers jumped out of a car and began kicking and hitting her. One yelled, "Hey, this is a girl!" They left her bleeding and badly bruised. She would later learn that some Miami teenagers assaulted homeless people for fun. Hernandez made her way to an emergency room. A nurse called a homeless shelter, and it sent a van to fetch her. That night, she took a shower, was given a meal, and had a cot to sleep on. But the next morning, she became convinced the shelter workers were plotting to murder her, so she returned to the same storefront where she'd been attacked. Two nights later, she was gang-raped by three men. Hernandez needed a less conspicuous place to sleep. She crawled under some bushes near a beachfront hotel. One morning, she was panhandling on Ocean Drive when she saw a boy bending over a homeless man who had passed out. "This kid had a permanent marker in his hand and he was tagging [writing graffiti] on the man's neck—like this man was a piece of trash."

Hernandez yelled, "I'll fucking kill you!" and she chased him away.

"People don't think you're a human being when you sleep on sidewalks and talk to yourself. They would see me talking to myself and just walk by. I felt worse than an animal. I knew they were making fun of me. But I couldn't control my crazy self." A week after the first rape,

Hernandez was dragged from her hiding spot in the bushes and gang-raped again by four men. They were part of a construction crew building a high-rise condominium in the neighborhood. They'd seen her earlier that day crawling into the shrubbery. She became pregnant during that attack.

In the two months that she had lived on the streets, she had been gang-raped twice and assaulted, and now was pregnant. "The streets had beat me."

She called Jackie.

Unbeknownst to Hernandez, Jackie had gotten a judge to sign a commitment order that authorized the police to arrest her daughter and force her into a hospital. Jackie had not used the Baker Act this time around. Instead, she had used a similar commitment law called the Marchman Act. It allowed families to intervene if they could show that their loved one was an alcoholic or a drug abuser. Its commitment criteria were easier to meet.

Jackie took a police officer along when she went to rescue her daughter. He handcuffed Hernandez and drove her to a hospital ward. She was forced to remain there for sixty days.

"I hated my mom," Hernandez told me, "but by the time I got out, I thanked her. She'd saved my life." Hernandez had an abortion, and a social worker arranged for her to begin receiving federal disability payments. That same worker helped her move into a rent-subsidized apartment.

One afternoon, Hernandez bumped into a former high school classmate. "This woman was married, had a baby, and lived in a nice house. In school, I had better grades than this girl. I was more popular. I went out more than she did. But now I was living in a shitty apartment, taking medicine because I was crazy and a recovering drug addict. I felt like I was a throwaway person." Hernandez was told that she would lose all her federal benefits if she got a job, which was an unlikely prospect anyway because of her checkered past. With nothing to do during the day, she began hanging out at the "circle," a gathering spot for oddballs on Lincoln Road. It was a cinder-block planter near the center of the pedestrian mall. Hernandez knew most of the other hangers-on there only by their nicknames—Pencil, Niglet, Kato, Icebox, Fire, and Moochie. All of them smoked pot or used harder drugs. She spent her days sitting on the perimeter of the circle, chain-smoking cigarettes, watching tourists, and gossiping with her street friends.

One morning, Hernandez was arguing at the circle with a drug addict named Afreea when a man walked by.

"Hey, handsome, what's the rush!" Afreea yelled. Hernandez had been embarrassed, but Jason Gilly had stopped and introduced himself. The next afternoon, he asked if he could sit next to Hernandez while he ate his lunch. He had just moved to Miami Beach from Buffalo, New York, and didn't know anyone.

"He was so cool and interesting," Hernandez recalled, "and I was shocked he wanted to talk to me because the circle was full of a bunch of losers." It turned out that Gilly had an ulterior motive.

At this point during my interview with Hernandez in her apartment, Gilly put aside his guitar and joined in our conversation.

"I thought she was cute and everything," he said, "but I wanted to buy some marijuana and I knew the woman [Afreea] that I'd seen the day before was a crack whore. It was really obvious."

Gilly eventually got around to asking Hernandez to buy him pot. She agreed, and they soon were smoking it together every night after he got off work. He was a cook in a Thai restaurant, but a few weeks after they met, he got into an argument with his boss and quit. Hernandez invited him to move in with her. They'd been living together about a month when I'd knocked on her apartment door.

I asked Hernandez if she had been afraid to tell Gilly about her mental illness. Before she could answer, Gilly said, "One night she just let everything out. And I said, 'Well, we're all a bit crazy. This is the here and now. I've done a lot of shit that I'm not going to tell you about. But you see how I am now and who I am, so if you are willing to take me at face value, I'm willing to do the same with you. As long as you don't try any silly shit with me, we'll be cool.'"

Their first days as a couple, however, had not gone smoothly. Gilly didn't like Hernandez hanging out at the circle. But the real problem was her sleep habits. "She would get up every couple hours to get something to eat or to use the bathroom and she'd wake me up," he explained. "Or she'd have these nightmares and she'd start beating on me while I was asleep. I'd wake up with her hitting me on the back."

Gilly blamed her antipsychotic medicine. "It is what made her hungry and made her act goofy."

"So how did you solve the sleeping problem?" I asked.

Gilly glanced at Hernandez, who was lighting yet another cigarette. Then he asked me how long it would be before this book was published. About a year, I said. "Good," he replied. Turning to Hernandez, he winked and said, "We can tell him our little secret then, because it won't matter by then."

But Hernandez still seemed reluctant. "Listen," she told me, "I want to be totally honest with you. I've told you everything that happened to me, even embarrassing shit, but I don't want you to tell my mom or my dad what I'm going to tell you now, okay? Do you promise to keep it secret?"

My first assumption was that she was pregnant or that she and Gilly were going to get married. "Okay, I promise to keep your secret," I replied.

"I'm not taking my medicine anymore," she blurted out.

Gilly jumped in. "I convinced her to stop because she doesn't need it. Doctors want everyone to believe they're crazy. They want everyone hooked on drugs. Look at how they push it on television. Try Lipitor.

Take Viagra. Doctors got a pill for everything. We've created a nation of hypochondriacs."

For the next several moments, Gilly talked about his childhood and how his parents had been cocaine addicts. He talked about how he was opposed to using all drugs, except marijuana. But I really wasn't paying attention to him. I was thinking about how Hernandez had just spent several hours telling me about her hellish life. I couldn't believe she had agreed to stop taking her medication.

"It's all about money," Gilly declared—his words snapping me back to attention. "Doctors really don't want you to be well, because then they couldn't charge you money to treat you. That's why I told her: You either stop taking the medicines and acting goofy or I'm out of here."

I looked at Hernandez and asked, "Aren't you worried that you might become psychotic again?"

"I was at first," she said quietly. "I really don't want to be crazy again." She glanced at Gilly.

"That's why I told her to cut her pills in half," he interjected. He added that he'd come up with his own treatment plan for her. Each night they got a minimum of nine hours of sleep and they both had stopped smoking marijuana. Because Gilly was a bodybuilder, he understood nutrition. He had designed a strict high-protein diet for them. "She doesn't need any freaking pills. Now that she's eating right and sleeping right, she's doing fine."

I asked her how long she had been off her medication.

"About two weeks." Then she added, "I stopped when I found out I was pregnant."

At least part of my assumption had been correct.

She said she had hallucinated only once since then. She had thought the models in the advertising posters displayed in bus shelters were watching her. But she had ignored their stares.

"Are you hearing strange voices?"

"No."

Gilly walked over to where Hernandez was seated and knelt down next to her. "Everything is going to be fine," he said, wrapping his toned arm around her shoulders. "I'm not going to let you go crazy again. I promise. Besides, you're a lot more talkative and fun now that you're off that shit."

After I interviewed Hernandez and Gilly, I met with her mother, Jackie. She told me the same stories that her daughter had.

"When she was homeless, I thought I'd open the newspaper one morning and read that a young girl had been found murdered in South Beach," Jackie said. "And if I'm being totally honest, I must tell you there were many times when I thought it would have been better if she *were* dead and *had* died. As horrible as that sounds, it would have been easier to grieve about her death than to know my beautiful daughter was completely out of her mind and performing oral sex on groups of men in an alley."

I asked her if she liked Jason Gilly.

She broke into a huge smile and said, "I love him! When my daughter first told me about him, he sounded too good to be true. I honestly wondered if he really existed. I mean, here was this man who had a good job and was not doing drugs and was not crazy and he wanted to move in with her. I invited them to dinner at my house, because I really wanted to see if he was real. And he does exist and he is just wonderful for her."

I began feeling uneasy. It was obvious that she didn't know as much about Gilly as I did. Nor had she learned that her daughter had stopped taking her antipsychotic medicine. If our roles had been reversed, I would have wanted to be warned that Mike had gone off his pills. I assumed that Jackie would want to know about her daughter's decision, too. Hernandez was taking a huge, huge risk, and I suspected that deep down, even she didn't believe that Gilly's well-intentioned health plan was going to prevent her from going nuts, she simply didn't want to lose him.

The more Jackie gushed about how great her daughter was doing, the more uncomfortable I became. She deserved the truth. But I'd promised Hernandez that I wouldn't reveal what she was doing. As a journalist, I could rationalize my silence. Promises in my profession are a sacred trust. As a reporter, I was also curious about what was going to happen next to Hernandez. But as a parent, I felt required to tell Jackie while she could still intervene.

When our interview ended, Jackie gave me a friendly hug. It was the knowing embrace that one parent shares with another when you are both dealing with sick children. Her tenderness made me feel even guiltier because I had decided *not* to tell her. I had kept her daughter's secret.

Back in my motel that night, I thought about Hernandez. I thought about Mike. I thought about Jackie, and how angry I would be if someone withheld information about my child from me. I stewed over it a long, long time, and when exhaustion finally kicked in, I closed my eyes not feeling any better about what I had done.

J udge Leifman invited me to attend a Partners in Crisis meeting that he was conducting in the courthouse with representatives from private, county, state, and federal agencies. All of them dealt regularly with the mentally ill in Miami-Dade County, and he called these meetings periodically so the different groups could discuss ways to coordinate and improve their efforts. About sixty people showed up.

The judge began by describing an initiative that he hoped would force the owners of assisted-living facilities (ALFs) to raise their standards. There were 647 boarding homes in Miami that together housed 4,568 mentally ill patients. Most of the patients were former residents at state mental hospitals who had been booted out during deinstitutionalization. The judge explained that only 250 of these ALFs had been licensed by the state. The other 397 had failed to meet Florida's *minimum* standards for boarding homes. Even so, the state paid them to take care of mentally ill boarders. The ALFs were issued "limited licenses," though the conditions in some were unsafe and even abysmal. The state claimed it had no alternative, because there was simply no place else for the mentally ill to live.

Judge Leifman and his colleagues didn't have any control over boarding homes. But as judges, they did have a say when it came to deciding where mentally ill inmates, who'd gotten into trouble, would be sent from the jail. At this point in the meeting, he introduced Alina Perez, a former prison psychologist, and explained he had hired her to inspect ALFs for the Eleventh Judicial Circuit. She had prepared five pages of requirements for an ALF to satisfy if its operators wanted judges to send them tenants. So far, she had given only eighteen of the 647 rooming homes her seal of approval. They were the *only* homes Judge Leifman and his fellow jurists would deal with. It was the judges' way of trying to strong-arm the boarding homes into providing better care.

In addition to Perez, the judge said he had hired a "super case manager" to keep track of mentally ill inmates after they were paroled. Her job was to make certain the parolees received follow-up services after they moved back into the community. Again, this was a job that the state was supposed to do but didn't do.

Judge Leifman then announced that he had been awarded a federal grant to develop a computerized system to track mentally ill offenders who were on probation. If one of them stopped attending a day treatment program or didn't pick up his monthly supply of antipsychotic medication, the computerized monitoring system would alert the court, the social workers, and the "super case manager" so they could intervene before the parolee got into trouble and was arrested again.

After Judge Leifman finished outlining his recent accomplishments, it was the Florida Department of Children and Family Services' turn to give a progress report. Its spokeswoman stood, announced that her report would not be as "optimistic" as Judge Leifman's, and then described how her agency was completely overwhelmed when it came to monitoring ALFs. She said there were only two inspectors in Miami-Dade County and they couldn't possibly police all 647 boarding homes. She warned the group that a frightening trend had been unmasked at ALFs. In order to maximize profits, ALF owners were hiring newly arrived immigrants to run their boarding homes. They were paid less than minimum wage, but didn't complain because they also were given room and board. Some were undocumented workers. Nearly all of them were women. Part of their job involved cooking meals and dispensing medications. But most of them didn't speak English, and none had any special training when it came to working with mentally ill residents. Tenants frequently were given the wrong pills, were fed diets of mostly rice and beans, and were being physically abused. "I'm not as optimistic as Judge Leifman that these ALF conditions can be improved," she said.

I was stunned by the frankness of her comments. But no one else in the room seemed surprised. As soon as the meeting ended, I cornered Judy Robinson and asked her why. "Everyone knows what is happening in these dreadful ALFs," she said. "These poor souls are simply being warehoused in them. There is no treatment. Everyone admits it. Everyone knows it. Some of these ALFs are so bad, you wouldn't want to keep your family pet in one."

Then Robinson surprised me. She lashed out at Judge Leifman. "Judges shouldn't be telling us how to run these programs," she said. "This interference is dangerous no matter how well intentioned Leifman's motives might be—because we're setting up a system where a mentally ill person has to go to jail if he wants help. Judge Leifman and the courts need to butt out of this process. He's creating a redundant system."

Judge Leifman was still standing at the front of the courtroom when I broke away from Robinson. He was talking to Carol Ann Ferrero, an attorney with the public defender's office, and as I stepped toward them, the judge nodded warily at me. I discovered that Ferrero had been grilling him about me, demanding to know why I was being permitted on the ninth floor.

"I don't think anyone in my office feels comfortable about you being there," she declared. She was worried that an inmate might say something incriminating in front of me, and she said my presence violated the inmates' privacy rights. Jail officials should never have allowed me inside without first clearing it with the public defender's office, she announced. Turning her attention back to Judge Leifman, she added that she was concerned about his plan to set up a computer monitoring system to keep track of the chronically mentally ill. It sounded a like a Big Brother operation.

I glanced around at the few people still filing out of the courtroom and noticed that no one had said anything to the state Department of Children and Family Services spokeswoman. After Ferrero left, I said, "Judge, doesn't it seem a bit odd to you that you are being chastised for trying to help the mentally ill and change the system—and the representative from the state, who just admitted that her office is not doing its job, is walking out of this meeting without anyone complaining?"

Judge Leifman shrugged. "Criticism comes with the job," he said.

Even so, the irony seemed painfully telling.

PART

FOUR

SEARCHING FOR
A SAFE PLACE

"Wherever I go, I take myself with me, and that always spoils it."

—as quoted by Susan Sheehan in
Is There No Place on Earth for Me?

Mike had been told by his psychiatrist and his therapist that he needed to take his antipsychotic medication every day. But deep down, I wasn't certain he really believed that. Not long after I returned home from Miami, he came by my office to use my computer. He wanted to buy a book that he'd found on the Internet. When he mentioned it was about mental health, I was happy, because I wanted him to learn as much as he could about his condition. But when he told me the book's title, I became irritated. It was written by an author who had been active in the antipsychiatry movement, and his spiel was clearly antimedication. I didn't say anything until after Mike had finished it. Then I explained how some activists in the 1970s had claimed that mental illness really didn't exist. A few even suggested that schizophrenia was simply an "enlightened way" of thinking. This was before MRI scans showed that the brains of many patients with bipolar disorder and schizophrenia were different from other, "normal" brains, proving that mental illness was a biological disorder.

"I had an MRI and it showed my brain was fine," Mike replied. "And this author says you can control mental illness without using chemicals."

I knew his psychiatrist had said Mike's MRI hadn't shown any anomalies. But I also suspected that the scans didn't always detect early cases of mental disorders. *The ones that I'd studied in medical journals had been performed on chronic schizophrenics who had been severely ill for years.*

"I'm not a doctor," I said, searching for words, "but I've seen in Miami what happens when mentally ill people don't take their medication. I love you. I'd never ask you to do anything I didn't believe was good for you."

"But you could be wrong," he replied. "What if you are wrong and this author is right? What if I really don't need medicine? Why does everyone have to think the same way, anyway? Maybe I just think differently. Maybe I'll never be 'normal,' whatever that is."

A few nights later, I saw A Beautiful Mind, *the powerful movie based on the life of John Forbes Nash Jr., who struggled with schizophrenia. According to the film, Nash overcame his disease because of his wife's unswerving love and his own willpower. The next day when I saw Mike, I knew where our conversation was heading.*

"He beat his illness on his own," Mike said.

"Son, I've interviewed families in Miami who love their children just as much as John Nash's wife loved him. And it didn't make their illness go away. Love can't fix a chemical imbalance. And you can't use willpower to fix a broken leg."

Mike didn't argue, but I sensed that he wasn't convinced. I decided to show him a transcript of a tape-recorded interview that I had done with a high school mathematics teacher in Miami whose son had become mentally ill during his first year in college.

Question: What happened when you learned your son was mentally ill?

Answer: I didn't believe it. I went to the library and began reading books about mental illness. Then I went into a week of mourning. I was crying and then I thought, No, I'm going to fix this.

That is your first instinct as a parent. You're going to fix it. I thought, "I can get him help. I can get him cured."

Mike was beginning to fidget, but I continued anyway.

Q: What happened after your son got out of the hospital that first time?

A: Our son did great. He took his medication and he went back to school and after several months, I thought, "Hey, we're out of the woods. He's going to make it. He won't be like those other mentally ill patients I'd read about." Then my son stopped taking his medicine and things got bad. I began keeping a record of the number of times he was arrested or had a breakdown, and at one point I showed it to him. It seemed so damn logical to me. I said, "When you are on your medications, you do okay. But when you are off them, you get into trouble. So why don't you just stay on your medication?" My wife laughed at me. I was trying to convince a person who had no insight because of his mental illness. It was like telling a paraplegic to get up and run in a footrace.

Mike had heard enough. "Dad," he said impatiently, "I'm not this man's son. Just because he had trouble when he stopped taking his medicine doesn't mean I would. I really don't want to discuss this anymore." He started to leave.

"Wait," I said. "I want to show you something else."

I removed a sheet of paper from a file and handed it to him. It was a copy of the chronology that the math teacher had made and shown his son.

12/94 First psychotic episode led to arrest in Chicago.

12/94 Diagnosis of schizoaffective disorder. Required two months of treatment.

1/95 Stopped taking meds, arrested in confrontation with the police, declared incompetent by court. Three months rehabilitation in hospital.

5/95 Returns to college, seems to have recovered.

2/97 Stopped taking medication. Second breakdown. Arrested for carrying a concealed weapon and assaulting a police officer. Forced into hospital.

4/97 Stopped taking meds. Arrested in confrontation with police. Forced into treatment program.

10/98 Refuses to take meds. Third breakdown. Used Baker Act to force him into hospital.

1/99–12/01 Gets a job. Takes medication. Lives independently. Seems much improved.

1/02 Stops taking medication after two years. Fourth breakdown. Hospitalized.

4/02 Fifth breakdown. Baker acted to Jackson Crisis Center for threatening a fellow condominium resident with knife.

5/02 Sixth breakdown after he stopped taking medication. Baker acted to Palmetto General Hospital.

6/02 Seventh breakdown. Baker acted to Citrus Hospital.

11/02 Stopped taking medication. Eighth breakdown. Baker acted to Larkin Hospital.

1/03 Stops taking medication. Ninth breakdown. Baker acted to Jackson Hospital.

"Look what happened every time his son stopped taking his medication," I said. Before Mike could argue, I told him that the math teacher's son had become so psychotic that he'd threatened to kill his own father and had shown up late one night outside his front door, waving a butcher knife. A judge had reacted by ordering the troubled youth to be injected each month with antipsychotic medication.

I scooped up the Q&A transcript and read:

Q: Is your son angry at you—angry that you went to court and got
   a judge to force him to take his medication?
A: What you discover is that if you really want to help someone,
   then you have to be willing to have them hate you. That is a
   really hard thing for most parents to accept, but if you aren't willing to take that step, then you will never be able to help them.

*"The reason why I wanted you to see this," I explained, "is that I want
you to understand just how important it is for you to continue taking your
medication. I don't care how many books you read. Or how much you want
your illness to go away. Just look at what happened to this man's son."*

Mike left.

*Later that same week, he landed a job. A temporary employment agency
sent him to work in an office, and the manager hired him full-time. As far
as we could tell, there was no background check, no questions raised about
his two misdemeanor convictions, no need to disclose his mental illness. The
salary was only a few dollars above minimum wage, but Mike reported each
day without complaint. Eventually, he qualified for health care coverage.
He had been paying insurance out of his own pocket. His employer used an
HMO, which meant Mike had to switch psychiatrists. He dragged his feet.
Mike resisted change. But when his supply of Abilify ran low, he finally
made an appointment.*

*After their first session, Mike told me, "My new doctor said she doesn't
know anyone who Abilify really helps. She called it a placebo."*

I thought he was joking, egging me on. But he wasn't.

"She ended up writing me a prescription for it anyway," he added.

"She told you that Abilify was a placebo?" I repeated.

"Yeah."

I was so angry I could barely speak. Mike had spent months in a daily treatment program whose main purpose had been to convince him to take his antipsychotic medication. What sort of irresponsible psychiatrist would tell a patient with bipolar disorder that the medicine he was being given had no therapeutic effect?

"What's this doctor's name?" I demanded.

"Why?"

"Because I'm going to call her and ask her what the hell she's doing."

"I don't want you to do that. It's okay."

"No, it's not okay! This is your life she's playing with. Listen, you've got to stay on your medications. You have a chemical imbalance."

"This is my problem," Mike said. "I'll deal with it."

As soon as he left, I sat down to write a letter of complaint against the psychiatrist, but I stopped mid-sentence. I didn't finish it.

Mike's mother called me three days later. She said Mike, who was still living at her house, had left his prescription bottle of Abilify next to a bathroom sink and she had noticed it was empty. It had been sitting there for several days. She also told me that he'd been staying up late at night and seemed to be acting odd.

I telephoned him at his job and asked him to stop by my house that night. I knew he'd be angry when I confronted him. But I didn't care. I had read a statistic in a government bulletin that said most patients with bipolar disorder stopped taking their medication after two and a half years. Within weeks, most had a mental breakdown.

Mike arrived at my office in a good mood.

"Are you taking your meds?" I demanded.

"Why?" he replied.

I told him what his mother had said.

"That's an old bottle by the sink," he explained. "I got my prescription refilled, but I keep my pills in my bedroom."

He could tell I was skeptical, so when he drove to his mother's house, he showed his refilled bottle to her.

"He's taking his medicine," she announced when she called me. "It was just a misunderstanding."

Later that night, Mike came by to talk. "Is this how it's going to be between us from now on?" he asked. "Are you going to freak out all of the time—worry all of the time whether or not I am taking my medication, whether or not I'm going to go crazy again?"

"No," I said. But it was a lie. Every time the phone rang late at night, my first thought was of him. Each time I went to Miami, I worried about him. I was afraid. I never wanted to see him out of his mind again. So I told him the truth. I explained how terrified I really was. I told him about the people whom I'd met in Miami—Ted Jackson, Freddie Gilbert, Alice Ann Collyer, and April Hernandez. I didn't want him to end up like any of them.

"Dad," he said, "those people—what's happening to them—it isn't going to happen to me. You worry too much. What happened happened. It's the past. You've got to let it go."

I wished that I could. I did. I wanted to believe Mike would never go off his medication, never have another relapse. But I knew too much now to be so confident. I'd seen too much in Miami. I'd talked to too many other parents. Every one of them had also wanted to believe that their child would beat the odds, that everything would work out for the best, that their son and their daughter would be different. But none of them had.

I told Mike it was going to take time for me to learn how to not worry.

"Just stay on your meds," I pleaded. "Please stay on your meds."

Chapter 26

I t was midmorning and I was working in my office when my cell phone rang. The caller ID showed that it was an out-of-state call from Ted Jackson, my "on the brink" inmate in South Beach.

"You've got to help me!" he exclaimed.

Jackson had been awakened that morning by knocks on his apartment door. When he peered through its peephole, he saw a Miami Beach police officer. He could see the outline of another through the apartment's drawn window shades. Jackson had backed away and remained perfectly still.

"I wasn't going to answer," he explained. "They knocked a couple times and then left."

"Have you been writing 'Jesus 2007' graffiti again?" I asked.

"No. I don't know why them cops are harassing me."

"Why don't you call and ask them?"

He didn't want to risk that.

"Then contact an attorney and have him find out if they have issued an arrest warrant for you."

At 6 P.M., Jackson called me and explained what he had done since our morning talk. He had spent much of the day telephoning lawyers whose names he had plucked from the phone book. Most had asked him to come into their office for a conference, but he hadn't wanted to risk leaving his apartment, so he'd simply hung up on them and moved down the list in the yellow pages. He had finally reached one who'd agreed to contact the police. Jackson had waited fifteen minutes and then had called the attorney back to ask what he had learned. The attorney's secretary explained that her boss was meeting with clients and hadn't had time to speak to the police yet. So Jackson waited another fifteen minutes and then telephoned again. He kept calling every fifteen minutes until the exasperated secretary ordered him to stop. Her reaction made him suspicious.

"I got to thinking: If this attorney is so buddy-buddy that he has friends at the police department, then he might be in cahoots with them. I called that secretary and said I didn't want her boss doing anything for me. Not a dang thing."

After that failed attempt, Jackson resumed his search and found another lawyer willing to contact the police. This time when Jackson telephoned him fifteen minutes later, the attorney had an answer. The Miami Beach police had refused to discuss Jackson or explain why they had come knocking on his door.

Jackson had remained sequestered in his apartment and had formulated a plan. "How about if I call you every night at eight o'clock?" he asked me. "If I hang up after one ring, that means everything is okay. If I let it ring three times, that means I need to speak to you. If I don't call you at all, then you'll know I've been arrested and you'll need to call my attorney lickety-split because I'm in jail again." He gave me the name of the attorney who had agreed to represent him if he was arrested.

"Isn't there someone in South Beach you can call each night?" I asked.

"No," he said, sounding hurt. "My attorney said I couldn't call him."

I was waiting the next evening, and at 8:10, when I still hadn't heard from him, I decided to give him a call.

"Hello," a groggy Jackson said after several rings.

"Are you okay?"

"I'm s-o-o-r-r-r-r-y," he said, slurring his words. He sounded drugged.

"Have you taken something?"

Jackson said he had. He'd upped his antipsychotic medication on his own. I knew he'd been prescribed 600 milligrams of Seroquel per day, just under the maximum 750-milligram amount. I asked him how much more he'd taken.

"I just doubled everything."

"Everything?" I did the math. That meant he had taken 1,200 milligrams of Seroquel. He'd also been prescribed 800 milligrams of clozapine, which had a maximum dose of 900 milligrams.

"How about clozapine? Did you double it, too?" I asked.

No, he replied. He knew clozapine was supposed to keep him from having delusions, so he'd *tripled* its dose. That was 2,400 milligrams of clozapine, or 1,500 milligrams more than its recommended maximum amount. He had then doubled the lithium that he'd been prescribed.

"I just want to go back to sleep," he said. He hung up.

I called a psychiatrist in Miami and asked him if Jackson had taken a lethal overdose. "No," he replied, "but those pills will definitely knock him out for a while."

Jackson telephoned me the next night at eight, but hung up after one ring. He did the same for three more nights. Finally, we spoke the next evening. During our conversation, I urged him to cut back on his medications. He promised he would.

"I'm supposed to be leaving in two weeks to visit my mother in Ohio for a month," he said. "If I can get out of Miami without them cops busting me, then I can go see a doctor and I should be okay." Meanwhile, he planned to remain holed up in his apartment. By this point, he had already stayed indoors a week.

"I think I know why they're hassling me," he volunteered. "There's a lot of Jews in Miami Beach and some of them are cops and they don't like me talking about how Jesus is coming back in 2007."

When he called the next night, he let the phone ring only once, so I didn't pick up. But at 3:13 A.M. my cell phone rang. I grabbed it, thinking something had happened to my son. But it was Jackson. He'd been studying the Book of Revelation in the Bible and he had found a scripture that he said confirmed Jesus would be returning in 2007. "You've got to hear this!" he exclaimed. He began reading it, but I cut him off and went back to sleep.

Jackson didn't call at eight the following day, so I decided to check on him, thinking that he might have been arrested. When he answered, he told me that he'd been attacked and beaten.

"By the police?"

"No, hit men hired by them Jews."

He had been unable to sleep the previous night after he had called me. He said he had been too excited because of the scripture that he'd discovered. So he had decided to slip out of his apartment to buy groceries. After checking to make certain there were no Miami Beach police officers lurking outside, he'd dashed to an all-night market a few blocks away. Three young men had been buying cigarettes at the counter when he rushed inside. After he paid for his supplies and left the store, he spotted the men loitering at a street corner. As he approached, one of them blocked his path, called him a "fag," and punched him in the face. The other two started hitting him. The clerk inside the market heard the ruckus and yelled out, "I'm calling the police!" That sent the three men running. Jackson had scrambled to his feet, scooped up his groceries, and dashed off, too.

"I'm sure they were hired by Jews to attack me."

I urged him to contact his VA psychiatrist, but he said he wasn't going to go outside again or call anyone except me, because his line might be tapped.

For the next several days, my cell phone rang at eight each evening. On the night before he was scheduled to leave for Ohio, I answered his call and he assured me that he was okay. He told me that he had arranged for a taxi to drive him to the Miami airport, but he had warned the cab company that its driver would have to show him an ID before he would come out of his apartment.

Jackson called me the next night from his mother's house. His trip had been uneventful, but he had not felt safe until the aircraft had lifted off, and even then he had been worried that the FBI might be waiting for him when the plane landed in Ohio.

During the flight, he had thought of a way to earn some money to pay off the mounting debts that he still owed. While he had been hiding inside his apartment, he had watched the Jack Van Impe Ministries from Canada. The television evangelist's sermons contained many of the same predictions that he'd discovered in the Bible. "People send him millions of dollars and, shoot, he don't know as much as I do, because I know the exact date when Jesus is coming back. Now, here's my plan. I'm going to write up a new flyer. I'm going to lay it all out, man, explain everything, and when I get back to Miami, I'm hitting the streets again. I've identified fifty-four verses in the Bible that absolutely prove Jesus will be returning during, after, or on the dot, in 2007 in Jerusalem," which he spelled out to me as Jer-USA-lem.

"Do you really think that's a smart idea?" I asked. "Writing graffiti and handing out flyers is what got you into trouble."

He didn't answer, so I continued: "Have you ever thought that maybe God didn't talk to you—that your mental illness just makes you think he did?"

There was another long silence and then Jackson said, "I've got to believe God spoke to me. It's what makes me special. What else do I have, if I don't have that in my life?"

Chapter 27

I returned to Miami on a Sunday afternoon and the first person I called was April Hernandez. Seven weeks had passed since I had interviewed her and her boyfriend, Jason Gilly, and been told that she had stopped taking her antipsychotic medication. No one answered at her apartment, so I left a message. A few hours later, Gilly telephoned. "April is in the hospital," he said.

I met him at a Starbucks on the Lincoln Road pedestrian mall, not far from "the circle," which is where he and Hernandez first met and where she had once spent her days loitering with her dope-smoking buddies.

Gilly was visibly upset. He said Hernandez had been feeling okay after she stopped taking her pills. In fact, he thought she was much more alert. Not long after they had met with me, Hernandez's mother, Jackie, had driven them to a craft show, where they had bought $50 worth of fifty-cent earrings. The next day, Hernandez had spread out a blanket on Lincoln Mall and had sold the wire-and-bead trinkets to tourists for $5 each. She told them that she'd made them. "It really gave her ego a big boost," he recalled. "It was good because she had something to do during the day besides hang around the circle with those losers." Gilly, meanwhile, found a job as a laborer at a construction site.

By this point, both of them had started having second thoughts about her pregnancy. She was afraid her baby might be mentally ill. She'd also started complaining about Gilly's constant flirting. She didn't want him to abandon her with a newborn if he decided to end their relationship. They went to a free clinic, where Hernandez underwent an abortion. Afterward, she became depressed. He thought it was a normal reaction, but when Hernandez told him that she didn't want to sell earrings anymore, he began to suspect something else was wrong.

"I couldn't stay home and watch her because of my job," he explained, "so I left her alone in our apartment, and that turned out to be a big mistake. I think the walls started closing in on her."

Gilly left early for work and didn't get back from his laborer job until after 7 P.M. on most days. One night when he came home, she was gone. He found her sitting at the circle with her old chums. Gilly didn't like that, and they got into an argument. He went back to their apartment alone, and she stayed out all night. The next day when he got home from work, he found her still sitting at the circle, "dancing and acting goofy."

"I told her, 'We need to get back on our health plan. You haven't been eating right or getting enough sleep.'"

They got into another loud dispute, but Hernandez went back to their apartment with him. That night, she had trouble falling asleep. She kept giggling. An exhausted Gilly finally asked, "What is so damn funny?"

Hernandez said she wasn't giggling.

"Then who is?"

It was one of the voices in her head making that noise, she said.

Gilly got scared and urged her to take one of her antipsychotic tablets. He kept badgering her until she went into the bathroom and swallowed one. In the morning, Gilly told her the abortion had thrown her hormone system out of whack. He thought she should begin taking her pills again until they could get back on their high-protein diet. He made her promise that she'd spend the day in their apartment. She promised that she would but when he got off work that night, she was gone. He walked to the circle, but she wasn't there either. Around 4 A.M., he spotted her in a South Beach neighborhood popular with crack addicts. When he confronted her, she refused to go home with him. Instead, she spent the night wandering the streets.

After work the following day, Gilly bought a bag of "cribbie," a potent form of marijuana, and used it to lure Hernandez back to their apartment. He'd never seen her act so crazy. But when they got to the efficiency, she changed her mind and insisted they smoke the drug in a park at Second Street and Ocean Drive. Gilly began rolling two joints as soon as they got there, and within seconds, a police car appeared and he was arrested. An undercover cop patrolling the park had spotted him. Gilly was taken to the Miami-Dade County jail, and by the time he posted bail, Hernandez had disappeared.

Not knowing what else to do, Gilly telephoned Jackie. She drove to South Beach and the two of them began hunting for Hernandez. Jackie saw her walking on the Lincoln Road mall and coaxed her into the same Starbucks where Gilly and I were now talking. Jackie told her daughter that she needed to check herself into a hospital. But Hernandez insisted there was nothing wrong. Gilly, meanwhile, went outside the coffee shop and waved down a policeman. The officer asked Hernandez if she wanted to go to an emergency room. She said no, and the officer told Jackie that there was nothing he could do to intervene, because Hernandez wasn't threatening anyone and was not in any imminent danger. Jackie claimed that Hernandez had threatened to kill her. But the cop could tell that she was exaggerating. He left. After about an hour, Jackie and Gilly persuaded Hernandez to return to her apartment. But neither of them could convince her to go to a hospital. As soon as Jackie left that night, Hernandez ran away from Gilly.

The next morning, Jackie took a psychiatric nurse with her to South

Beach to find Hernandez. They trolled through the streets until they saw her standing at a corner, yelling obscenities. Jackie called the police while the nurse took notes. The police decided the nurse's written statement was enough for them to take Hernandez to an emergency room for observation. Jackie then threatened her daughter with the Marchman Act, which allows a parent to have an adult child locked up for sixty days as a drug addict. At that point, Hernandez voluntarily checked herself into the hospital for treatment.

"I quit my construction job," Gilly told me, "so I could visit her every day in the hospital. She's been in there three days now and is supposed to be discharged tomorrow morning."

"What happens then?" I asked.

He said they were moving in with Jackie, who lived in another section of Miami.

"We've got to get away from the circle and streets," he said.

I asked him if he blamed himself for her breakdown, since he had insisted that she stop taking her medication.

"I never thought this would happen," he replied. "I think we would have been okay if her hormones hadn't gotten all screwed up. If we try it again, we'll do it with a doctor watching, so we can make sure she doesn't go off the deep end."

Despite everything they'd been through, he still believed she could stay stable without medication. I offered to go with him to the hospital in the morning when she was discharged. We met in the hospital lobby, and Gilly was clearly nervous. As soon as Hernandez appeared, he broke out into a big smile and embraced her. But she seemed distant. Her voice was robotic and her demeanor reminded me of how Mike had been when he had first been released from the hospital. She was obviously sedated.

I felt sorry for her, but Gilly was optimistic. "We won't be staying at your mom's for long after we get you back on your feet," he said. "I want to get out of Florida. We can go north. Get a new start." He wanted to move to Manhattan. "I'll enroll at NYU and become a lawyer. I'm getting too old for this rock-and-roll and bodybuilding bullshit." Turning to Hernandez, he said, "How about that, baby, me being an attorney? You can go to school there, too. It'll be great. We'll put all of this behind us. You'll see, I'm going to make it happen."

Hernandez smiled wearily and lit a cigarette. She glanced at it and told me, "I was down to one a day, but not now."

Gilly left us for a minute to run an errand and I asked Hernandez if she was angry at him for pushing her to go off her medication.

"It was my fault," she said. "I should have known I'd go crazy again."

"Did you realize you were losing it—while it was happening?"

"No, I just felt this urge to be back on the streets again."

"Would you like to go to New York and go to college?"

"No, not really. Okay, well, maybe. Sure, I guess. Why not? But I don't know. I don't want to go too far in case this happens again. I don't want to get too far from my mom. I don't want to end up on the streets again. I need someone to watch over me."

"Are you looking forward to moving in with her?"

"Everyone says it's a good idea and we need to get away from the circle. But in a way, it really doesn't matter."

"What do you mean?"

"The circle. It changed. It's not like most of the people I knew are still there anyway, you know?"

"They're not?"

"No, they went to jail or went home to live with their parents or they're dead."

"That's sad."

"Really? You think so? I mean, I don't know, I just think that's what happens to people like me. There's jail, there's your parents, or you die."

Chapter 28

D r. Poitier seemed unsettled when we met in his ninth-floor office. The night before, a deranged man had been arrested for causing a ruckus at the emergency room in Jackson Memorial Hospital. The prisoner had collapsed a few hours later in his jail cell. He'd been rushed back to the same emergency room but had died moments later. "I've got to find out what happened," Dr. Poitier explained.

He spent the entire morning investigating, and by noon he had an answer. The inmate had brain cancer. He'd gone to the hospital to get pain medicine and had become frustrated and angry at how long it was taking. He'd caused a scene, and the police had assumed he was crazy. It was the tumor in his brain that had killed him. Nothing had happened while he was in the jail that had contributed to his death.

"Whenever someone dies in the jail, I want to know why," Dr. Poitier said. Then he repeated a statement that he had told me during every one of my earlier trips to Miami. "This is no place for someone who is mentally ill. I worry a lot about what can happen in a place like this to someone with mental problems."

About a year earlier, a psychotic prisoner named William Weaver Jr. had been brought into the jail. "This man's father called me to make sure his son was safe, and I assured him we were doing everything we could to help his son get better," Poitier said. Not long after that call, Weaver climbed onto the top bunk in his cell and dove off. His head struck the cell's steel commode, breaking his neck. He was paralyzed.

An internal review by jail officials had determined that no one was to blame. But that report hadn't soothed Dr. Poitier. "The bottom line is, that man didn't belong in a jail setting. A hospital doesn't have bunks for patients to dive off. He should have been taken somewhere better equipped to handle the mentally ill."

I wanted to learn more about the Weaver incident, so I located his father, William Weaver Sr., a retired postal worker who was in his late seventies when we talked. "I could've bailed my son out," he told me, "but I thought leaving him in jail was the smart thing to do, because I couldn't handle him at home. He needed help and I thought he'd get it in jail."

Weaver's next comment caught me off guard. "That wasn't an accident that hurt him, you know. Them guards broke his neck."

"He didn't jump off a bunk and hit the toilet?" I asked.

"No, them guards broke his neck fighting with him."

Weaver gave me the address of a nursing home where his forty-five-year-old son was living. I drove there, found his room, and introduced myself. According to the jail's booking sheet, Weaver had weighed 337 pounds and stood six feet, three inches tall when he was arrested. Although he was draped by a sheet from the neck down in his room, he still looked huge. He asked if I'd wipe his face with a towel, because he was perspiring. Then he said, "My dad is angry and wants me to sue the jail—that's why he told you them guards beat me up—but I'm a Christian and I don't believe in lying and that's not true."

"What did happen?"

"I jumped. I was out of my head."

Weaver told me that he had suffered his first psychotic breakdown when he was twenty years old. His parents had driven him to a hospital, but while they were waiting to see a doctor, Weaver had become convinced they were plotting to kill him. He ran outside and commandeered a car. When his parents got home, he was hiding in a room and attacked them with his fists. The police were called and Weaver was jailed. He was diagnosed with bipolar disorder and spent three months in a treatment facility. Luckily, antipsychotic medication kept him stable, and he had lived a seemingly ordinary life for the next twenty-three years.

"For *twenty-three years* you didn't have any mental problems?" I asked.

"I took my medication every day and didn't even think about it."

"What caused your relapse?"

"I got a new boss and we didn't get along."

Weaver had worked as a butcher in a local grocery store, but he couldn't handle the extra pressure after his new boss arrived, so he quit. Not long after that, he stopped taking his medication because his health insurance coverage expired. "I thought I'd be okay because I hadn't had any problems for all of those years."

He soon began acting so strange that his wife asked him to leave their house because she was afraid. He moved in with his father, and one night, he attacked him while the senior Weaver was sleeping. The police arrested him, and he was put into a cell on the ninth floor that had two bunks in it. One was about five feet above the floor.

"A guard told me I was going to be sent to prison for what I did to my father, and that really scared me. I'd heard awful stories about what happens to men in prison. I thought, 'If I hurt myself, then they'll have to take me to Jackson Hospital—not prison.' I climbed up on the bed and jumped off headfirst because I wanted to hurt my head enough they'd have to take me to the hospital."

After doctors said Weaver would be a quadriplegic for the rest of his life, all the charges filed against him were dismissed and he was moved into a long-term-care home. His thinking had been restored as soon as he began taking antipsychotic medication again.

"I don't blame the doctor in jail or even the guard who told me I was going to prison," he said. "I shouldn't have jumped. I just wish I could take it back now, because I'm going to be like this forever."

There was a drawing next to his bed that his ten-year-old daughter had given him. For financial reasons, his wife was divorcing him so he'd become a ward of the state. "My daughter's birthday is next week," he said, "and I can't even sign a card for her." He became emotional and asked me to wipe his eyes with a towel. On impulse, I offered to mail his daughter a card with his name signed to it.

"Oh, that'd be so great!" he exclaimed.

When I returned to the jail, I told Dr. Poitier that Weaver didn't harbor any ill will toward him. Even so, Dr. Poitier said he still felt bad. "This man was not a criminal. He was mentally ill, and now he is paralyzed because he was brought into our facility. There should have been some way for this man to continue getting his medication." Repeating himself yet again, he declared, "Jails are not where the mentally ill belong!"

C wing had been freshly painted since my previous visit. The fresh-up had been ordered by jail officials because Judge Leifman had invited a *Miami Herald* reporter to tour the ninth floor. The new paint, however, didn't impress reporter Joe Mozingo. He likened C wing to a dungeon in his feature story, and he quoted Dr. Poitier saying, "I don't even try to describe to people what's going on up here. It's beyond talking about."

Not long after Mozingo's story was published, an inmate began choking another prisoner in C wing. Officer Clarence Clem ran to the cell front and yelled, "Let him go!" The inmate freed his grip and the gasping prisoner stumbled toward the door just as Clem unbolted it. He pulled the injured inmate out and slammed the door closed. Inside, the angry inmate paced back and forth.

Sergeant Alonso asked Dr. Poitier if he would give the prisoner who'd started the fight a sedative to calm him down. Alonso and Officers Clem, Roosevelt Jackson, and Michael Urbistondo then gathered outside the cell as a show of force.

"You need some medicine," Clem yelled.

"There's going to be problems," the inmate replied.

"Listen," Clem said calmly, "we don't want no problems. We don't need no problems. We're just going to give you a little medicine that will help settle you down."

Alonso ordered the prisoner to step forward to the door to be handcuffed so he could be taken to Dr. Poitier and given a shot. The inmate hesitated, but then eyeballed the beefy officers and did as he was told. After the prisoner got his sedative, he slept for a few hours. And then, without any warning, he leaped up from his bunk and charged into the glass cell front, causing a loud *blam* to echo through the wing. Backing up, he rammed the glass again at full force with his head. Clem ordered him to stop, but he refused and instead began baiting the officer to come inside to fight him.

Alonso sprayed OC spray into the inmate's face as he began to charge the wall again, and the powerful pepper spray stopped him in his tracks. Clem immediately burst inside and tackled the inmate. During the wrestling match that followed, several of Clem's fingers were twisted backward and he heard a snap, although later it would not be clear whether they were bent by the prisoner or by the other officers during the confusion. As soon as the prisoner was immobilized, he was given another shot and Clem was taken to Cedars Medical Center, where an X-ray revealed that his little finger was broken and several ligaments torn. He was still being treated there when the four-o'clock ninth-floor shift ended.

The officers who worked with Clem left the jail together and walked to the hospital, which was only a block away. Although Clem's fractured finger was not a life-threatening injury, they went to check on him and pay their respects. "It's what you do when a fellow officer is hurt," Urbistondo explained.

Officer Clem took the attention and broken finger in stride. "This stuff happens on the ninth floor," he said. "It can get violent real fast."

L ater that night, I pulled into a drugstore and bought a Happy Birthday card. I signed William Weaver Jr.'s name to it and addressed it to his daughter. It seemed the least I could do.

Chapter 29

I'd seen how Judge Leifman's diversion program moved mentally ill prisoners who had been charged with minor crimes off the ninth floor and into community treatment centers. But these inmates were a minority. Most of the mentally ill prisoners in the jail were accused of much more serious crimes, and they often spent months waiting for their felony cases to be resolved. In an average year, some 3,000 such inmates would be booked into Miami's jails. I wanted to find out what happened to these prisoners, so Judge Leifman introduced me to Terry Chavez and Bart Armstrong. They worked for the state's attorney general's office and specialized in cases filed against the mentally ill.

Energetic and no-nonsense, Chavez was only a few days away from celebrating her fiftieth birthday when we met early one Thursday morning outside the courthouse. Officially, she was the state's mental health coordinator, but that tag really didn't convey the clout that she wielded. Chavez decided—largely on her own—which mentally ill felons would be released to treatment programs through plea bargains and which would be put on trial and possibly sent to prison. Her protégé, Bart Armstrong, had only recently been assigned to help her. He was lanky and serious-minded, just a few years out of law school.

"Most judges have no training in mental health, so they often don't know the difference between bipolar disorder and schizophrenia," Chavez explained as we entered the courthouse. "The average judge here gets four hundred and fifty mental evaluations *each month* from court-appointed psychiatrists. A lot of them simply don't have time to read them, so they depend on us to offer them advice."

As Chavez passed through the metal detector at the doorway, the security guard greeted her with a cheery "Good morning, Ms. Zoom-Zoom." I soon understood why. "I hate wasting time," she said as she walked briskly through a crowded lobby. Chavez skipped the elevators and began climbing the steps of a nearby escalator.

Although Armstrong was a prosecutor, Chavez didn't have a law degree. She was a former social worker. Even so, she was afforded the same privileges as attorneys in the courthouse and, in many instances, appeared to be even more respected by judges.

"Bart and I both have fifteen cases to track today," she announced.

"Fifteen?" I asked. That seemed like a lot.

"Some days we have twice that number."

As soon as Chavez reached the sixth floor, a square-framed man in his sixties came rushing over. "This is Sam Konell," Chavez said. He sized me up with a hurried glance, handed me his business card, and told Chavez, "I've got a problem."

His card identified him as the "court liaison and forensic program director" for the Westchester Health Care Network. But I'd already heard stories in the jail about Konell and knew that job title was a euphemism. Konell was a "patient broker," the most successful in Miami. Each morning, he scoured police, court, and jail records, looking for felony cases that involved psychotic defendants. He picked *only* the defendants who had health insurance. In most cases, Konell could get a felony charge reduced, suspended, or even dismissed by promising the court that he would personally take responsibility for getting the accused into a hospital. In return, Konell required defendants to "voluntarily" enter treatment programs that were run by the Westchester network. Those facilities paid Konell's salary.

Depending on whom you spoke with, Sam Konell was either a vulture or a saint. Judy Robinson, Rachel Diaz, and several other NAMI members claimed his hospitals kept patients only until their insurance benefits ran out. Then they shipped them back to the jail. But Judge Leifman and Chavez both defended Konell. Even if inmates got to stay in his hospitals just for short periods, at least they received some therapy, and that was better than having them languish in jail.

Konell opened his notepad and read Chavez the name of a ninth-floor inmate. "You remember him, don't you?" he asked.

Chavez nodded. A few days earlier, she'd agreed to reduce a felony charge filed against him. In return, Konell had promised to get him into one of his programs. But before he could, the prisoner had gotten into a fight in jail, and now a new felony charge had been lodged against him.

"Can you get it dismissed so I can get him into the hospital like we planned?" Konell asked.

"Sam," Chavez replied, "I checked this guy's sheet this morning and I've got a problem." The inmate had a history of going off his antipsychotic medication and getting into scuffles.

"Ah c'mon!" Konell snapped. "You were willing to turn him loose yesterday. This was a done deal!"

"Well, now it's undone," Chavez retorted.

For the next several moments, Chavez and Konell argued. Neither cared that they were standing in a busy hallway while lawyers, witnesses, defendants, and jurors scurried by them.

"This goes on every morning," Armstrong whispered to me. "Sam is the first person we usually see, and he and Terry will go through a half dozen cases just like this."

Seconds later, Chavez agreed to "abate" the new charge—put it on hold—but only after Konell promised that he would keep an eye on the prisoner for sixty days to make certain he stayed out of trouble. If the inmate screwed up, Chavez would reinstate the felony charge and have him arrested. In effect, Chavez was forcing Konell to act as the defendant's parole officer.

Konell was about to walk away, but Chavez wasn't done. A bipolar prisoner on the ninth floor had been charged with what the plain-speaking Chavez called "a bullshit felony." He'd never been in trouble before, and Chavez wanted Konell to admit him into one of his hospitals. Konell recognized the inmate's name and said, "Sorry, I got no place for him."

Now it was Chavez's turn to cajole. The reason Konell didn't have space was that the prisoner belonged to an HMO, and none of Konell's hospitals accepted HMO patients.

"How about giving him a scholarship?" she asked.

Each month Konell awarded a handful of "scholarships" to inmates without medical insurance. They were freebies—cases the hospitals took knowing they wouldn't be paid. Konell had been pressured by judges into awarding them after the courts were criticized for giving him so much business.

"I don't have any scholarships left this month," he said.

Chavez dug in. "Help me out here, Sam. It's a good case."

"Oh, so now *you* want a favor from me?" he asked. "I'll think about it."

He walked away. But Chavez was confident. "He'll come through. I can tell. We argue so much, I can tell. He wants me to sweat awhile because I pushed him on that other case. But he'll cough up a scholarship."

I asked her how much income she thought Konell generated for his hospitals. Rolling her eyes, Chavez said, "Sam Konell rains money." On an average day, judges released as many as *thirty* defendants to him. Doctors at his hospitals charged their insurance companies between

$7,000 and $80,000 *each*, depending on what sort of treatment the patients required. ·

I didn't understand why Konell was earning money performing a job that—it seemed to me—either the courts or various state agencies should have been doing. When I asked, Chavez was blunt: "Sam is making big bucks off a hole in our system. But when your resources are as low as ours in this state, then someone such as Sam becomes a godsend. He's a workaholic, you can trust him to do what he says he'll do, and I believe he really does care about helping these people. Yes, he's in it for the money, but if I have to balance the scales of justice, I'd say Sam does more good than bad."

She paused and then added, "A few years ago, an elderly man stabbed his wife seventeen times one night while she was sleeping. This couple had been married for more than fifty years, and the woman—who, incredibly, survived—didn't wanted to press charges because she knew her husband had dementia. This was a sad, sad case. The woman loved him, and her husband was a good man who had never been in trouble."

Chavez hadn't seen any reason to send the defendant to prison or to an overcrowded state forensic hospital. But he was too unstable to be turned loose. "Sam agreed to take responsibility for him. Okay, so the couple had money, but still, it was Sam who got him into an ALF and monitored him." The man lived six more years without causing any trouble. "I didn't think society needed to punish the husband because he'd developed dementia, but that's what would have happened if Sam Konell hadn't agreed to take him in."

Moments later, Chavez and Armstrong separated. I followed Chavez into a nearby courtroom, where a prosecutor was waiting for her. He'd just been handed a case and wanted to know what Chavez thought. "I think the defendant is faking it," she replied. The accused had already been convicted of two felonies, and Chavez suspected he was trying to avoid Florida's three-strikes mandatory sentencing law by acting crazy.

That way he could be sent to Chattahoochee rather than prison. "His attorney wants to work out a deal," she added, "but I don't." When the judge called the defendant's name, the prosecutor said the state wanted to schedule the case for a jury trial. There would be no plea-bargaining.

Checking her watch, Chavez scooted across the hall, where an attorney was asking a judge to change the conditions of his client's probation. A month earlier, the defendant had pleaded guilty to beating his wife during a psychotic episode. He'd been ordered to attend a daily mental health treatment program as part of his probation. But he didn't like going. His attorney told the judge that the husband and his wife had reconciled and were now seeing a marriage counselor. "My client doesn't have time to attend both—marriage counseling and group therapy," he explained, "so we'd like permission to have him continue with only the marriage counseling."

Chavez jumped in. "Your Honor, there's a big difference between marriage counseling and mental health therapy. They're not interchangeable."

The judge denied the request.

Chavez darted back across the corridor into the same courtroom where she had been earlier.

"Welcome back, Ms. Chavez," the judge said. She used his greeting as an opening to ask him about another case. A defendant had just been brought back to Miami from Chattahoochee, and Chavez wanted to get his case scheduled for trial before he decompensated.

"Sorry," the judge replied. "My dance card is full." The earliest opening on his calendar for a trial was two months away.

"He might not last that long, " Chavez warned.

"Then he'll just have to go back to Chattahoochee again," the judge replied.

When Chavez slipped outside the courtroom, I said, "That defendant—do you really think he's going to be sent back to Chattahoochee?"

She nodded. "It happens all the time. I've got defendants going back and forth and back and forth because the courts are so crowded. By the time we're ready to put on our case, they'll no longer be mentally competent."

Chavez tugged open the door to yet another courtroom and said, "This is my most important case of the morning." The hearing was being held because Dr. Poitier wanted the court's permission to forcibly medicate an inmate in C wing. Chavez had warned me that this case had been "bungled" from the start. A police officer had spotted the defendant walking alone late at night and had stopped to ask him what he was doing. They had gotten into an argument, and the policeman had accused him of "attempted battery of a law enforcement officer," a catchall crime frequently used whenever the police simply want to arrest someone. Rather than taking the defendant, who had bipolar disorder, to a hospital, the angry cop had booked him into jail.

What happened next turned the situation into a real catastrophe. *The officer left on vacation without filing an arrest report.* Because of his oversight, no one in the prosecutor's office knew the prisoner was being held in the jail. He had slipped in under the radar, Chavez said.

Dr. Poitier had interviewed the prisoner during his morning rounds on the ninth floor and had asked if he was willing to take antipsychotic medicine. The inmate had refused, which was his legal right, and his mental condition had started to deteriorate. By the end of three weeks, he had stopped talking and eating. It was at this point that Dr. Poitier had contacted the state's prosecutor's office and asked it to file a motion in court so he could force the inmate to begin taking antipsychotic drugs. Dr. Poitier was afraid the inmate would soon become catatonic if the state didn't intervene.

Dr. Poitier's request had set off an alarm. The prosecutor's office suddenly realized it had a mentally ill inmate in jail who had never been charged with a crime. Worse, he'd been there nearly a month.

The public defender's office also found out about the inmate. It immediately sent a social worker to interview him, and it also contacted his mother. She had been looking for her son since the night when he'd disappeared. The police had told her that he had *not* been arrested. They hadn't been lying. They hadn't known.

Had it not been for Dr. Poitier's concern, the accused would have remained on the ninth floor without *anyone* in the prosecutor's or the public defender's office knowing he was in jail.

When Chavez and I entered in the courtroom, Robin Bengochea, a public defender, was explaining the situation to the judge and was demanding that her client be released. As expected, Prosecutor Jeremy P. Leathe disagreed and pointed out that Florida statutes gave his office thirty days to file formal charges. The inmate had been in jail for twenty-nine days, so the state's attorney's office still had until the next day—a Friday—to either charge or free him.

Bengochea told the judge that the arresting police officer was still on vacation and wouldn't be back in Miami until Monday. "You might as well release my client now," she argued, "because the state can't possibly meet its Friday deadline."

Prosecutor Leathe asked for a short recess so he and Chavez could huddle together in the hallway. Chavez had told me before the hearing that she believed the prisoner should never have been arrested. But he had been, and now he was in such horrible mental shape that she didn't feel it was safe to simply turn him loose. He needed to be admitted into a hospital, and there was no guarantee that he'd get help if the state released him. It was Chavez who came up with a delaying tactic.

When court resumed, Prosecutor Leathe announced that the state wanted the inmate evaluated by two psychiatrists to see if he was mentally competent to stand trial. Chavez knew it would take a minimum of three working days for two doctors to evaluate the prisoner and report back to the judge. That meant the earliest the judge could read their reports would be next Wednesday. The prisoner would have to stay in jail while those examinations were being done. By Wednesday, Chavez would have buttonholed the vacationing police officer, gotten his arrest report, and completed all the paperwork so the inmate could be formally charged. That would solve the problem.

Bengochea saw through Chavez's ruse and objected. But Judge Ivan Fernandez went along with the ploy. He warned Chavez, however, that if the state hadn't charged the defendant by Wednesday, he would be freed regardless of his mental condition.

Having resolved that thorny issue, Judge Fernandez said he was ready to decide if the inmate needed to be forcibly medicated. Prosecutor Leathe called Dr. Poitier as a witness and asked if he thought the prisoner was in "imminent danger."

> *Dr. Poitier: Yes. At one point in the jail, he was almost catatonic.*
> *Leathe: But didn't he take his medicine this morning?*
> *A: Yes. He took it today because he knew we were coming to court.*
> *Q: What will happen if he stops taking his medicine again?*
> *A: He will decompensate.*
> *Q: And what will happen if he decompensates?*
> *A: He could ultimately die, because when he doesn't take his medicine in jail, he stops eating.*
> *Q: Why won't he take his medicine?*
> *A: He has a lack of insight and doesn't realize he needs it.*

Now it was Bengochea's turn.

> *Bengochea: Did the defendant get out of bed today to come to court?*
> *Dr. Poitier: Yes, he did.*
> *Q: Well then, he can't be catatonic, can he, if he came to court?*

A: *He's been taking his medicine off and on this week because he knew he was coming to court, but I'm afraid he will stop taking it again after this hearing.*

Q: *Can you read minds, Dr. Poitier?*

A: *No.*

Q: *So you can't be sure he will stop taking his medicine?*

A: *I can only tell you he has refused to take them most of the time he's been in jail.*

In their closing arguments, Leathe and Bengochea sniped at each other. Bengochea called Dr. Poitier's request an "outrageous violation" of her client's civil rights. Leathe argued that Dr. Poitier was simply trying to save the prisoner from his own destructive behavior.

Judge Fernandez ruled in favor of the prosecution. He said Dr. Poitier could forcibly medicate the inmate, but *only* if he refused to take his pills and if his health continued to deteriorate to the point that his life was being "seriously threatened."

I glanced at the inmate, who was sitting in the jury box with a correctional officer beside him. The prisoner seemed completely unaware of what was happening in court.

Within seconds, Chavez was on her feet. I followed her into another courtroom, where a judge was conducting a competency hearing. A fifty-year-old man had been accused of masturbating in public. But two court-appointed psychiatrists had decided he was so severely mentally ill that he wasn't responsible for his actions. One of them was testifying when we arrived. "This man is not only mentally ill, he is mentally retarded," the doctor said. "In my opinion, he will *never* be competent to stand trial because of his mental retardation."

"So, doctor," the judge said, "where am I supposed to send someone like this—if he can't be put on trial?"

Instead of answering directly, the psychiatrist told the judge where he shouldn't send the accused. "Because of his low IQ, he should not be kept in the jail, because he will be preyed on by other inmates. You will be condemning him to a life of victimization if you keep him there." But he also cautioned the judge against sending him to a boarding home for the retarded. "In that environment, he will become the bully who preys on those who are weaker than him, because he has criminal tendencies." Finally, he warned the judge not to free the prisoner. "His total lack of control will cause him to commit more sexual crimes. Much like a small child, he needs constant supervision, because he doesn't understand what is appropriate behavior when it comes to his own sexuality." To press that point, the psychiatrist said the defendant had been arrested more than three dozen times for masturbating in public.

The doctor's testimony clearly exasperated the judge.

"If he can't be put on trial because he's not competent," he said, "and I can't keep him in jail or place him in a home for the retarded or release him, then where exactly is he supposed to go?"

The doctor shrugged. "There really is no place for this man to live safely in our society. There was a time before deinstitutionalization when he could have been locked in a state mental hospital, but those institutions have all been closed."

Even though the psychiatrist had just testified that the defendant was so severely retarded that he would never become mentally competent, the judge ordered him sent to Chattahoochee to be "made" competent.

"At least he will be kept in a secure setting there for a couple more months until someone figures out what to do with him," the judge said.

As I listened to that rationalization, I thought about Alice Ann Collyer, the chronic schizophrenic who also was being shuffled between the jail and the state forensic hospital. She had been waiting for more than three years to be put on trial for pushing an elderly woman at a South Beach bus stop. When Chavez and I left the courtroom, I asked her if she recalled Collyer's case. Of course, she replied. "That woman refuses to take her medicine when she is on the streets, and she's dangerous. The way I see it, the longer we can put off her case and not go to trial, the safer the public is, so keeping her on a bus going back and forth to the hospital is not such a bad thing."

By one P.M., Chavez and Armstrong had finished their courtroom duties and retreated to the courthouse cafeteria to discuss the next day's schedule.

"I became a prosecutor because you can do more good as one than, say, a defense attorney," Armstrong said. "A public defender can sit up there and yell and scream all day long, but unless he can convince the prosecutor to go along with him, he's screwed. A prosecutor can decide to dismiss a case, plea-bargain a case, or put a case on trial. Prosecutors wield the power."

Armstrong said he had a personal reason for wanting to help the mentally ill. An uncle of his had had schizophrenia and had been put into a state mental hospital years ago. One day his uncle had been taken by an attendant on an errand and left locked in a car for several hours on a blistering day. He was dead when the driver returned. "That affected me," Armstrong said. "Most of the mentally ill defendants whom we deal with are *not* criminals. They didn't have any concept of what they were doing when they committed a crime. If the point of prison is punishment and rehabilitation, then what are these people being rehabilitated from—their mental illness? What are they being punished for—their mental illness? It's in society's best interest to help them get treatment, not lock them up."

"The question we ask ourselves every day on every case is: Was there criminal intent?" added Chavez. "That's the most difficult part of our job. You can't assume every mentally ill defendant should go free. Some burglars and armed robbers are mentally ill, but they deserve to be punished because crime is how they make their living. I think we do a good job of sorting them out."

Sam Konell waltzed over to where we were sitting. "I've decided to do the scholarship you wanted for the bipolar kid," he told Chavez. Without waiting for an invitation, the patient broker pulled out a chair, sat down, and opened his notebook. "Now I've got a few cases I'd like to discuss."

I excused myself and walked outside the building. I'd been impressed by Chavez and Armstrong. Both were sincere and hardworking, and clearly had the best of intentions. Still, I felt a sense of anger—not at them but at the randomness of what I'd just witnessed. If an inmate had health insurance, Sam Konell stepped in to rescue him. If not, the inmate lingered in jail. That was hardly blind justice. The system also seemed topsy-turvy. The public defender's priority had been to get his clients released no matter what their mental state. It was the prosecutors who had been working to get them treatment.

But there was something that bothered me even more. Chavez and I had chosen today to meet by random. Yet I'd stumbled into a court hearing where a mentally ill man had been arrested, apparently for little reason, and imprisoned on the ninth floor for nearly thirty days without anyone except Dr. Poitier noticing. I'd seen a judge become frustrated because he didn't have anywhere to send a mentally ill and mentally retarded defendant who couldn't stop masturbating in public. *If I'd happened upon these two cases completely by chance, how many others like them were out there? How many went unnoticed every day in the courthouse? How many other mentally ill inmates had slipped into jail under the radar or were being shuffled between the jail and forensic hospital simply because no one knew what else to do with them, or, as the psychiatrist had so aptly put it, because there really was "no place" for them "in our society"?*

I crossed the street from the courthouse to the jail. I wanted to talk to Dr. Poitier about what I'd observed, but before I reached the ninth floor I bumped into a social worker.

"Hey, you're back," she said. "I guess you heard what happened while you were gone this last time around?" Without waiting for my reply, she filled me in. As soon as she finished, I spun around, left the jail, and drove immediately to South Beach.

My conversation with Dr. Poitier would have to wait. There was someone there I had to see.

Chapter 30

was looking for Freddie Gilbert.

I Because of Judge Leifman's interest in him, Gilbert had received the finest care available at the Jackson Memorial Hospital Mental Health Center. The results had been dramatic. Arrested originally for panhandling and trespassing and because he was a "sanitary nuisance," the homeless chronic schizophrenic had been transformed. Six months of intensive treatment had turned him into a well-groomed and coherent patient. Everyone at the center understood how important his recovery was. If someone as severely mentally ill as Gilbert could be rescued, there was hope for the city's other homeless psychotics.

When Gilbert's forced treatment ended, the charges filed against him had been dismissed and a hospital case manager had arranged for him to move into an ALF. Expectations had been high on his discharge day at the hospital, and Gilbert had seemed eager to please. He had assured his therapists that this time he was going to continue taking his antipsychotic medicine, and he also promised them that he would not return to living on the streets.

But three days into his newfound freedom, Gilbert went for a walk and didn't return to his room inside the boardinghouse. A short while later, Judge Leifman was told that Freddie Gilbert had been seen loitering at the same South Beach corner where he had first been arrested. Within a month, Gilbert had reportedly decompensated and was as mentally disturbed as he had been before he had been treated. Six months of intensive treatment and a cocktail of powerful antipsychotic medicines hadn't kept Gilbert from regressing. The criticism that Dr. Poitier had gotten for testifying at Gilbert's Baker Act commitment hearing and the expense, time, and efforts of Gilbert's doctors and therapists had been for naught. Judge Leifman's attempt to help him had failed.

I stopped at a South Beach convenience store on my way to find Gilbert and bought a carton of cigarettes. He had asked me repeatedly for smokes when I'd interviewed him midway through his treatment protocol, and I thought he might be willing to speak to me again if I arrived with a gift. Moments later, I spied him entering an alley. His clothes were filthy, his hair unkempt. I parked, grabbed the cigarettes, and went after him. When I turned the alley's corner, Gilbert was searching through a trash Dumpster.

"Hello," I called out, stopping about ten feet away.

Gilbert glanced at me, but there was no friendly hint of recognition.

"Remember me? We talked in the hospital. I met you in jail on the ninth floor. I'm writing a book."

He didn't reply.

"I have cigarettes." I held up the carton. "They're for you."

But Gilbert didn't reach for them.

"How'ya feeling today?" I wasn't sure he could still speak. He had only grunted when he was psychotic in the jail.

"Go away," he said. He closed his eyes.

"Freddie, here, take the cigarettes." I placed them on the pavement and stepped away. He peeked through half-shut lids. Stepping forward, he snatched the carton and immediately recoiled.

"I'd like to talk to you," I explained.

Gilbert lifted his forefinger to his lips. "Sssh." He squeezed his eyelids shut. "Go away!"

"Don't you remember seeing me in the jail? Or in the hospital?"

"Go away!" he said. His eyes were still closed.

Because Gilbert was keeping his eyes closed, I wondered if he thought that I was one of the "ghosts" he saw whenever he was hallucinating.

I backed out of the alley and returned to my car for the drive to my Miami motel. I was staying in an older two-story building near the airport with rooms that had outside entrances. I climbed the concrete staircase and unlocked the door to my unit. By this point, I had made a half dozen trips to Miami and had stacks of notepads filled with interviews. I thought about some of the mentally ill characters whom I'd met. Ted Jackson was still calling my cell phone each night at eight o'clock from his mother's house in Ohio to let me know that he hadn't been arrested. April Hernandez and Jason Gilly had moved into Jackie's house. William Weaver Jr. was in a long-term-care facility just down the street from my motel. I'd recently spoken to Susan Wagner, whose sister, Deidra Sanbourne, had died after being discharged from a state hospital.

From the start, I knew I would have a difficult time finding a "success" story in Miami. I had, after all, chosen the ninth floor as my base. But of all the inmates whose lives I had been shadowing, Freddie Gilbert had seemed the best positioned for a dramatic transformation. He had been severely and chronically mentally ill for years—but he had also received the very best treatment available.

It hadn't worked. And that bothered me.

I stepped out onto the balcony and drew in a breath of Florida's sultry night air. It wasn't exhaustion that was causing the sense of sadness that I felt. It was a lack of hope. I wanted to find a glimmer of promise—not only because I wanted to include an inspiring story in this book, but because I wanted to believe that my son was not doomed to the grim realities that I'd found here.

I thought about Renee Turolla and how she had spent two years studying the mentally ill in the Miami jail during the early 1980s. Had she discovered something that I was missing?

Think.

I remembered one of the footnotes in her thick analysis. Turolla had mentioned a treatment program called Passageway. I had been curious about it because she had written that the program had been created to help the most feared and most hated of all the mentally ill. Its clients were deeply troubled prisoners who had committed horrible crimes, and yet Passageway had helped them safely reenter society.

I returned to my room and called Rachel Diaz. She had helped launch the Miami NAMI chapter in 1980, five years before Turolla had published her findings. I figured Diaz probably would have heard about Passageway and could tell me more about it. I explained what I wanted as soon as she answered.

Diaz laughed. Had she heard about Passageway? "I'm on its board of directors," she said.

Chapter 31

lthough I had been given directions, I drove by Passageway twice without spotting it. There was no sign outside
its dull-looking building, which was tucked between old
warehouses and vacant lots in an industrial area in
Miami. I rapped on a metal door and was buzzed in and led to Tom Mullen's office. He was the program's founder and director.

Mullen was wearing worn denim jeans, an inexpensive cotton turtle-
neck, and a navy-blue sports jacket with badly frayed sleeves. In his late
fifties, he already had snow-white hair that tapered into an all-white
beard. He had a reputation for having a dry wit and strong opinions
about nearly everything, and for being esoteric when he spoke.

I asked about his background and why he had started Passageway.
He said he'd been reared in a tough Irish Catholic neighborhood in the
Bronx. When he was fifteen, his father had been swept overboard and
drowned during a nor'easter while fishing with friends in the Atlantic
Ocean. Afraid that her teenage son might become a hooligan, Mullen's
mother had sought help from the Marist Brothers, a religious order
whose members dedicate their lives to helping the underprivileged. The
group took Mullen under its wing, and he eventually joined the order
and was sent to teach in Miami.

In 1968, a chance meeting with Father Daniel Berrigan changed Mullen's life. At the time, Berrigan was awaiting sentencing for using homemade napalm to destroy draft board records in protest of the Vietnam War. He urged Mullen to put his life "at risk" in service to his faith. Mullen quit his job, returned to New York, and began working in soup kitchens. Two years later, the archdiocese in Miami recruited him to run a methadone clinic that it operated for heroin addicts.

Almost from the start, Mullen proved difficult to control. When church leaders learned that he was allowing social workers at the clinic to discuss the pros and cons of abortion with pregnant drug abusers, there were calls for his resignation. Although Mullen was not a priest, firing a Marist brother was not something the archdiocese wanted to do.

At about this same time, Florida was in the midst of emptying its state mental hospitals, and psychotic inmates started showing up in jails. The city ran several halfway houses for ex-offenders, but none was equipped to deal with disturbed inmates. The city turned to the federal government for help, and it gave Miami a $100,000 grant to open a halfway house specifically for mentally ill ex-offenders. The city passed that grant along to the archdiocese, and it asked Mullen if he would resign from directing the methadone clinic and take charge of opening the halfway house.

He agreed. But a few weeks later, the church's lawyers began getting nervous—not about Mullen but about the entire halfway house idea. What if a crazed ex-offender living there committed a violent crime? His victims or their heirs might sue the church. To protect itself, the archdiocese asked the city to indemnify it from all future lawsuits. When the city refused, the church decided to return the $100,000 and scuttle the project.

Mullen was incensed and also out of a job. So he began searching for a way to go forward with the halfway house project on his own. He contacted Mel Black, a local attorney who specialized in mental health law, and in 1981 the two of them incorporated Passageway. The city awarded Mullen the $100,000 federal grant, but even with that burst of cash, he was flying without a safety net. Passageway had no insurance to protect it from lawsuits, and after the archdiocese backed out, Mullen had trouble finding a landlord willing to rent him space. Finally, he got one to lease him a dilapidated building in one of the city's most dangerous areas. One of his mentally ill parolees was mugged the first week Passageway opened. Things didn't get any easier.

No banks would loan Mullen money, and start-up costs quickly ate through the $100,000. Still, he somehow found a way to limp along. In 1982, he caught a break. Governor Bob Graham had promised residents in Pembroke Pines that if they voted for him, he'd shut down a state forensic unit in their community. He offered to pay Passageway $90,000 to take responsibility for the prison's sixty patients. Those funds kept the fledgling halfway house open, and Mullen made certain the new arrivals stayed out of trouble. Passageway was soon winning accolades from the courts and state agencies for Mullen's handling of the mentally ill. "It's a model for the state, maybe even for the nation," a Florida official boasted after a state-run inspection. "It's one of the few programs that really work."

Word quickly spread across Florida, and judges, jails, forensic hospitals, and prisons began asking Mullen to take in more clients. He decided to move into a bigger and safer building in northern Miami. By chance, a *Miami Herald* reporter heard about Passageway. She contacted Mullen, and he granted her an interview and also allowed her to talk to several ex-offenders in the program. But first, he made her promise not to reveal the halfway house's new address.

The *Herald* published her account in April 1984 under the headline "Halfway House for Insane Draws Praise, Protests." The reporter described how two murderers convicted of sensational crimes were being groomed by Mullen to reenter the community even though they both were still mentally ill. She then quoted an angry local police chief who accused Mullen of sneaking into his jurisdiction. Much to Mullen's horror, she also revealed where Passageway was located.

The halfway house's unsuspecting neighbors were aghast. They held an emergency community meeting and pressured Passageway's landlord into evicting Mullen. He was forced to stash his residents in hotels while he searched for another building. He found an old motel on the outskirts of town that seemed perfect. But before he could finalize the deal, word leaked out.

"We don't want the thing here," an upset neighbor told the *Herald*, which was following up on the ongoing controversy. "If one of these screwballs were to get loose, God knows what would happen!"

Angry protesters showed up at the county zoning board when Mullen asked it for a variance so he could move into the motel. It rejected his request. Mullen appealed, and the dogfight eventually ended up before the Miami-Dade County Commission, the elected body that governs the entire county. Mullen brought letters of support from several psychiatrists to a public hearing about his request. His opponents arrived with a petition signed by more than *ten thousand* voters. They were not only opposed to Passageway's moving into the motel, they didn't want the halfway house to operate *anywhere* in the entire county. The commission voted six to two against Mullen.

Mullen went back to knocking on doors, but no landlord would rent him space. The situation became so desperate that state officials finally were forced to step in. They agreed to let his few remaining clients live in a state-run hospital in Lantana, sixty miles north of Miami, for three months while he continued his search. If Mullen didn't find a new facility by then, Passageway would be closed.

As soon as the Lantana hospital's employees heard the news, they threatened to strike unless they were given "hazardous duty" pay. Meanwhile, protesters in Miami asked the county commission to pass a law that would ban Passageway from lodging its clients in hotel rooms or using meeting halls to conduct its rehabilitation program. They were trying to tighten the noose around Mullen's neck and make certain he couldn't slip back into town.

It looked as if Passageway's vocal opponents were going to succeed in shutting down the halfway house, but just before time was about to run out, Mullen received help from an unlikely source. Janet Reno was the prosecutor in Miami-Dade County, and she told Mullen about an undeveloped piece of land that the county wasn't using. She then pulled political strings so the property fell into his hands. With Reno's backing, Mullen was able to raise enough money through a private bond issue for Passageway to erect its own building. When it was finished, he held an open house and invited Reno. But he didn't tip off the *Herald.* Although two decades had passed, Passageway still didn't post any signs outside its doors, and I was the first reporter to be let inside since the controversy.

The halfway house operated from a two-story, U-shaped building, encircled around its back by a tall chain-link fence topped with razor wire. The ground level held offices, classrooms, a lobby, a dining area, and a kitchen. The second floor was a dormitory designed to accommodate thirty-eight residents. Only sixteen were allowed to live there, however. This was an arbitrary federal restriction that was known nationally as the "sixteen-bed rule." Simply put, the federal government would not pay Medicaid or many other federal benefits to mental patients who lived in a facility that contained more than sixteen beds. The restriction had been adopted as part of the government's campaign to shut down large state mental hospitals through deinstitutionalization. It forced patients to move into smaller treatment facilities. Mullen thought it stupid.

For years, Passageway had been allowed to ignore the sixteen-bed restriction. Inspectors had turned a blind eye because they knew how desperately Florida needed the halfway house. But in 2003, Mullen had been told to comply. He'd been given a month to move twenty-four residents out of Passageway and into low-income housing.

Mullen was still bitter about that forced exodus. Passageway now had empty bedrooms that couldn't be used. Meanwhile, the federal government was paying rent to keep twenty-four former Passageway residents in apartments that weren't nearly as comfortable or as safe as their old dorm rooms. "I've got judges who want to send clients to us," he explained, "but I can't accept them even though I've got empty rooms. It's frustrating."

Despite the hysteria that had nearly driven Passageway out of business in the 1980s, Mullen said the halfway house had never had a client commit a serious crime against anyone in its neighborhood. That didn't mean Passageway's clients weren't dangerous. Most were. But Passageway had several safeguards built into its program to protect the public from the so-called "criminally insane."

The first was a thorough screening process. Passageway accepted only residents who voluntarily took antipsychotic medication. If a client stopped or refused, he was immediately sent back to the hospital, jail, or prison where he'd come from.

"This isn't a civil rights issue here," Mullen explained. "People with serious mental disorders are sick and they must take their medication. They have to comply. Otherwise, we won't take them."

Newly arrived clients also were required to live inside Passageway's locked compound until the staff decided they were ready to move into an outside apartment with another resident. Even then, they were required to report to Passageway every day.

"It takes time for a person who's been taking medication to decompensate," Mullen explained. "There are warning signs. We should be able to see in advance when someone is beginning to lose it." Passageway's psychiatrist kept a close watch on all residents, and if Mullen decided one of them had become dangerous, he was sent packing.

"The *Miami Herald* article and the problems it caused were a clear reminder to all of us about how much our clients are loathed in the community," Mullen said. "We can't afford a single mistake."

Passageway's safeguards sounded straightforward to me. Clients had to take and stay on their antipsychotic medications, and they had to be carefully monitored. "Is the therapy here different from other treatment programs?" I asked. "Is that why your program is so successful?"

"No," Mullen replied. "Our therapy is pretty standard stuff."

"Then why is Passageway unique? You've got to be doing something different from other programs. What makes your halfway house succeed when others fail?"

Mullen suggested that I find out that answer on my own. He had already agreed to let me spend several weeks at Passageway. He led me out into the courtyard, where a therapy group was in session. I took a seat in a plastic patio chair and began listening to a resident describe what it feels like when a voice in your head tells you to kill yourself.

Dunja Patriski-James, a young social worker, distributed a worksheet to students in her morning Passageway therapy class. The instructions said:

Most major mental illnesses can be divided into two major categories. 1. Disorders of mood/affect. 2. Disorders of thought/perception.

"Depression and bipolar disorder," Patriski-James explained, "are mood disorders, because you either feel very happy or feel very sad. But schizophrenia is a thought disorder, because it makes you hear and see things that aren't really there." She told her students to write down three symptoms of a mood disorder on the left side of the worksheet and three examples of a thought disorder on the right side. At the bottom, they were instructed to list three symptoms that they had personally experienced. After they finished, they were supposed to compare the lists and decide if they had a mood or a thought disorder. I had already spent several days in Patriski-James's class, so I knew the clients by their first names. Angela raised her hand and said, "My doctor said I'm schizoaffective. What's that?"

"It's both," Patriski-James replied. "It's a mood and a thought disorder. People who have it go through drastic mood swings and also hallucinate."

Angela seemed pleased to learn her illness bridged the gap. I was sitting next to Carl, a thin man in his mid-thirties. I had asked him earlier if I could spend the day with him. Under "Examples of a Mood Disorder," he wrote: *"Sad, can't sleep, anxiety."* Under thought disorder, he scribbled: *"Hearing voices, thinking you got magic powers, can fly."* In the bottom space, he listed three symptoms that he had personally experienced: *"Being cut in half, having eyes gouged out, seeing dead people rise out of sidewalk."*

At the bottom of the worksheet, he concluded that he had *schizophrenia*. Carl finished faster than most. During the six years that he'd lived at Passageway, he'd filled out dozens of similar worksheets. He had another five years to go before he could be released. Carl had been sent to Passageway from a state forensic hospital after he'd been found not guilty by reason of insanity of an attempted murder.

Robert and Allaf were seated at the same table as Carl and I. At age twenty, Robert was Passageway's youngest client. He also stood out because he was from a well-connected Palm Beach family. Unlike the other residents, he was dressed in pressed khaki pants, a designer Polo shirt, and leather boat shoes without socks. Carl had told me earlier that he didn't believe Robert was mentally ill. Robert had a drug problem. But his parents had used their political connections to get a judge to put him in Passageway rather than prison. No one knew much about Allaf. His head was tilted back, his mouth was gaped open, and he was snoring. He'd been asleep every morning that I'd been in the class. Allaf had just arrived at Passageway, and its psychiatrist, Dr. Maraima Trujillo, was still trying to adjust his medication so he wasn't always drowsy.

"Okay, let's go over your answers," Patriski-James said. "What'd you write, Guy?" Guy was a big man in his early thirties who had played a year of college football in Alabama before his breakdown. Carl had met Guy on the ninth floor at the jail, but they hadn't become friends until they both were sent to Passageway. "My disorder is severe depression," Guy told the group. "It's a mood disorder. It makes me not care if I'm alive." He glanced up from his worksheet and said, "When I get sad, I don't even care about my daughter, and she's the most important part of my life. Why's that?"

"No one really knows what causes you to be sad," Patriski-James replied. "All the doctors can do is treat your symptoms with medications." She asked him, "What red flags do you need to recognize?"

"If I get sad for no reason—that's a red flag."

"That's right," Patriski-James said. She spent several minutes explaining how it was okay to feel sad if something bad happened. But feeling depressed for no reason was a signal to Guy that his illness was seeping back into his thoughts.

"What should you do, Guy," she asked, "if you begin to feel sad for no reason?"

"Talk about it to someone I trust."

"Yeah," Carl volunteered. "If you're hearing voices in your head, then you need to ask someone if they're hearing 'em too, and if they're hearing 'em too, then both of you are nuts."

Carl laughed at his joke, but Patriski-James didn't. She said, "It's important for everyone to have a buddy who can be your sounding board. Someone you can check with if you begin to see red flags. Now, what do you do, Guy, if your buddy tells you that you're becoming depressed?"

"Tell the doctor," Guy replied.

"Tell Tom Mullen or someone else in Passageway," Carl volunteered. After his last comment, he didn't want Patriski-James to think he wasn't taking the class seriously.

"Very good," she replied.

There were eight other students sitting in the courtyard. John was at a table across from ours. He was wearing black combat boots and army fatigues and had a dozen gold-plated chains dangling from his neck. John liked to dress in a different outfit each day. Yesterday, he'd worn his football ensemble: an oversized Miami Dolphins jersey, sweatpants, and sneakers. Although he liked to participate in class, he couldn't read. That's why John always sat at the same table as Henry—because Henry helped him decipher words. Henry had spent fifteen years in Passageway, making him its longest-held client. Angela had been here eight. She and Henry lived together in an apartment several blocks from the compound. Angela was here because she had murdered one of her own children. Henry had lit himself on fire. The gasoline had felt cold on his skin, he told the group, until he'd struck a match. His neck and arms were still badly scarred, but his face hadn't been burned.

Julio was sitting at a third patio table. He was from Chile and always carried a book with him. His favorite subject was philosophy. He had been on a vacation in Florida with his parents when he'd attacked a child. Julio had thought the boy was Satan in disguise. Next to him was Mary. She was shy and rarely spoke. But she liked to paint, and several of her pictures were hanging in the lobby. Thomas and Paul were sitting with Julio and Mary. They were roommates outside the compound and were about to be released from the program. Thomas had attacked his father and sister seven years before; he thought they were plotting to kill him. Now he attended classes at the University of Miami. Paul already had earned a degree in psychology during his time in Passageway. He'd been there for five years, since he had tried to murder his mother.

It was just about Carl's turn to read his worksheet out loud when Tom Mullen interrupted the class to introduce a potential new class member. Fidel was in his sixties and was spending several days visiting Passageway to see if he fit in. Although Mullen was introducing him to the group for the first time, word had already spread through Passageway about Fidel, and everyone knew that he had murdered his brother, his brother's wife, and a neighbor during a schizophrenic hallucination. Fidel sat down at our table between Carl and me.

Patriski-James had everyone introduce himself to Fidel, and by the time all were finished, it was nearly 11:15 A.M. and class was over. I followed Carl into the kitchen, where Passageway's meal supervisor, Randy Flowers, was adding taco spices to ground beef left over from yesterday's lunch of hamburgers. Carl had kitchen duty, which meant that he was responsible for helping serve lunch. He liked Passageway's food, although he would have preferred more dishes like his mother made, such as collard greens and chitlins. His parents had been sharecroppers in Mississippi. "I think only us blacks here would like greens," he volunteered. "We got some blacks, some whites, some Hispanics, no one knows what Allaf is—some kind of Arab—but all of us are crazy just the same," he said.

Carl said he had been a picky eater when he was a youngster, but that ended after he spent nine years living under Miami's Interstate 95 highway bridges. "I was always hungry—always—when I was homeless, and I was afraid, too."

"Of what?" I asked.

"Of damn near everything—being arrested, being beaten up by the cops. Two times, I was attacked by teenagers who thought it was funny. Living on the streets is rough!"

There had been one night, however, when he had felt a magical experience. He'd been sleeping in a cardboard box when he heard someone call him. He'd crawled out and looked around, but didn't see anyone. Then he heard his name again.

"Carl." He glanced up at the sky. "There were no clouds," he said, "and the stars were brighter than anything I'd ever seen. It was God talking to me."

Carl stayed awake the rest of the night to see what God wanted. But God didn't talk to him.

In the morning, he went looking for food, and when he got back, the cardboard box was gone. "I always wondered if God only talked to whoever was sleeping in that box." Mullen came through the kitchen, and everyone working there stopped what they were doing and said, "Hello, Tom." He said hello and called each of them by their first name. Saying hello was encouraged at Passageway. Sometimes Carl said hello to the same person more than a dozen times during the day. If he saw Guy in the courtyard, he said hello. If he bumped into Guy a few moments later in the lobby, he said hello again. Saying hello showed you were not retreating into your own delusional world. Whenever Carl said hello and someone didn't say hello back, he wondered why.

After lunch, everyone had "open time," so Carl went into the lobby to play eightball at a tired old pool table with warped cues. On a good day he could beat almost everyone. Julio was sitting on a sofa nearby, reading his book. Allaf was sleeping in an oversized chair. Robert was listening to a tape about the Kabbalah.

Life in Passageway was intentionally kept slow-paced and routine. Each day was scheduled to be much like the day before. Between 8:30 and 9 A.M., clients did their morning chores. Tasks were assigned based on capabilities. Some jobs were as simple as brushing the pool table. A kitchen assignment was more demanding. Therapy sessions began at 9:30 A.M. and ended at 11:15 A.M., with a cigarette break in between. Nearly everyone smoked, including the staff. The clients were divided into three morning therapy classes, but the same material was used in each. The lessons focused on teaching residents how to recognize "red flag" warnings and how important it was for them to *always* take their medication. At least once a week, the three groups joined together for a field trip. The social workers used the excursions to teach basic living skills: how to shop, how to budget.

After lunch, clients had three hours of open time. They were expected to socialize during this period. They could play dominoes, watch television, smoke, listen to music, or chat. But they were supposed to do it in the lobby or courtyard with other residents. This was also when they could meet with their case managers, and with Passageway's psychiatrist, Dr. Maraima Trujillo.

Carl always shot pool, and after he won his eightball match, he went to see his case manager, Steve Henderson. Before Carl was arrested, he had fathered a child, and the state had sent him a letter last week informing him that he owed $19,000 in child support payments. His case manager was helping Carl draft a letter that explained why he hadn't been paying support—since he'd been sent to jail right after the baby's birth.

Passageway's ultimate goal was to help its clients move into the community and live on their own. But that didn't mean they would be able to support themselves by working at full-time jobs, marry, or have families. For most of them, that American dream was too far of a reach. They would survive on federal and state assistance, which they'd use to pay for their medicines, rent, food, and clothing.

After Carl finished with his case manager, I followed him into the courtyard, where we sat down next to Henry. We were soon joined by Albert Jones, who, at age sixty-eight, was the oldest client in the program. In the 1960s, he'd done a stint in California's San Quentin prison and he'd spent most of his life locked either in jails or in mental institutions because of his paranoia and schizophrenia. Albert was wearing a dark-wine-colored felt derby that he'd bought for five bucks at a secondhand shop. He'd found a ruby-red shirt for seventy-five cents a couple of days later that matched, giving him what he described as a "Superfly" look—a reference to a 1972 blaxploitation movie.

I was curious about some of the answers I'd seen Carl write on his worksheet that morning in class, so I asked, "What did you mean when you wrote you'd been cut in half and had your eyes gouged out?"

"I was walking down this sidewalk—when I was homeless and really crazy—and I saw a big black vertical line directly in front of me," he said. "It was one of them saw blades like they use to cut them big logs and it was aimed directly at me. I tried to get out of the way, but my feet wouldn't move, so I couldn't do anything but take it."

He paused to collect his thoughts and then said, "That motherfucker cut me right in half. I could feel it cut through my skin and my bones and my heart and my lungs. It cut my head plum in half."

I started to grin, but Henry and Albert remained stone-faced.

"Now, I know I am sitting here today all in one piece, but I'm telling you I know what it *feels* like to be chopped in half, because in my crazy head that was exactly what happened. It was no different than if you'd grabbed a knife and stabbed me with it right now. I'd feel the pain just like I felt then because my mind told me it was happening."

When no one said anything, Carl continued. "Another time, I was walking down the street and peoples I'd knowed who were dead started rising up from the sidewalk. They just lifted out of the ground like they was in some Michael Jackson 'Thriller' video. These people were like zombies and they started coming after me, so I started running. Now, this shit sounds funny now, but in my head it was just as real as the four of us sitting here."

"Carl," I said, "if the police had taken you to the hospital and asked if you wanted to be given medicine, would you have gone willingly?"

"Hell no! When you're crazy like that, your paranoia sinks in and you think everyone's trying to poison you."

"Would you have fought them?"

"Absolutely, and I got several ass-kickings to prove it."

"So you would have rather been left alone on the streets than forced to take medicine?"

"Yes and no. I would have been angry and fought, but if they had stuffed pills down my throat, I would have kissed their asses and thanked them once I got my mind back, because no one wants to be crazy like that."

Carl had smoked his last cigarette and he wanted another one, but he'd already bummed several from Henry. For several moments, no one at the table said anything. This wasn't unusual at Passageway. Most clients had a difficult time making small talk, even Carl. I'd discovered that they were afraid they might say something stupid.

"Hey," Carl said, addressing Henry. "Blow some smoke over here, will you? I know you can't spare another cigarette, but you can at least give me a taste, can't you?" Henry blew a puff toward him.

"Don't be a bitch," Carl said, waving his palms toward his face, fanning the smoke closer. "Give me more. More."

Albert pulled a cigarette from his shirt pocket and offered it to Carl. "Praise the Lord!" Carl declared.

At three o'clock, free time ended and everyone was required to report inside the dining hall for a daily meeting. The staff generally made a few announcements, and then the clients who lived outside the compound were free to go. Some went to night school. But most walked or rode the bus home, fixed dinner, and went to bed around five o'clock. This was largely due to the sleepiness from the medications they took.

The sixteen residents who stayed behind in the dorm were on their own for the rest of the evening, but most of them went to bed right after dinner, too.

Henry and Albert left the building after the three-o'clock meeting, so Carl returned to the courtyard. He spotted Robert listening to music through headphones. Carl said his obligatory "Hello, Robert," but kept on moving. He bummed a cigarette from a resident named Rick and went to the back of the building, where he sat down in an old metal folding chair and stared through the chain-link fence at the world outside.

"People don't understand how ashamed you feel because you're so different—ashamed and embarrassed and damn angry, too. I hurt people who I loved when I was crazy, and now they're all scared of me. All them doctors say it's chemicals in your brain and what you got is no different than that disease old President Reagan had. But that's bullshit! People aren't afraid of someone who has whatever it's called."

"Alzheimer's disease," I volunteered.

"Yeah, I mean, I even felt sorry for that old bastard myself. But they don't feel sorry for someone who is schizophrenic. You know what I hate? I hate it whenever I hear someone say they acting 'schizo.' What they mean is they are acting like they got two different personalities. Being schizophrenic ain't anything like that."

"What's it like?"

The afternoon temperature was in the high nineties, and beads of sweat had started to dot Carl's forehead. "It's fucked up, man. You want to know what it's like? How do I know you are here right now? How do I know I'm not imagining all this? Close your eyes. What if when you opened your eyes, you discovered you was now in New York City instead of at Passageway in Miami? Then you closed them again and when you opened them you were in Los Angeles? Or maybe New Orleans? Or Russia? What if every time you opened your eyes it was like you were somewhere else? That's what it's like sometimes for me. You ever have a dream where you flew? Them's the kind of things my brain tells me is true and I can't tell."

He sucked on his cigarette as long as he possibly could, and when he finished it, he said, "Damn it, I got to find someone to give me another one." He wiped his face with his palms. "Don't tell Tom this, but I still hear voices sometimes. I take my medicine, but I hear them. What you got to understand is people like me—it's just bad, man. We have fucked-up brains, and when your own goddamn brain starts fucking with you, you're not just fucked up a little bit, you're totally fucked up."

Albert Jones was dead. The oldest client in Passageway, who loved to wear colorful derby hats, died in his sleep. Jeffery Turner's end was not so peaceful. The Miami police found his body floating in a canal. They initially thought he might have been murdered, but when they learned he was a client at Passageway, they ruled it a suicide.

Both men's deaths hit the other residents hard, especially Turner's. In his mid-thirties, he had been at the halfway house thirteen years and had frequently been held up as an example to the others as someone who had overcome the symptoms of bipolar disorder. His death undercut everyone's confidence. *If he had killed himself, what chance did they have?*

Tom Mullen wanted to know why Turner had committed suicide. It didn't take him long to find out. Turner had gotten a job bagging groceries at a supermarket and had begun dating a coworker. He'd kept their romance secret from the Passageway staff because he was afraid his case manager would force him to tell his girlfriend about his mental illness. After several weeks, the woman had ended their romance. That same night, Turner had drowned himself.

Turner's mother asked Mullen to give the eulogy at her son's funeral, but she told him not to mention that Turner was mentally ill. Some of her relatives didn't know.

Dunja Patriski-James talked about both men's deaths in her morning therapy session. Carl didn't say much during the discussion. He and Turner hadn't liked each other. "I beat him playing pool and people wouldn't talk to me for days around here because he was so popular," Carl confided to me. "No one was supposed to beat the mighty Mr. Turner at anything. People were holding him up to be somebody really important, but he was just like the rest of us loony birds."

Carl had felt differently about Albert Jones. "That old man had style. I'll miss him."

Patriski-James used Turner's suicide to warn her students about how stressful romantic relationships could be. A few days later, she handed out a worksheet. It was illustrated with a drawing of a soldier riding in a World War Two tank. The sheet explained that soldiers used weapons to fight in a war. It asked what tools a mentally ill person needed in his ongoing battle. Life in Passageway was gradually returning to normal.

Angela entered the hospital because doctors were worried she might be developing diabetes. Guy moved into Angela's empty chair during therapy class to be near Henry, which was good, because they both suffered from severe depression and they could watch for each other's red flags. Julio finished a book about Descartes and was disappointed the only person with whom he could discuss it was Mullen. John found a Nehru jacket in a secondhand-clothing shop and began wearing his new outfit to class. Allaf was finally able to stay awake. Fidel joined the class permanently but still didn't say much. Robert got into trouble for stealing medication to get high. And Carl kept bumming cigarettes.

One morning, Thomas told the class that this would be his last day in Passageway. The judge overseeing his case had signed an order releasing him. His sister and her husband had agreed to let him live with them in Virginia. She'd gotten him a job at a landscaping company. After class, Carl, Guy, and Henry invited Thomas to smoke a cigarette with them in the courtyard. Because he was leaving, Thomas was a celebrity. Carl asked if he was nervous.

"I'll be okay if I stay away from the beer," Thomas said. Passageway didn't allow anyone to drink or use illegal drugs. But once Thomas was released, he could drink alcohol without violating his parole. That worried him, since he had a drinking problem as well as schizoaffective disorder. "It's like they say at my AA meetings, 'One beer is too many and a thousand is not enough,'" he explained.

"What's the first thing you're going to do when you get to Virginia?" Carl asked.

"Earn enough money to buy a car. I'd like to get a girlfriend, but my sister's already told me I can't bring girls into the house. She's real religious. I'll need a car if I want to go on dates."

Carl laughed. "The faster you get a car, the faster you can get some sex."

"Yeah, but I don't want to do anything to upset my sister."

Thomas said he still felt badly about how he'd punched her in the face when he'd been paranoid, drunk, delusional, and certain she was plotting to murder him seven years ago. "I don't think she's afraid of me anymore, but I wouldn't blame her if she was. I'll just take my medication, stay away from the beer, and take things slow."

Another client came outside into the courtyard and challenged Thomas to a game of eightball. As soon as he was gone, Carl said, "I think he'll make it."

Henry said, "As long as he stays away from beer."

Guy said, "And women. If he gets involved with a woman, then he'll definitely start drinking beer."

The three of them laughed. And then Henry added, "I'm glad he's getting another shot."

"Yeah," Carl replied. "Hey, let me bum a cigarette."

The next afternoon I was talking to Sadie Sands, who was in charge of interviewing prospective clients, when we both heard a loud commotion in the lobby. It was Mullen arguing with a visitor. The outsider was a representative from the Bristol-Myers Squibb company who'd stopped by with samples of Abilify.

"How dare you make money off these people's illnesses," Mullen snapped. "You should be giving this medicine to these people for free."

Sands wasn't surprised. She had worked for Mullen since 1983, two years after he opened Passageway. "Tom feels passionately about our clients," she told me when we stepped back into her office. "Once a client asked if he could wash some of the staff members' cars. Tom said, 'Hell no!' He wasn't going to put a client in a position where he might be manipulated or taken advantage of by anyone. I've seen him well up in tears when he talks about how our clients are stigmatized. The *only* reason Passageway has survived is because of Tom, and the only reason it works is because of Tom."

Later, I stopped by Mullen's office. He was talking on the phone to a social worker at the jail. He was checking on a former Passageway client named LeRoy Clarkson who had been sent back to the ninth floor. When Mullen finished the call, I asked him what Clarkson had done that had gotten him booted out of Passageway.

"His story takes some explaining," Mullen replied.

In 1982, Clarkson was homeless, psychotic, and living on the streets of Miami. He became convinced one day that he was being spied on by a man who frequently walked by the highway underpass where Clarkson slept. He attacked the man and nearly beat him to death. Clarkson was found not guilty by reason of insanity and sent to a state mental hospital and then to Passageway. In 1988, a judge released him. He met a woman named Daphne and fell in love, and the two of them moved into an apartment.

Three years later, Clarkson showed up unexpectedly one morning at Passageway and asked to talk to Mullen.

"I did something last night," Clarkson told him.

"What'd you do?"

"I murdered Daphne."

Clarkson said he'd beaten her to death because she had been "putting roots" inside him. She was hiding "magic seeds" in his food at night. It was voodoo. Clarkson asked if he could move back into Passageway.

Sadie Sands kept an eye on Clarkson while Mullen and Lillian Menendez, Passageway's program director, went to check on Daphne. They found her lying on the couple's bed covered with blood. An iron bar was on the floor exactly where Clarkson said he'd left it. Mullen called the police and immediately launched his own investigation. He discovered that a psychiatrist had reduced Clarkson's medication from 80 milligrams a day to 20 milligrams. The doctor had wanted to see if Clarkson could get by on a lower dosage, but hadn't bothered to follow up and check on him, even after he had missed his next appointment.

Clarkson was charged with murdering Daphne but was found not guilty because he was insane. He was sent to Chattahoochee. Twelve years later, he asked if he could return to Passageway. Mullen sent Sands to interview him, and together they decided to let him come back. For the next three years, Clarkson lived inside the Passageway compound without causing any problems. In fact, he was a model client. But earlier this year, he started having problems with his medication again. He became aggressive. A week before I arrived at Passageway, Mullen had been forced to step between Clarkson and another client during an argument that had become heated. Mullen could tell Clarkson was losing control, so he called the police.

"Sending someone back is the hardest part of my job, but sometimes you simply don't have a choice," he said.

"What happens to him now?" I asked.

"He'll go back to the state forensic hospital and stay there until he's ready to come here again."

"You're going to take him back?" I asked in a shocked tone.

"Yes," Mullen said calmly. "If he meets our criteria, why wouldn't we?"

I said the obvious: Clarkson had already had two chances. He had spent six years in Passageway the first time around, had been released, and had killed his girlfriend. He'd come back twelve years later, done fine for three years, and then become threatening again. Sure, both of his mental breakdowns had been caused because of problems with his antipsychotic medication. But just the same, "Why risk taking him back?"

Mullen gave me a puzzled look and then said, "How many chances would you want us to give your son?"

My face turned bright red.

Mullen opened a desk drawer, removed an 8-by-10-inch sheet of white paper, and handed it to me. Every inch of it was covered with intricate scrawls that he'd made late one night when he had set out to diagram the "profound complexity of the human condition" based on the "external and internal forces that motivate and shape us."

He'd spent hours laboring on his chart, and when he'd finished, his scribbles had led him to a "fundamental truth" about life: *All of us are alone.*

"As each of us is confronted with our own complexity, then we are simultaneously confronted with the reality of our aloneness and isolation," he said. "To avoid being alone, human beings seek out relationships with others, either individually—as friends and lovers—or in families or by joining gangs, neighborhoods, clubs, or religious groups. The question then becomes, Where does the chronic mentally ill adult felony offender fit?"

Mullen's answer: nowhere.

"No group will accept him or her willingly into membership. What person wants to join with this mentally ill person in any kind of intimacy or trust? As a result, the most fragile of our brethren—mentally ill offenders—are the only ones without an escape from their aloneness. Among us all, they are the *most* alone, the *most* isolated."

This, in turn, had led Mullen to reach another conclusion. "The core, the bottom line, for Passageway, the rationale for the righteousness and the continuation of our service, is this: to help these mentally ill felons not be *alone*."

Mullen was just warming up. "What is a church? What is a parish?" he asked rhetorically. "A church is a group of people who congregate together to feel safe. A parish is a place where they can be inspired by one another and their leaders. It's a community where everyone is encouraged to follow a set of behaviors that will perpetuate their wellness. And that's what we have created here. Passageway is a parish. We *care* about one another. We are a community. That's our so-called 'secret to success.' Many of our clients have burned out everyone else who was part of their lives—their parents, their siblings, their spouses, their children. Who do they have left? No one. That's where Passageway comes in. It's that connection, that caring—the fact that we tell these people that their lives matter regardless of what they have done—that makes this program work. We're certainly not foolish about it. We're aware of the dangers and we watch for them. But we don't ever give up on anyone who is willing to work with us against their mental illness."

At Passageway, he concluded, "We never say anyone has run out of chances."

PART

FIVE

DÉJÀ VU

I attended a theater workshop to learn about playback theater: listening to true stories from the audience's lives and then having a group of performers reenact these stories on stage. Our leader got my story about my brother, Lee, out of me. The director had someone play me, someone else play Lee and someone else play Lee's schizophrenia. I watched as the actor playing Lee's illness stood on a chair perched alongside the actor playing Lee, whispering or yelling in his ear. When Lee moved, the actor playing the illness followed him, quietly hissing, sometimes roaring, sometimes talking sense and nonsense, never leaving his side. He never went to the other side of the room or sat politely in the background while Lee spoke. Even during quiet moments it was preparing for the next onslaught. It didn't back off. The actor playing Lee got really irritated. He tried to escape by turning, running or twisting and talking or yelling above the voice of the illness, but the illness didn't sit quietly. It didn't take turns and wait for other people to finish speaking the way actors in a play might. The illness knew its lines and relentlessly recited them. For me, it was a cognitive thump on the head to be confronted by the physical separation of Lee and his illness as embodied by the two performers. I saw and felt the disconnection. I understood a little better that Lee wasn't his illness. It wasn't his fault.

—*from "My Brother and Schizophrenia"*
by Susan Garrett

J	udy Robinson was fuming. She had sent Jeff to the pharmacy to get a refill of Zyprexa, his antipsychotic medication, but her son had returned empty-handed.

"They won't give me my pills," he said.

The NAMI advocate snatched up the telephone and called the pharmacist. He told her that a stop order had been placed on Jeff's prescription by Medicaid. Robinson knew the federal government was cutting back on how much it would pay for drugs. Several members of her monthly support group had received notices that said Medicaid would no longer pay for anything except the cheapest generic brands. An advocacy group called Florida Legal Services had filed a lawsuit, but it hadn't been able to stop the new cost-cutting rules. But the suit had forced Medicaid to create a grievance process. Patients could call a toll-free number and plead their case to an ombudsman if they felt the restrictions were going to harm their health.

Robinson dialed the ombudsman's number and listened to it ring. Finally, a recording came on telling her to call back during normal business hours between Monday and Friday. That made her even angrier. If a mentally ill patient needed medicine on a weekend, how was he supposed to get it? Luckily, Jeff had enough pills to carry him over.

A still-irked Robinson called again on Monday. She was told that Jeff wasn't being denied Zyprexa. His prescription had been stopped because he had asked for *two* different doses.

"But he needs two," Robinson protested. She told the ombudsman that Jeff's psychiatrists had spent months fine-tuning his prescription and had learned that the best dosage was exactly 12.5 milligrams. If he took less, he became anxious. If he took more, he became droopy. Unfortunately, Zyprexa didn't come in a 12.5 milligram pill. Jeff had to split a 5-milligram pill in half and take one piece of it with a 10-milligram tablet. While the ombudsman sounded sympathetic, she said there was nothing she could do. Medicaid had installed a new computer program that identified waste in its system and it had caught Jeff's double order and replaced it with a single one: a prescription for 15-milligram tablets.

"How are we supposed to break two and a half milligrams off of a fifteen-milligram pill?" Robinson asked.

The woman didn't know. Robinson asked to speak to her supervisor, and during the next four hours, she continued to plead her case to more than a dozen bureaucrats. But she got nowhere. Next she called the Eli Lilly company to learn if it could suggest some way Jeff could split 12.5 milligrams off a 15-milligram pill. No one from the company returned her calls.

"These are the irritants that drive me to conniptions," she said. "What these decisions do to a mentally ill person's life is secondary to Medicaid saving a miserly few dollars. Of course, if Jeff's stability is threatened, he could end up back in jail or in the hospital, and that will cost a lot, lot more. But you can't get anyone to listen. They figure you are just some excitable and overly concerned mother!"

A few days later, Robinson got more troubling news.

Jim DeFede, the *Miami Herald* columnist who frequently wrote about the mentally ill, called to tell her that the Miami-Dade County police had killed another psychotic suspect. The last time Robinson had spoken to DeFede was when he asked her to comment about that same department's fatal shooting of Robert Steven Mills III—Renee Sherman's son—outside his girlfriend's house. DeFede quickly outlined to Robinson what had happened in this new incident.

A forty-nine-year-old black man named Randy Carlos Baker had been walking home from visiting his cousin—on a sidewalk in a poor neighborhood—when a squad car pulled up next to him. There had been a robbery a few blocks away, and the patrolman asked Baker where he was going.

"I ain't done nothing. I'm going home," Baker replied, according to witnesses. The officer ordered Baker to stop walking and to answer his questions. At that point, Baker began to yell and wave his hands wildly in the air. The patrolman jumped out of his squad car and grabbed the mentally ill man. A neighbor standing across the street yelled, "He's not in his right mind!" But it was too late. The two began fighting.

Within moments, two female police officers arrived and joined the fray. All three cops were hitting Baker with their nightsticks. His cousin ran up to them and tried to intervene, but couldn't. Baker grabbed one of the batons and swung it at the two women, drawing blood. The patrolman drew his handgun, pointed it at the back of Baker's head, and fired. After he collapsed, the officer fired two more times into his body.

Columnist DeFede told Robinson that it appeared to be another example of a shooting that could have been avoided if the Miami-Dade County Police Department's officers had undergone Crisis Intervention Team training. Robinson agreed.

In his column the next day, DeFede unleashed his anger. He told readers that Baker did not have a criminal record and had not broken any laws when the police decided to question him. "Randy Baker should be alive today," he declared. But the columnist directed his harshest criticism not at the three officers but at their boss, Miami-Dade police director Carlos Alvarez, who had stubbornly refused to institute CIT training. DeFede noted that nearly all of the thirty-four municipalities in the county that operated their own police departments had added CIT training—except Alvarez's. He ended his column by quoting Robinson: "All the Miami-Dade police have done is drag their feet and now this is the result—another person is needlessly killed. And this is going to happen over and over again until they change their way of thinking."

A spokesman for Alvarez fired back the next day. "Are we now, as police officers, required to go, 'Excuse me, sir. While you're bashing my head in, can you tell me if you are mentally ill?'" he declared indignantly.

Baker's death and DeFede's column did little to hurt the police director's popularity. On November 2, Alvarez was elected mayor of Miami. His replacement's feelings about CIT differed from Alvarez's. He announced that one of his first acts as the new police chief would be to implement CIT training. Robinson was asked to help teach it.

At least six years had passed since Robinson had first learned about the Memphis CIT program and had begun knocking on doors, trying to get police departments in Miami to adopt it. During that same time period, five mentally ill men had been killed—four by Alvarez's department. She believed all five had died needlessly.

Why, she wondered, do changes that involve the mentally ill always have to be so difficult? "Why?"

J   udge Steven Leifman was feeling optimistic when I stopped at the courthouse to see him. A lot of "positive steps forward" had been taken during the twelve months that I had been coming to Miami, he said.

In a hard-fought battle, the Florida legislature had recently voted to "reform" the Baker Act. The campaign to change the state's commitment statute had been led by the Treatment Advocacy Center, the Washington, D.C.–based lobbying group started by Dr. E. Fuller Torrey.

Just as it had done in New York with Kendra's Law and in California with Laura's Law, TAC played a key role in changing Florida's statute. The "human face" in this case was Deputy Sheriff Eugene Gregory, who had been fatally shot when he responded to a landlord's complaint in Seminole County. Alan Singletary had a long history of mental illness and had barricaded himself inside his apartment when Gregory arrived. Singletary murdered Gregory, and during the next thirteen hours, he wounded two other deputies before he was killed. Previously, Singletary's family had tried unsuccessfully to get him medical help.

Judge Leifman and Rachel Diaz had both endorsed TAC's campaign and had written letters to newspapers supporting the Baker Act reforms. But the most dramatic testimonials had come from Seminole County sheriff Donald F. Eslinger; the fallen deputy's widow, Linda Gregory; and Singletary's sister, Alice Petree. The trio had toured the state, urging lawmakers to reform the law. All the state's major newspapers endorsed TAC's campaign. The new statute gave judges permission to involuntarily treat mentally ill patients if they had a history of violence or multiple hospitalizations.

While Judge Leifman was thrilled by TAC's success, he was even prouder of another coup. He had finally found a way to move mentally ill prisoners off the notorious ninth floor. On November 2, voters had passed a sweeping *$3 billion* municipal bond issue in Miami-Dade County to pay for 334 civic projects. Tucked inside those bond funds was $22 million that Leifman had requested to move the mentally ill out of the jail and into a special "holding facility" specifically designed for handling disturbed prisoners. "We are finally going to be able to move out of the dark ages," he proudly proclaimed.

The judge already had his eye on a possible site for the facility. He'd heard a rumor that the state was going to "privatize" the South Florida Evaluation and Treatment Center in Miami. A private firm was going to be paid to treat the criminals who were currently being hospitalized there. If that deal went through, the private company was planning to erect an entirely new forensic facility, leaving the old center's seven-story hospital and its maximum-security compound empty. Constructed in 1968, the center could hold as many as 220 inmates. "It would be perfect for us to remodel," Leifman explained. It was only a few blocks from the courthouse and could be used as both a holding facility and a hospital treatment center. It was an ambitious plan, but Leifman felt confident he could pull it off.

After speaking to the judge, I walked over to the jail and polled the correctional officers on duty in C wing. None of them believed Judge Leifman would be able to shut down the ninth floor. *The Miami Herald* had reported that the $3 billion in bond funds would be doled out on a "priority" basis during the next four decades. "A lot can happen in forty years," Officer Michael Urbistondo warned, "and the inmates here have never been a priority."

Like other county judges, Leifman faced reelection every six years. His current term was scheduled to end in twelve months, and there was no guarantee that voters would reelect him despite all that he'd accomplished for the mentally ill. "Judge Leifman is championing these inmates' problems," an officer explained, "but that's for right now. If something happens to him, if he isn't reelected, then this place will go right on like it's always gone on and that bond money will end up being spent on something else." A third officer chimed in: "Come back here in forty years. My guess is you'll still find crazy prisoners locked in this shithole."

S everal days later, a fistfight broke out on the ninth floor where A, B, and C wings came together. Three inmates, who were being moved to different cells, got into a scuffle. The four officers working in C wing rushed into the lobby to help end the disturbance. It took about ten minutes. When Officer Lynne Grant returned to her post in

C wing, she noticed that one of the prisoners in cell number sixteen had draped a blanket over his head and shoulders. He was standing with his back to the cell front, leaning against the wall near where the top bunk was bolted into the concrete. Grant thought there was something odd about how his shoulders were slumped. She also knew the inmate had tried to kill himself earlier in the week. Grant pounded on the glass cell front and called his name. But the prisoner didn't respond. She quickly unlocked the door and darted inside to investigate.

While the officers had been distracted by the fistfight, the inmate had hanged himself. There was a piece of a bedsheet wrapped tightly around his neck and attached to the top bunk. The prisoner had lifted his feet off the floor to tighten the noose enough to cut off his airway. The bedsheet was hidden by the blanket draped over his head.

Grant hollered for help and felt for a pulse. Officer Michael Urbistondo cut the sheet while Grant and officers Roosevelt Jackson and Clarence Clem held on to the unconscious prisoner and then carried him into the center corridor, where Dr. Poitier began administering CPR. While the doctor applied mouth-to-mouth resuscitation, Urbistondo pushed on the inmate's chest. After several minutes, the prisoner began breathing again. "He was as close to being dead as you can get," a relieved Urbistondo said. The inmate was taken by paramedics to a hospital emergency room. Five days later, he was brought back to the ninth floor and put under suicide watch once again.

T he elevator doors on the ninth floor opened, and a correctional officer led a prisoner in handcuffs and leg chains toward C wing. The inmate was a huge man, and he shuffled his feet as he walked past Dr. Poitier's office. The newcomer was ordered to strip out of his filthy clothes, was issued a blue Ferguson gown, and was taken to a cell.

He stepped inside it, turned around so that he was now facing the

cell front, and stared blankly through the glass at the correctional officers, nurses, and social workers working in the center corridor. Because
he was nearly catatonic, he couldn't speak, so there was no way to know
what he was thinking. He was homeless and chronically mentally ill, and
had been arrested in South Beach, where he'd been charged with panhandling, trespassing, and being a sanitary nuisance.

Freddie Gilbert was back where he had been a year earlier, when I
had first seen him.

Chapter 35. Solutions

My job as a journalist is to go places where others can't and come back and tell what I have seen. I am a fact gatherer, and I've always been content to let the pundits on Sunday television talk shows argue about solutions to society's problems. But I realized when I returned from Miami that I could not be dispassionate about what I had seen.

Every police department in America should implement Crisis Intervention Team training. CIT saves money and, more important, lives. Most police forces already have speciality units, such as hostage rescue teams or SWAT or bomb squads. They also need officers who have been taught how to deal with the mentally ill. The killing by a Miami-Dade County police officer of a mentally ill man who was walking home from his cousin's house and had not been disturbing anyone should alarm us all. It was a preventable tragedy.

Unfortunately, as Judy Robinson's tireless six-year campaign in Miami shows, getting police departments to accept CIT training can be difficult. "No one thinks they need CIT officers until either an officer or a mentally ill person ends up dead," Memphis lieutenant Sam Cochran warned me. "That's how it always happens—how it always works."

I was lucky that my son had not been shot by the Fairfax County

Police Department when he was arrested. Its officers sent a dog into an unoccupied house to subdue him, but even after it locked its teeth into Mike's arm and dragged him to the floor, my son had struggled. In his deluded mind, Mike believed the police had come to murder him. It had taken five officers to wrestle him down. Thankfully, they did it without using their nightsticks or a handgun. At this writing, I've been told that Fairfax County is considering implementing CIT training. I hope it does so quickly.

An important benefit of CIT is that it changes attitudes. "One of the things we learned," said Lieutenant Cochran, "is you can't talk about mental illness without talking about stigma and prejudice, because that is what is out there in our society—a real prejudice against the mentally ill. Unfortunately, the police mirror that, and Hollywood magnifies it by always showing mentally ill persons as violent and dangerous and sadistic. When we began CIT training, I began to see these people differently. If you saw a man with a white cane trying to cross a busy street, I can guarantee you that most Americans would help that person cross safely. But every day we pass people who have a mental illness on the street, often they're ranting, and we don't see them with our eyes and we sure don't see them with our hearts. I have a problem with that."

Seeing the mentally ill differently is something that not only the police but also prosecutors, judges, and the public need to do. The National Institute of Mental Health has confirmed that people with severe depression, bipolar disorder, schizoaffective disorder, and schizophrenia have a chemical imbalance in their brains that distorts their moods and impairs their thoughts. They need treatment. They do not belong in jails.

During my first visit to the ninth floor, a frustrated Dr. Poitier compared the nude men cowering in freezing cells in C wing to the lunatics whom the Reverend Louis Dwight and reformer Dorothea Dix had stumbled on in Boston's jails in the 1800s. Dr. Poitier noted that we were going backward in our handling of the mentally ill. He called jail-ing them a national disgrace. Yet it is happening every day across our country. This is not just a Miami problem. A study by NAMI and Public Citizen's Health Research Group released more than a decade ago named the Flathead County Detention Center in Flathead County, Montana, as being the "worst jail" in America for the mentally ill. It had faced "stiff competition" from equally deplorable conditions found in jails in Idaho, Kentucky, Mississippi, and New Mexico. Before I settled on Miami, I spent several days in the Twin Towers, the Los Angeles city jail, and the conditions that I observed there were every bit as unsettling as what I later saw on the ninth floor in Miami.

As this book documents, jails and prisons are simply not safe or humane places for the mentally ill. William Weaver Jr. is a quadriplegic today because he dove headfirst from a jail bunk into his cell's toilet. Was Weaver dangerous when he was arrested? Absolutely. But he should have been taken to a secure hospital setting, where he could have been held safely and received medical treatment—not locked in a jail cell that was designed to inflict punishment.

Our jails and prisons have become our nation's new asylums because there is nowhere else for the mentally ill to go. The reason is deinstitutionalization. The ninth floor exists today because Florida did what every other state was doing and what the federal government pressured it to do: it began emptying its state mental hospitals. Because deinstitutionalization was done without a community safety net, a huge gap in the mental health system was created.

In Miami, Judge Leifman is trying to fix this by opening a "holding facility" to get inmates out of jail. Other jurisdictions are experimenting with jail diversion programs and with mental health courts. But while these ideas are encouraging, they are *reactive steps*. As Judy Robinson put it: The mentally ill should not have to be arrested and go to jail in order to get mental health services and treatment.

And it is a lack of fundamental services and adequate treatment that has added to our current problems. Obviously, the federal government needs to make good on the unkept promise that President Kennedy and Congress made in the 1960s when they pledged to create a national network of community mental health centers. Programs such as the Northwest Center for Community Mental Health in Reston, Virginia, where my son was treated, need to be fully funded and should not have to beg each fiscal year for scraps to stay open. Every community needs a local facility where someone with mental problems can go for help *before* he ends up in trouble.

But no matter how well funded and well run these centers are, they will still not be able to accommodate the chronically mentally ill, who are the most likely to become stuck in our jails' revolving door. Community mental health centers are not designed to deal with severely schizophrenic or violent patients. And that is why it's time we admitted what has become painfully obvious to nearly all of the prosecutors, judges, and jail psychiatrists who talked to me. We need to rethink our understandable dread of state mental hospitals. Despite their horrific past, asylums are not intrinsically evil. They are buildings made of bricks and steel. They became giant warehouses because of neglect, ignorance, prejudice, and wanton indifference. But they didn't have to be that way and they shouldn't have been that way. Dr. Morton Birnbaum did not intend to dismantle the state mental hospital system when he first proposed his "right to treatment" argument. He was trying to force state legislatures to provide decent care in them.

What is missing in our system today are modern, long-term treatment facilities where the chronically mentally ill can receive good medical attention and, if necessary, can live safely until they can be moved into less restrictive facilities.

Why do we need state hospitals for the most severely ill?

Look at how they are being dealt with today. They are locked in jails and sent to prisons. They are tucked away in so-called assisted-living facilities where they receive no treatment, often are physically abused, and live in squalor. Many are abandoned on our streets. Consider the fate of Deidra "DeeDee" Sanbourne. Look at the lives of Alice Ann Collyer and Freddie Gilbert. For them, deinstitutionalization was a cruel hoax, and the wholesale closing of state hospitals was abandonment, not freedom.

The chronically ill are not the only ones who have paid a price because of deinstitutionalization and our lingering fear of asylums. We have become indifferent. We walk by homeless, ranting psychotics in our cities and we soothe our consciences by convincing ourselves that they are choosing to live that way. They have become "throwaway people," as April Hernandez said. They are the butt of our jokes and an accepted part of our city landscape. Rather than see them as human beings who are suffering from serious brain disorders and who need medical attention, our laws defend their right to be crazy, as if having a chemical imbalance in your neurons is a choice. We live in the world's richest and most medically advanced nation in the world, yet we allow people who are chronically ill to defecate in their clothing, eat garbage, and crawl under bushes during rainstorms. April Hernandez was twice gang-raped. Chronic schizophrenics such as Carl, the Passageway client who was homeless, are savagely beaten.

In addition to rethinking our attitudes about the need for state hospitals, we also should reexamine commitment laws. Obviously, the civil rights of the mentally ill need to be guarded. But we have created a system that is heavily biased against intervention and treatment. Most commitment laws were passed thirty years ago in reaction to lax commitment standards and ghastly conditions in state-run hospitals. But in reacting to those wrongs, we have turned commitment hearings into adversarial confrontations where the relatives of persons with mental disorders and the doctors who wish to help them are assumed to be vicious co-conspirators intent on maliciously imprisoning a confused mark. Freeing a delusional defendant who has a long history of psychological problems does neither the patient nor the public any lasting good. Instead, it prolongs that person's misery and puts society at risk.

What makes this especially unfortunate is that 80 percent of the mentally ill can be helped with antipsychotic medication, yet civil rights laws are used daily to prevent patients from getting help. The doctors, judges, prosecutors, and defense attorneys involved in the commitment process know this. Yet we insist no one be compelled to take antipsychotic drugs until he becomes so deranged that he is in "imminent danger" and a judge has to intervene to save his life. If we really believed that forced treatment was an injustice and forced medication was cruel, then why would we allow a judge to impose it as a last resort to save a life?

The commitment process needs to be retooled so that doctors and a patient's loved ones can be brought back into the decision-making process, instead of immediately being viewed with suspicion. The courts should find a way to help defendants who can't think for themselves because of their brain disorders—rather than simply turn them loose to, as Wisconsin psychiatrist Darold Treffert put it, "die with their rights on."

Doctors, in particular, need to step forward and demand change. The emergency room physician who refused to treat Mike was obeying the law, but in doing so, he brought shame to himself, his profession, and the oath that he'd taken to help the afflicted.

While there are no easy answers, Tom Mullen's "secret" to helping deeply troubled and violent psychotics at Passageway safely reenter our society serves as a model of what can and should be done nationwide. Mullen created a parish, a refuge where patients are treated, cared for, and cared about. Passageway is an example of what a *real* asylum— defined in the dictionary as being a "safe place"—should and can be.

And in the end, Mullen himself stripped away the mystery of why Passageway works. The answer proved to be rather basic. He created a community where the mentally ill are not alone, a community that genuinely cares about how the weakest among us are treated.

M ike invited me to lunch. Now that he was working full-time, he wanted to show off his financial independence. We met at his favorite restaurant and sat on the veranda because it was such a beautiful afternoon. Mike had only a few months to go before his probation ended, and I was tremendously proud of him. He had come a long way from that panicky day when I had picked him up in New York City and raced him to the hospital. I had come across Oliver Stone's movie Heaven and Earth one afternoon by accident and had left it out on the kitchen counter. When Mike had seen it, he'd become embarrassed. He no longer believed it held secret messages.

During lunch, we talked about his future. He planned to go back to graduate school, and that meant moving to another state. He would be living on his own again, and that frightened me.

"If you move, the first thing you'll need to do is find a psychiatrist," I lectured, "and you'll have to make certain you can get Abilify."

Our entrées came, and for some reason our conversation turned to birthdays. He was the one who mentioned my fifty-first. We had celebrated it in a locked psychiatric ward at the height of his breakdown. I'd brought him a bucket of Kentucky Fried Chicken and he'd given me a hand-drawn birthday card.

"Do you remember how you made a list of fun things that we'd done together as father and son?" I asked.

"Yeah. I remember."

We had laughed at the hospital about how he had fallen from the edge of a cliff when he was little and we were fishing in South Dakota. He'd caught himself before he'd tumbled all of the way down the embankment and had screamed for help. I had climbed down the ravine and carried him back to safety.

For a few moments, neither of us spoke. I watched as he ate his steak. He was now twenty-five years old and a handsome man. Tests showed his IQ was higher than mine. Sitting there, I realized once again how fortunate we both had been. Despite everything that had happened, he had recovered from his breakdown, he hadn't been marked for life as a convicted felon, and he was doing well on his antipsychotic medication. It was impossible from looking and speaking to him to know that he had a serious mental illness.

I had gone to Miami because I wanted to save him. But I now realized that I had actually been searching for a way to save both of us. Judy Robinson had told me that parents with mentally ill children were given a choice: Either you could become despondent and wallow in pity, or you could have a good cry and start fighting back. I now understood that fighting back meant doing whatever was necessary as a parent, even if it meant having your own child hate you.

So what had I learned in Miami—not as Pete Earley the journalist but as Pete Earley the father?

Three simple truths. The first and second were intertwined. Nothing in life is guaranteed. And much in life isn't fair. There was a chance that Mike would never again be troubled by his disorder. But statistically, there was a better chance that he would stop taking his medicine at some point in the future because he would become convinced that he no longer needed his pills. He would have a relapse. His illness was not ending because I was writing the final chapter of this book. There would be no living-happily-ever-after sentence on the last page.

"You know what your problem is, Dad?" Mike said, as if he were reading my thoughts. "You worry too much. Just eat your steak and enjoy this lovely day. Everything is going to work out fine for me, you'll see. All the stuff that happened is in the past."

It was the blind optimism of his youth talking. And yet he was right. At that moment, everything was fine. My son was thinking clearly. He had a job, was making plans for his future, was enjoying life, and seemed genuinely happy.

Which led me to the third truth that I had discovered as a father.

Mental illness is a cruel disease. No one knows whom it might strike or why. There is no known cure. It lasts forever. My son Mike has it. And because he is sick, he will always be dancing on the edge of a cliff. I cannot keep him from falling. I cannot protect him from its viciousness. All I can do is stand next to him on that cliff, always ready to extend my hand. All I can do is to promise that I will never abandon him.

I took a bite of my steak and it tasted better than any I had ever eaten. I understood why. The sun was warm on my face and I was a fortunate man. I was a proud father. Mike was laughing. He was safe.

I had my son back.

ACKNOWLEDGMENTS

This book could not have been written without the consent of my son. I spent many restless nights worried about how it might affect his future. But he encouraged me because he believed his story could possibly help someone else. I appreciate his courage.

I would not have been able to write about Mike and my research in Miami had it not been for Neil Nyren, my editor at Putnam. When I decided to write about the criminalization of the mentally ill, several publishers expressed an interest. But most disappeared after their marketing departments cautioned them that a book about such a gloomy subject was risky. Neil recognized the importance of this subject matter and my need as a parent to describe my frustration about how my son was treated.

I am also indebted to Miami County judge Steven Leifman. He pulled strings to get me unlimited access to the ninth floor, because he believed the public had a right to see what was happening there. Miami's mentally ill are better off today because of his tireless efforts to help them. In my thirty years as a reporter, I've known only a select few politicians as altruistic as Judge Leifman. Miami-Dade County is fortunate to have him as a judge.

This was not an easy book for me to write, and I am indebted to two fellow authors and journalists who provided me with much-needed and appreciated editorial advice. My longtime friend and former *Washington Post* colleague Walt Harrington read my manuscript twice and each time offered insightful guidance. And a new friend, Philip Gerard, a professor of creative nonfiction writing, showed me how to give this book its spine by becoming its narrator, and also helped pull me back whenever my emotions ran roughshod over a need for evenhandedness. I would urge readers to learn more about them and their books by visiting www .waltharrington.com and www.philipgerard.com. Thanks also to Toni Rachiele, who did a fine job copyediting my manuscript.

In addition, I would like to thank Rachel Diaz, Tom Mullen, Dr. Joseph Poitier, Judy Robinson, and Renee Turolla for guiding me through Miami's mental health care system. I would also like to acknowledge the real people behind these four pseudonyms: Alice Ann Collyer, Freddie Gilbert, April Hernandez, and Ted Jackson.

This is a factual account of activities that happened during a two-year period. The material is based on interviews, hospital and court records, newspaper articles, books, and my personal observations. Close to a hundred people were interviewed face-to-face, including several whose names do not appear but whose comments proved helpful. While pseudonyms were used to protect most mentally ill characters, Deidra "DeeDee" Sanbourne, William Weaver Jr., and my son Mike were identified by their actual names. Events that I did not personally witness have been reconstructed based on interviews with the participants. Dialogue has been taken from public documents, court records, or personal observation and tape-recorded interviews. In cases where people remembered events differently, I've chosen to use the version that appeared to be the most logical. There are a few instances where I've written sentences that appear to be a character's actual thoughts. These are based on that person's recollections and were usually prefaced during interviews with "I remember thinking" or "I was feeling at the time."

I would like to especially thank Susan Wagner and her husband, Robert, for helping me investigate the final days of Deidra Sanbourne's life. I appreciate their determination to ferret out the truth.

The following people were helpful to me: Gregory Adams, V. Albert, Terrance Alden, Michael Alonso, V. O. Armel, Bart Armstrong, Joan Arruabarrena, Naomi Auerbach, Hilda Baldwin, Dedra Barber, Sal Barbera, Richard Barrantez, Robert Bernstein, Dr. Morton Birnbaum, Melvin S. Black, Gayle Bluebird, Russell Boley, Robert Brown, Yvonne Burke, Peter Carlson, Robert Cates, Terry Chavez, Lilly Chu, Clarence and Theresa Clem, Lieutenant Sam Cochran, Luis Collazo, Stephanie Costanza, Rebecca Cox, Susan Curran, Jose Dapena, Irene Darmstedter, Larry Davis, Joanmarie Ilaria Davoli, Nancy Domenici, Leonard Downie Jr., Mike Farrell, Mary Jane Ferdman, Marie Fleurmont, Randy Flowers, Dennis A. Fordenwalt, Lolita Francis, John Franklin, Diane Funston, Mark Gale, Mario Garcia, Sebastian Garcia, Fidel Gonzales, Lynne Grant, Randall Hagar, Janelle Hall, Stephen Henderson, Martha Hodge, Charles Jackson, Darrell Jackson, Doris Jackson, Roosevelt Jackson, Carla Jacobson, Sanford Jacobson, Steve Jacobson, Stephen Jaffe, Evelyn Johnson, Andrew Kersey, Louis Kilmer, Debra Kirsch, Thomas Klotz, Richard Knight, Martha Knisley, Sam Konell, Susan Kronberg, Paula Larson, Ray Leyva, N. McCarthy, Michael P. Maloney, Richard Mason, Lillian Menendez, Laura Millan, Marvin Minoff, Allan Monica, A. G. Montanari, Barry Morris, Alice Nelson, Ann Norman, Samuel C. Ormes, Dunja Patriski-James, Alina Perez, Peter Perl, Colleen Phipps, Maureen Reddy, Kim Reed, Alida Renoso, Frederick Robbins,

Jeff Robinson, Judith Rumreich, Anne Marie St. Charles, Sadie Sands, Marilyn Sawyer, Catherine Schofield, Joseph Seiglie, Roderick Shaner, Dennis and Renee Sherman, Addison Smith, Robert Smith, David Sofferin, Marvin Southard, Jon Stanley, Phillip Strander, Theodore Thomas, E. Fuller Torrey, Maraima Trujillo, Michael Urbistondo, Harry Vann, David Vise, Mike Wallace, Robert Ward, William Weaver Sr., William Weaver Jr., Howard and Magdalena Wechsler, Don and Gene Weiner, Richard Westin, Carter Wiggins, Tom Wise, Victor Wright, Pat Wyman, Mary Zdanowicz, and Ronald Zimmet.

Others, who can't be fully named, include these Passageway clients: Alex, Byron, Hubert, Jeffrey, Kenny, Lewis, Mike, Patty, Tim, and Tony. I'd also like to thank members of Judy Robinson's NAMI support group, particularly Lori, and, of course, the correctional officers in the Miami jail.

As always, I am grateful to my wife, Patti, who put up with my trips to Miami and my endless doubts and insecurities about this project. She was my rock during Mike's ordeal. I am thankful to my children—all seven of them—for their support.

Other family members whom I'd like to acknowledge: my parents, Elmer and Jean Earley, and Gloria Brown, James Brown, LeRue and Ellen Brown, Phillip and Joanne Corn, Donnie and Dana Davis, George and Linda Earley, William and Rosemary Luzi, Charlie and Donna Stackhouse, and Jay and Elise Strine. In addition, I want to thank Nelson DeMille, Keran Harrington, Marie Heffelfinger, Don and Susan Infeld, Reis Kash, Richard and Joan Miles, Mike Sager, Lynn and LouAnn Smith, and Kendall and Lynn Starkweather.

Finally, I'm grateful to Georgiana Atkins Havill for running her editing pencil through my first draft of this book and to my literary agents, John Silbersack, who believed in this book from the start and worked hard to get it published, and his partner, Robert Gottlieb, both of Trident Media Group.

(Readers are invited to post comments about this book on my website: www .peteearley.com. While I may not be able to respond to every message, I read all of them.)

HELPFUL RESOURCES

American Psychiatric Association
1000 Wilson Boulevard, Suite 1825
Arlington, VA 22209-3901

Telephone: 703-907-7300

The APA has more than 35,000 member physicians whose goal is to "ensure humane care and effective treatment for all persons with mental disorders, including mental retardation and substance-related disorders."

Website: www.psych.org

Bazelon Center for Mental Health Law
1101 15th Street, NW, Suite 1212
Washington, DC 20005

Telephone: 202-467-5730
Fax: 202-223-0409

For three decades, the Bazelon Center has been the nation's leading legal advocate for people with mental disabilities. Known until 1993 as the Mental Health Law Project, it was the driving force behind the mental health civil rights movement and was responsible for precedent-setting legal cases that have defined how the mentally ill are treated.

Website: www.bazelon.org

Depression and Bipolar Support Alliance (DBSA)
730 North Franklin Street, Suite 501
Chicago, IL 60610-7224

Toll-free: 800-826-3632
Fax: 312-642-7243

DBSA is a grassroots network of more than 1,000 patient-run support groups across the country. It is the nation's leading patient-directed organization focusing on depression and bipolar disorder.

Website: www.dbsalliance.org

Depression and Related Affective Disorders Association
2330 West Joppa Road, Suite 100
Lutherville, MD 21093

Telephone: 410-583-2919

Established with help from the Johns Hopkins University School of Medicine, this community group provides educational information to the public about mental illness.

Website: www.drada.org

GAINS Center for People with Co-Occurring Disorders
    in the Justice System
345 Delaware Avenue
Delmar, NY 12054

Toll-free: 800-311-GAIN (4256)
Fax: 518-439-7612

Part of the federal government's Department of Health and Human Services, the GAINS Center was created in 1995 to act as a clearinghouse for information about diversion and other programs aimed at getting the mentally ill out of jails and prisons.

Website: www.gainsctr.com

National Alliance for the Mentally Ill (NAMI)
Colonial Place Three
2107 Wilson Boulevard, Suite 300
Arlington, VA 22201-3042

Telephone: 703-524-7600
Fax: 703-524-9094
TDY: 703-524-7227
Information hotline: 800-950-NAMI (6264)

NAMI is a grassroots, self-help education and advocacy organization that bills itself as the "Nation's Voice on Mental Illness." It operates support groups in nearly every American city. Founded in 1979 by fifty-four people from around the country who felt the need to form a national organization focusing on people with mental illness, it acts as a referral service for patients and their families. Its website contains helpful information about mental illness and where families can turn locally for support.

Website: www.nami.org

National Alliance for Research on Schizophrenia and Depression
60 Cutter Mill Road, Suite 404
Great Neck, NY 11021

Telephone: 800-829-8289
Fax: 516-487-6930
E-mail: info@narsad.org

National Commission on Correctional Health Care
1145 West Diversey Parkway
Chicago, IL 60614

Telephone: 773-880-1460
Fax: 773-880-2424

The NCCHC was established by the American Medical Association to improve the quality of health care in jails, prisons, and juvenile correctional facilities. It sets minimum acceptable standards and regularly tracks conditions in correctional facilities.

Website: www.ncchc.org

National Institute of Mental Health (NIMH)
6001 Executive Boulevard
Bethesda, MD 20892-9663

Toll-free: 866-615-6464
Fax: 301-443-4279
TTY: 301-443-8431

Part of the National Institutes of Health, NIMH is the federal government agency charged with conducting biomedical research about the mind, the brain, and behavior. Its website contains detailed information about mental illnesses and the latest research into their causes.

Website: www.nimh.nih.gov

National Mental Health Association (NMHA)
2001 North Beauregard Street, 12th Floor
Alexandria, VA 22311

Telephone: 703-684-7722
Toll-free: 800-969-NMHA (6642)
Fax: 703-684-5968

Established in 1909 by former psychiatric patient Clifford W. Beers, NMHA is the country's oldest and largest nonprofit organization focusing on all aspects of mental health and mental illness. It has more than 340 affiliates nationwide. Beers set NMHA into motion after he was subjected to horrible abuse in state-run facilities.

Website: www.nmha.org

Stanley Medical Research Institute
5430 Grosvenor Lane, Suite 200
Bethesda, MD 20814

Telephone: 301-571-0760
Fax: 301-571-0769

The Stanley Medical Research Institute is the largest privately funded research organization investigating schizophrenia and bipolar disorder. Funded by Ted and Vada Stanley, it currently pays for half of all U.S. research on bipolar disorder and one-quarter of all research being conducted on schizophrenia.

Website: www.stanleyresearch.org

Treatment Advocacy Center
200 North Glebe Road, Suite 730
Arlington, VA 22203

Telephone: 703-294-6006
Fax: 703-294-6010

Founded by E. Fuller Torrey, TAC is dedicated to "eliminating legal and clinical barriers to timely and humane treatment for millions of Americans with severe brain disorders who are not receiving appropriate care." Its "preventable tragedies" page on its website lists fatalities that were caused because of mental illnesses that were not treated.

Website: www.psychlaws.org

HELPFUL BOOKS

A Brilliant Madness: Living with Manic Depressive Illness
Patty Duke and Gloria Hochman
Bantam Books, 1992

An Unquiet Mind: A Memoir of Moods and Madness
Kay Redfield Jamison
Vintage Books, 1997

Darkness Visible
William Styron
Vintage Books, 1992

I Am Not Sick, I Don't Need Help!
Dr. Xavier Amador with Anna-Lisa Johanson
Vida Press, 2000

Madness in the Streets:
How Psychiatry and the Law Abandoned the Mentally Ill
Rael Jean Isaac and Virginia C. Armat
The Freedom Press, 1990

Out of the Shadows: Confronting America's Mental Illness Crisis
E. Fuller Torrey, M.D.
John Wiley & Sons, 1997

72 Hour Hold
Bebe Moore Campbell
Alfred A. Knopf, 2005

Surviving Schizophrenia:
A Manual for Families, Consumers, and Providers
E. Fuller Torrey, M.D.
HarperCollins, 1983

The Noonday Demon: An Atlas of Depression
Andrew Solomon
Scribner, 2001

The Mad Among Us:
A History of the Care of America's Mentally Ill
Gerald N. Grob
The Free Press, 1994

And for parents and children:
Sometimes My Mommy Gets Angry
Bebe Moore Campbell
Puffin, 2005